PEOPLE'S PALACES

Victorian and Edwardian Pubs of Scotland

Rudolph Kenna · Anthony Mooney

PAUL·HARRIS·PUBLISHING

First published in Great Britain 1983
by Paul Harris Publishing
40 York Place
Edinburgh

© Copyright Rudolph Kenna and
Anthony Mooney 1983

ISBN 0 86228 027 3

Typeset in Great Britain by
Scotprint Limited,
Printed and bound in Great Britain
by Billing & Sons Limited, Worcester.

CONTENTS

INTRODUCTION

For centuries the Scottish pub had literally been a licensed house – frequently diminutive, evil-smelling and sparsely furnished, but occasionally clean, commodious and comfortable. It continued to be more house than shop until the nineteenth century when counter service was gradually introduced. In the Scottish equivalent of the early Victorian gin palace spirits were dispensed from painted and gilded casks, and beer, stored in the cellar to keep it in good condition, was raised to the bar by a beer engine. The most illustrious phase in the history of the Scottish pub was yet to come, however. This was the period 1880-1910, when licensed premises everywhere were made to conform to late Victorian and Edwardian standards of beauty and utility.

The pubs of the "golden age" vied for attention with elaborate wrought-iron signs, embossed or stained glass windows, and resplendent gas lamps. In gilt metal lettering or virtuoso signwriting the words "Wine and Spirit Vaults" designated many a hostelry. Some architects made a speciality of pub design, and there was no shortage of craftsmen to carry out their strikingly effective schemes.

Opulent pubs proliferated in the towns and cities where there were large numbers of "floating" drinkers whose allegiance could conceivably be won by means of a substantial outlay on carved mahogany, stained glass, and leather upholstery. The rural licence holder, with the support of a small but reliable clientele, was less interested in costly improvements, and often his sole concession to the spirit of the age was some fancy shelving or an etched advertisement mirror.

With their richly decorated interiors, the late Victorian and Edwardian pubs were the people's palaces. Their characteristic features would be extremely expensive to reproduce today; craftsmen are no longer a prolific breed and their work now commands respect in terms of hard cash. Unfortunately many surviving pubs of this period are now only partially intact; some have lost their massive and ornate display stands, others their wall paintings or their stained glass windows. By dint of timely exertions, preservationists have managed to save a representative selection of Victorian railway stations, warehouses, and even factories, but they appear to have neglected the no less worthy cause of Victorian pubs; these continue

6

to vanish utterly on the bidding of brewers or independent licence holders, and consequently – in Scotland at any rate – they are becoming something of a rarity.

At the turn of the century, however, they were numbered in thousands, much to the dismay of the nation's teetotalers – for the last quarter of the nineteenth century was also the heyday of the temperance movement, the adherents of which considered alcohol to be the root of all evil. On six days of the week, from eight in the morning until eleven at night, men of different backgrounds congregated in handsome bar-rooms where, as in the contemporary saloons of North America, all were equal in the sight of the fiercely mustachioed waiters. In many instances they also got thoroughly drunk, for the bar staff were dispensing the products of over a hundred independent Scottish breweries, as well as Scotch whisky which varied greatly in quality and in some instances was simply firewater. On Sundays the pubs remained closed, but the Scots were very resourceful when it came to avoiding the worst implications of the Forbes Mackenzie Act. In defiance of the law proscribing Sunday drinking the shebeens – unlicensed public houses – were well patronised, notwithstanding the fact that they usually supplied whisky of very dubious ancestry.

Even without the stimulating influence of alcohol it would have been easy to attune oneself to the extrovert character of the palace pub. In any street it was highly conspicuous by virtue of its elaborate frontage, and particularly so at night when light streamed from its etched and engraved windows. The handsome frontage was designed to command the attention of the occasional drinker (the habitual drinker would have patronised the meanest shebeen as readily as the most opulent pub). If, discovering a thirst, he then passed through the pub's swing doors, there was an interior that did not belie the promise of the exterior.

Late Victorian and Edwardian publicans were very often (in the popular phraseology of the day) self-made men. It is certainly true that many of them had been born and bred to the licensed trade, but a substantial number entered it only after trying their hands at other occupations. For the stonemason, the ship's carpenter, the coal miner or the crofter, a public house licence represented an opportunity to attain a modicum of independence and prosperity in a society which was still extremely conscious of social and class divisions.

The successful publican could expect to have his photograph reproduced in the National Guardian, the weekly newspaper of the Scottish licensed trade, and to be described in the accompanying article as a prince of good fellows and an ardent Freemason. He was not, as a rule, an educated man, although he was often an exceptionally shrewd one. His cultural horizon usually encompassed the works of Burns, and occasionally also those of Scott and Tannahill. When it came to the reconstruction of his licensed premises on larger and more opulent lines, however, he was generally content to leave matters in the capable hands of the architect and the contractors. Profit and prestige were no doubt uppermost in his mind when he spent large sums of money on bar furniture and fittings; a lavishly appointed pub invited more custom, and the expensive improvements were sure to be admired by the other gentlemen of the trade.

Everything had to be of excellent quality. Bar counters and display fitments were made of various woods – mahogany, walnut, cypress, sycamore, oak, teak.

Mirrors were embossed, coloured and gilded. Walls were wood-panelled, frescoed, tiled, or hung with heavy Lincrusta or Tynecastle papers. Whisky casks were girt with hoops of polished nickel or brass, or were painted and gilded. Colour, sparkle and variety were provided by innumerable glass, crystal or china containers. At the turn of the century, in defiance of temperance opposition, which assumed such Protean forms as the Good Templars, the Blue Ribbon Army, the Band of Hope, and Mrs. Carry Nation, the public houses of Scotland were more flamboyant than at any other period in their history.

Some pubs – those at the bottom of the league – were mere drinking dens, sordid enough in all conscience, but many others boasted an enviable standard of comfort and service. More than nowadays it would seem, there were individualistic publicans who took pride in their calling; they enhanced the appearance of their premises by means of paintings and engravings, knick-knacks, potted plants and curios. They provided the latest newspapers and periodicals. They occasionally even went to the trouble of preparing free snacks.

Scotland's late Victorian and Edwardian pubs grow fewer year by year, and they have been largely ignored by writers on architectural subjects. Of those which survive in whole or in part, many have been specially photographed for this work. Plans and elevations which the architects originally lodged with the Dean of Guild Courts or the Licensing Courts have also been reproduced, as these convey valuable information on pubs which have since been demolished, remodelled, or subjected to alterations of a more trifling character. It will be appreciated that while some Victorian or Edwardian plans are quite well preserved, others are in rather poor condition.

Much use has also been made of material from those informative and entertaining journals, the Scottish Wine, Spirit and Beer Trades' Review, the Victualling Trades' Review, the Scottish Licensed Trade, and the National Guardian.

Archives and libraries in several Scottish towns and cities kindly made books, periodicals, plans and other documents available, and the authors wish to take this opportunity of thanking the members of staff concerned for their help. Thanks are also due to numerous members of the Scottish licensed trade and their employees, whose co-operation outside the statutory licensing hours made the task of photographing the interiors of surviving Victorian and Edwardian pubs a relatively easy one.

Rudolph Kenna
Anthony Mooney

1983

Part One

1 Ancestry

The Scottish public house as we know it today evolved in the latter part of Queen Victoria's reign. At the beginning of the nineteenth century, the tavern's hospitable interior was hardly distinguished from the kitchen or parlour of the humbler sort of private dwelling. There was no serving counter; instead, depending on the class of the establishment, there was a greater or lesser preponderance of household objects such as tables, chairs, cupboards, pictures and ornaments.

The gin shops of the 1830s familiarised Anglo-Saxons with fancy display shelving, decorated mirrors and other features of the new-fangled urban public houses, and in due course the ornate dram shop, the precursor of the late Victorian palace pub, took root in Scotland.

By all accounts the old Scots taverns – and the eighteenth century ones in particular – made up in conviviality for what they may have lacked in salubrity. During the day, much business was transacted in them, and at night all classes flocked to them for recreation. At this period drinking customs permeated the business and social life of the nation to an extraordinary degree. Ale and stout were cheap beverages, as universally popular with young and old alike as tea and coffee are today. Originally, ale had been brewed in every village, usually by womenfolk, but by the eighteenth century commercial brewing was well under way.

The famous Edinburgh taverns live on in the literature of the eighteenth and early nineteenth centuries. Johnnie Dowie's Tavern, in Libberton's Wynd (a steep lane leading from the High Street to the Cowgate), had become something of a tourist attraction by 1834, the year in which it was demolished to make way for the King George IV Bridge. It was so badly situated that all of its sitting rooms were windowless with the exception of two, into which light filtered from the gloomy Wynd. The largest room could accommodate fourteen people, more or less, while the smallest – nicknamed the "coffin" – was little more than a closet. Despite these inadequacies, Dowie's Tavern was frequented by some of the most distinguished Scottish artists and literati of the late eighteenth and early nineteenth centuries, including Hume, Raeburn, Fergusson and Burns. The speciality of the house was Archibald Younger's Edinburgh ale, a potent fluid which, if surviving accounts can be relied on, had a tendency to glue the lips of the imbiber together.

Tavern dissipation, now so rare amongst the respectable classes of the community, formerly prevailed in Edinburgh to an incredible extent, and engrossed the leisure hours of all professional men, scarcely excepting even the most stern and dignified. No rank, class, or profession, indeed, formed an exception to this rule. Nothing was so common in the morning as to meet men of high rank and official dignity reeling home from a close in the High Street, where they had spent the night in drinking. Nor was it unusual to find two or three of His Majesty's most honourable Lords of Council and Session mounting the bench in the forenoon in a crapulous state.

Robert Chambers' *Traditions of Edinburgh,* the source of the above, quotation, was first published in 1824, by which time the moral tone of Edinburgh society was almost Victorian, and the solid citizens were more decorous.

Prior to the late Georgian expansion of Edinburgh, most of the population lived in cramped and insanitary conditions in a miniature Manhattan of multi-storey flatted skyscrapers. The towering tenement "land" was occasionally a microcosm of the contemporary urban order, with aristocrats and artisans sharing a common entrance and turnpike stair. This democratic state of affairs was ultimately terminated by the construction of the spacious but exclusive New Town. The cellars of the great stone hive sheltered the wretchedly poor, including those engaging tatterdemalions, the caddies. The ground floor usually consisted of shops, while the first one or two floors above ground level were occupied by citizens of modest means, shopkeepers, clerks and the like. Flats on the third and fourth floors fetched the highest rents; the fortunate tenants were isolated from the noises and odours of the street, but at the same time they did not have too many stairs to climb. There dwelt the judge, the dowager countess, the physician and the clergyman. The upper storeys and the garrets were let at very moderate rents to people endowed with the fortitude and stamina to scale interminable flights of dark winding stairs.

In the claustrophobic conditions of mid-eighteenth century Edinburgh, the taverns were homes from homes for their habitues. Lawyers or physicians could be tracked down to their favourite howffs, and Cleriheugh's Tavern – the Star and Garter in Writers' Court – was as good a place as any to look for the magistrates and town council. In Sir Walter Scott's Guy Mannering, Colonel Mannering and Dandie Dinmont went thither in search of Councillor Pleyell. They found the lawyer and his cronies engaged in the sort of jovial drinking bout which, in the following century, would be increasingly frowned on as "tavern dissipation." Scott's description of this celebrated Edinburgh tavern is a vivid one.

Besides the miserable entrance, the house itself seemed paltry and half ruinous. The passage in which they stood had a window to the close, which admitted a little light during the day-time, and a villainous compound of smells at all times, but more especially towards evening.

Corresponding to this window was a borrowed light on the other side of the passage, looking into the kitchen, which had no direct communication with the free air, but received in the day-time, at second hand, such straggling and obscure light as found its way from the lane through the window opposite. At present, the interior of the kitchen was visible by its own huge fires – a sort of pandemonium, where men and women, half-undressed, were busied in baking, broiling, roasting oysters, and preparing devils on the gridiron; the mistress of the place, with her shoes slip-shod, and her hair straggling like that of Magaera from under a round-eared cap, toiling, scolding, receiving orders, giving them, and obeying them all at once, seemed the presiding enchantress of that gloomy and fiery region.

Some of the most convivial retreats of old Edinburgh were situated in the long, narrow, steep and malodorous closes (passageways) leading off each side of the Lawnmarket and the High Street. The tavern's dingy little rooms preserved the autonomy of the various groups of patrons. Stolid tradesmen were able to "talk shop" over their moderate draughts of ale or porter, oblivious of the ribaldry emanating from a bevy of drunken law-clerks or the wit and wisdom exuded by a coterie of impecunious men of letters. Shortly before noon, at the sound of the music bells of St. Giles, the good citizen left his work and repaired to his favourite hostelry for a restorative dram, known as the "meridian." At eight o'clock in the evening the working day was over for merchants, artisans and apprentices, and as the welcome bell, familiarly called the "tinkle sweetie," rang out, men's thoughts lingered on the prospect of minced collops or rizzared haddocks, washed down with claret or porter. This was the genial hour, immortalised by the poet Fergusson, when the taverns filled up and hard-working folk took their ease.

> Whan auld Saunt Giles, at eight o'clock,
> Gars merchant lowns their shopies lock,
> There we adjourn wi' hearty fouk
>   To birle our bodles,
> And get wharewi' to crack our joke,
>   And clear our noddles.

In the Edinburgh of the early eighteenth century, by order of the magistrates, no one was permitted to linger in the taverns after ten o'clock, and the drum-tattoo of the city guard, like the modern publican's "time gentlemen, please," would brook no denial. Later in the century the ten o'clock drum still sounded its ultimatum, but only the casual drinker was likely to call for his "lawin" (reckoning) and make his way home. Serious topers, magistrates among them, stayed on; perhaps they were wise to do so, for the drum was also the signal for the inhabitants of the tenements to empty the tubs of human excrement from their windows, with warning cries of "gardy loo" (gardez l'eau).

Robert Fergusson was as familiar with the pleasures and perils of "tavern dissipation" as any of his contemporaries, but his constitution was not of the strongest, and he was only twenty-four when he expired in the Bedlam attached to the Edinburgh Poorhouse. His well-known poem Auld Reikie is a fascinating evocation of old Edinburgh, with due emphasis on conviviality.

> Now, some to porter, some to punch –
> Some to their wife, – and some their wench, –
> Retire; – while noisy ten-hour's drum
> Gars a' your trades gae danderin home.

Now, mony a club, jocose and free,
Gie a' to merriment and glee:
Wi' sang, and glass, they fley the pow'r
O' Care, that wad harass the hour:
For wine and Bacchus still bear down
Our Thrawart fortune's wildest frown;
It maks you stark, and bauld, and brave,
Even whan descendin to the grave.

The Edinburgh clubs, of which there were a great many, also met in the taverns. The members of the Sweating Club were a thoroughly nasty set; that is, unless they have been grossly libelled. According to Chambers:

After intoxicating themselves, it was their custom to sally forth at midnight, and attack whomsoever they met upon the streets. Any luckless wight was chased, jostled, pinched, and pulled about, till he not only perspired, but was ready to drop down and die with exhaustion.

The Spendthrift Club evidently tried to live up to the national reputation for frugality, for they had a rule that not more than 4½d per member was to be disbursed for an evening's entertainment!

Emerging from an Edinburgh tavern, the Georgian toper had to make his way home through an obstacle course of dark, narrow, refuse-strewn closes and wynds. In that age of heavy drinking it seems likely that he would have been none too steady on his feet, and he may have stumbled several times before he reached the security of his lodgings. An entry in James Boswell's Edinburgh Journal for 1774 is revealing in this respect.

I went to Fortune's; found nobody in the house but Captain James Gordon of Ellon. He and I drank five bottles of claret and were most profound politicians. He pressed me to take another; but my stomach was against it. I walked off very gravely though much intoxicated. Ranged through the streets till, having run hard down the Advocate's Close, which is very steep, I found myself on a sudden bouncing down an almost perpendicular stone stair. I could not stop, but when I came to the bottom of it, fell with a good deal of violence, which sobered me much. It was amazing that I was not killed or very much hurt; I only bruised my right heel severely.[1]

Boswell preferred to drink wine, but immoderate doses of Younger's Edinburgh ale would very likely have produced similar results. In eighteenth century Scotland, claret was consumed in huge quantities. It was shipped from Bordeaux to Leith, and when a new, duty free, consignment arrived, a hogshead was trundled around Edinburgh on a wagon – anyone could have a generous draught of wine, by way of a sample, for sixpence. It was also dispensed in a similar fashion in the streets of other Scottish towns. Claret was virtually the national drink, its ready availability being one of the advantages of Scotland's "auld alliance" with France; there was almost invariably a cask on tap in the most wretched Lowland tavern. It was also the favourite tipple of the intelligentsia – the famous judge Lord Newton considered that he was at his best after drinking six bottles. As the elder Allan Ramsay – wig-maker, bookseller and poet – observed:

> Good claret best keeps out the cauld,
> And drives away the winter sune;
> It makes a man baith gash and bauld,
> And heaves his saul beyond the mune.

Subsequently, a tax on claret and war between France and the United Kingdom conspired to diminish its popularity.

Fortune's Tavern was situated in the Stamp Office Close, and it was a favourite resort of high society in the Edinburgh of the 1760s and 70s. Dinners at Fortune's were showy and expensive affairs; it was probably a most comfortable establishment by the standards of the times, for it had originally been the town mansion of the Earl of Eglintoune. Dawney Douglas's Tavern in the Anchor Close was also a public house of the better sort, for it had a separate entrance leading to a fine apartment called the Crown Room. This was lit by two large windows, and the proprietor, sensible of having something out of the ordinary in the way of drinking parlours, reserved it for special occasions. A far less reputable hostelry than either of these was James Clark's Tavern in Fleshmarket Close, frequented by the remarkable Deacon William Brodie, respectable burgess by day, housebreaker by night.

Whisky, today the pre-eminent Scottish liquor, was an almost exclusively Highland beverage until the second half of the eighteenth century, when it achieved popularity in the Lowlands as the drink of the common man. Although praised by Fergusson and Burns, it did not become a prestigious stimulant until the late Victorian period. Eighteenth century whisky was fiery and pungent, and lacked the golden colour which was later to be induced by maturing the liquor in sherry casks or, more prosaically, adding gooey caramel; such whisky, one suspects, would not enjoy world-wide popularity today. Captain Edward Burt, an English officer of engineers employed on General Wade's road-making work, gave an account of whisky that was unlikely to commend it to his compatriots.

> Some of the Highland gentlemen are immoderate drinkers of Usky, – even three or four quarts at a sitting; and, in general, the people that can pay the purchase, drink it without moderation.
>
> Not long ago, four English officers took a fancy to try their strength in this bow of Ulysses, against the like number of the country champions, but the enemy came off victorious; and one of the officers was thrown into a fit of the gout, without hopes; another had a most dangerous fever, a third lost his skin and hair by the surfeit; and the last confessed to me, that when drunkenness and debate ran high he took several opportunities to sham it.[2]

Captain Burt also described twopenny, or small ale, as sold in the Highlands of Scotland in the early eighteenth century. It had little in common with ale as we know it today, nor did it bear much relation to the fine Scotch ales brewed in Edinburgh and elsewhere from the mid-eighteenth century onwards.

> This liquor is disagreeable to those who are not used to it; but time and custom will make almost anything familiar. The malt, which is dried with peat, turf, or furzes, gives to the drink a taste of that kind of fuel: it is often drank before it is cold out of a cap, or corf, as they call it: this is a wooden dish, with two ears or

handles, about the size of a tea-saucer, and as shallow, so that a steady hand is necessary to carry it to the mouth, and, in windy weather, at the door of a change,* I have seen the liquor blown into the drinker's face. This drink is of itself apt to give a diarrhoea; and therefore, when the natives drink plentifully of it, they interlace it with brandy or usky.[3]

If Highland ale left much to be desired, certain Lowland localities were in the process of developing brewing skills second to none. By the late eighteenth century the ales of Edinburgh, Alloa and Falkirk were justly celebrated, while Glasgow's specialities, stout and porter, were also much in demand. An immensely popular beverage for more than a hundred years, porter is reputed to have made its debut in 1772 when Ralph Harwood, a Shoreditch brewer, decided to produce a beer resembling "three threads" (this was a much requested mixture and was drawn from barrels containing three different qualities of ale). Harwood called his happy invention "entire butt" beer; it came to be known as porter because it rapidly established itself as the favourite drink of heavy manual workers, and of the London market porters in particular. Brewed from brown malts and quite heavily hopped, porter or entire was dark in colour with a distinctive bitter-sweet flavour. London porter was matured in large wooden vats over a prolonged period and was a potent and sustaining beverage.

In the 1770s porter was brewed in Glasgow by Murdoch, Warroch, and Company at the Anderston Brewery, and also by John Struthers whose brewery was situated in the Gallowgate, on the site of the present Kent Street. When first introduced, around 1760, the Glasgow equivalent of porter fell far short of perfection; whether or not it contained a strong infusion of liquorice, as many people believed, it was undoubtedly inferior to the porter produced by London brewers such as Richard Meux, Samuel Whitbread and Sir Benjamin Truman. Determined to brew porter similar to the best porter from London, Murdoch, Warroch, and Company obtained the services of one Nathaniel Chivers, a London-trained brewer. Chivers came to Glasgow in October 1775; within a year, thanks to his expertise, Murdoch and Warroch were able to market a beverage of the requisite flavour and quality. Having succeeded in their aims, the proprietors of the Anderston Brewery then saw fit to dispense with the services of Chivers; he was handed his fare to London and politely shown the door. Predictably, he travelled only as far as John Struthers' brewery in the Gallowgate. Chivers' contract with the Anderston Brewery Company had stipulated that he should not reveal the mystery of London porter brewing to the proprietors of any of the other breweries in Glasgow and its environs, and so when it came to the notice of the Company that he was brewing porter on Struthers' premises the machinery of the law was put in motion. In due course a Court of Session interdict prevented Chivers from disseminating his knowledge of London methods, but not before John Struthers had acquired a sufficient understanding of the London process to successfully compete with Murdoch, Warroch, and Company.

Oyster cellars were public houses of the most rudimentary sort, and the oyster beds of the Forth provided abundant supplies. One of the most popular of the Edinburgh oyster cellars was kept by Luckie (i.e. – ale-wife) Middlemass. Fergusson was a regular customer.

> Whan big as burns the gutters rin,
> Gin ye hae catcht a droukit skin,
> To Luckie Middlemist's (sic) loup in,
>   And sit fu' snug
> Owre oysters and a dram o' gin,
>   Or haddock lug.

In the late eighteenth century, fashionable society took to frequenting the oyster cellars, delighting in the simple pleasures of the lower orders. Anglican Captain Edward Topham, sojourning in Edinburgh during the winter of 1774-75, was duly invited to rendezvous with a gentlewoman of his acquaintance in an oyster cellar. Knowing nothing of the modish Scottish predilection for "High Life below Stairs" he felt justified in looking forward to a romantic and clandestine assignation or, as he put it, "a partie tete-a-tete." On being ushered into the cellar, Topham was more than a little surprised to find, not one lady as he had expected, but "a large and brilliant company of both sexes."

The large table, round which they were seated, was covered with dishes full of oysters, and pots of porter. For a long time, I could not suppose that this was the only entertainment we were to have, and I sat waiting in expectation of a repast that was never to make its appearance. This I soon verified, as the table was cleared, and glasses introduced. The ladies were now asked whether they would choose brandy or rum punch? I thought this question an odd one, but I was soon informed by the gentleman who sat next me, that no wine was sold here; but that punch was quite "the thing." The ladies, who always love what is best, fixed upon brandy punch, and a large bowl was immediately introduced. The conversation hitherto had been insipid, and at intervals: it now became general and lively. The women, who, to do them justice, are much more entertaining than their neighbours in England, discovered a great deal of vivacity and fondness for repartee. A thousand things were hazarded, and met with applause; to which the oddity of the scene gave propriety, and which could have been introduced in no other place. The general ease, with which they conducted themselves, the innocent freedom of their manners, and their unaffected good-nature, all conspired to make us forget that we were regaling in a cellar; and was a convincing proof, that, let local customs operate as they may, a truly polite woman is every where the same. . . The bill for entertaining half a dozen very fashionable women, amounted only to two shillings a-piece. If you will not allow the entertainment an elegant one, you must at least confess that it is cheap.[4]

Ambrose's Tavern, demolished in 1864, but immortalised in John Wilson and James Hogg's "Noctes Ambrosianae" (1822-1835), exemplified the old style of Edinburgh hostelry at its best. A three-storeyed vernacular building, it stood in Gabriel's Road, on the approximate site of the present Cafe Royal. The Blue Parlour in Ambrose's was a favourite haunt of the three literary convivialists – "Christopher North" (Wilson), the "Ettrick Shepherd" (Hogg) and "Timothy Tickler" (Robert Sym, W. S.).

16

In general, the inns and taverns of eighteenth and early nineteenth century Glasgow were just as basic as those of Edinburgh. A notable exception was the famous Saracen's Head in the Gallowgate, which was frequented by the elite of the town. In 1754 the magistrates and town council of Glasgow disposed of the disused churchyard of Little Saint Mungo to one Robert Tennent, gardener and vintner, and empowered him "to build thereon a commodious and convenient inn . . . all of good hewn stone, three storys (sic) high," in conformity to a plan which they provided. Tennent was given permission to "pull doun" the old Gallowgate or East port (gateway) and take the stones for his own use on the understanding that he paid the town treasurer the sum of £10 sterling. Within a year the site of the burial ground was occupied by the Saracen's Head; it was constructed on "the most modern principles," for whereas the bedrooms in other Glasgow inns were interconnected, those in Tennent's hostelry were self-contained and opened onto corridors. When the proprietor duly inserted an advertisement in the Glasgow Journal he laid stress on the novelty and convenience of this arrangement.

Robert Tennant (sic), who formerly kept the White Hart Inn, without the Gallowgate port, is removed to the Saracen's Head, where the port formerly stood.

He takes this opportunity to acquaint all ladies and gentlemen, that at the desire of the magistrates of Glasgow, he has built a convenient and handsome new inn, agreeable to a plan given him, containing 36 fine rooms, now fit to receive lodgers. The bed-chambers are all separate, none of them entering through another, and so contrived that there is no need of going out of doors to get to them. The beds are all very good, clean, and free from bugs. There are very good stables for horses, and a pump well in the yard for watering them, with a shade within the said yard for coaches, chaises, or other wheel carriages.

As the said Robert Tennant has been at a very great expense in building this inn, and making it commodious for his guests, he hopes to have the countenance and encouragement of all his old friends and customers, who may depend on their being rightly accommodated and well used.

*There is a large room where 100 people can be entertained at one time.[5]

Tennent did not in fact recoup the "very great expense" of the Saracen's Head, for he died bankrupt in 1757. The inn, which at that time consisted of "twenty-five fine rooms and beds . . . a neat and well finished stabling, with stalls for 20 horses, a coach-house, and a large new billard (sic) table," was then let at 50 guineas a year to Katherine Tennent, widow of the deceased Robert. On her death it was sold to James Graham, landlord of the Black Bull in the Westergate (the rival hotel at the opposite, West End of the town; the Westergate is now known as Argyle Street). Among the many distinguished visitors who enjoyed the amenities of the Saracen's Head over the years were James Boswell and Samuel Johnson, on their return from the Highland jaunt.

On our arrival at the Saracen's Head Inn, at Glasgow, I was made happy by good accounts from home; and Dr. Johnson, who had not received a single letter since we left Aberdeen, found here a great many, the perusal of which entertained him much. He enjoyed in imagination the comforts which we could now command, and seemed to be in high glee. I remember, he put a leg up on each side of the grate, and said, with a mock solemnity, by way of soliloquy, but loud enough for me to hear it, "Here am I, an ENGLISH man, sitting by a COAL fire."[6]

In 1792 the Saracen's Head was converted into a tenement of shops and flats. At the beginning of the nineteenth century a new Saracen's Head Inn was built on the opposite side of Gallowgate; to this hostelry the old inn's hanging sign – a colourful representation of a wild-eyed Saracen warrior – was duly transferred. In the early 1900s part of the original Saracen's Head property consisted of a public house, the licence of which was held by a Mrs. MacPhail. In 1905, shortly before the historic building was demolished, she removed to a handsome new pub at the corner of Saracen Head Lane. This pub, inevitably, was called the Saracen's Head; it is still in existence (1983), albeit in a very dilapidated condition. The frontage incorporates two interesting painted panels, depicting the Old College in the High Street and the first Saracen's Head Inn.

The taverns and dram shops of late eighteenth and early nineteenth century Glasgow were commonly located in "pends" or closes, like the Black Boy and the Elephant, both of which were situated in the Gallowgate. Patrons made themselves at home in one of several sitting rooms, the refreshments of their choice being brought to them by the landlord or one of his assistants. At their best, these hostelries were snug parlours where the firelight played over sturdy furniture, china ornaments, copper utensils, and the quart pewter flagons known as "tappit hens".

Advertising in the Glasgow Courier (January 1, 1823) William Menzies, proprietor of the Three Tun Tavern, 19 Trongate and 173 Saltmarket, thanked his friends and the public for their "very liberal encouragement" and assured them that he would "ever make it his most anxious and unremitting study to merit a continuance of their patronage." Menzies had "constantly on hand an excellent stock of old wines, spirits, ales, and porter, from houses of the first respectability," and also served "soups, dinners, &c. on the shortest notice, and in the most elegant style." The following year the Three Tun Tavern had a new landlord, John Lemon from Carlisle, who announced that he had "laid in a stock of excellent old wines, spirits, ales, &c., of the first qualities and flavours," in the hope that these, along with "strict attention and moderate charges," would "entitle him to a share of public patronage." (The Glasgow Courier, June 10, 1824).

In 1824 the Eagle Inn and Renfrewshire Hotel in Maxwell Street, Glasgow, was taken on lease by James Frazer, who respectfully announced to "the nobility, gentry and commercial gentlemen, and the public in general," that he had fitted up the establishment "in an elegant style, with every attention to internal comfort and convenience." (The Glasgow Courier, June 19, 1824). As a recommendation to families visiting the city it was intimated that the Eagle Inn was "contiguous to the River Clyde, and in a very retired situation." The original inn was demolished at the turn of the century, owing to the extension of St. Enoch Station. A pub of Edwardian origin called the Old Eagle Inn stood in Howard Street until 1977 when the St. Enoch Station Hotel was demolished.

A newly-built tavern at 173 Dowhill's Close, "near the head of the Saltmarket," was advertised in the Glasgow Courier of Saturday, August 21, 1824. Consisting of "seven rooms and bar, with kitchen and extensive cellars in the sunk storey," it awaited "a respectable tenant" who was invited to apply to John Weir, architect, of 5 Great Hamilton Street.

Some Glasgow taverns had cock-pits and rat-pits in the back courts. Dog fights, cock fights and ratting with terriers were favourite pub entertainments, as popular then as darts, dominoes or music nowadays. Sparring matches were a popular diversion at a tavern kept by former prizefighter Jock Goudie – the Zebra at the foot of the High Street.

Rather more exclusive than the Zebra Tavern was the Crypt, located in the sunk storey of Thomas Hamilton's neo-classical Royal Exchange (now Stirling's Library) in Royal Exchange Place. Frequented by Glasgow's mercantile elite, it consisted of a bar, four comfortable private rooms – known as the "Ship," the "Star," the "Sun," and the "Globe" – and a row of dining compartments which were named after some of the better known capital cities of the world. The snugs were considerably more popular than the stalls, since it was felt that the latter – separated only by scarlet curtains suspended from brass rods – were conducive to eavesdropping.

Under the Home Drummond Act of 1828 (9 Geo. IV c.58) the would-be proprietor of a "common inn, alehouse, or victualling house" required, in addition to an Excise licence, a certificate from the local licensing authority. The justices of the peace for the counties and the magistrates of Royal or parliamentary burghs were authorised to grant certificates and hold half-yearly general meetings for the purpose of considering applications. The applicant usually had to convince the authorities that he was of good moral character; in Glasgow he was obliged to produce a certificate to that effect, signed by his minister or elder, or by two responsible householders. If, in spite of these references, he failed to obtain a certificate, he was at liberty to appeal against the decision of the magistrates or the justices in petty sessions to the assembled justices in Quarter Sessions. There was only one form of certificate for all kinds of licensed houses, and it was valid for a year or six months, according to whether it had been issued in the spring or in the autumn. Certificate holders were obliged to observe certain conditions and faced penalties if they neglected to do so. If convicted of using illegal weights and measures, permitting "unlawful" games "whereby the lieges may be cozened and cheated," or knowingly allowing "men or women of notoriously bad fame" or "dissolute girls and boys" to frequent his establishment, the licence holder was liable to be fined or imprisoned.

The Home Drummond Act allowed the publican considerable latitude with regard to "permitted hours," although he was not expected to dispense liquor at "unseasonable" hours or during the two periods of divine service on Sundays. The licensee who did not wish to incur the displeasure of the justices or magistrates kept what were then considered to be reasonable hours, opening at six o'clock in the morning and closing at midnight. The proprietors of low-class tippling shops were notoriously reluctant to close even for a few hours out of the twenty-four, and although they dutifully locked their doors during the hours of religious observance on Sundays, they allowed their customers to carry on drinking on the premises. The 1828 Act also gave the licensee the right of appeal at Quarter Sessions against summary convictions or the refusal by the magistrates or justices to grant, confirm, transfer or renew a licence.

In the 1840s the licensing authorities of Glasgow, Edinburgh and Dundee were strenuously endeavouring to reduce the quantity and improve the quality of licensed houses in their respective towns. Between 1834 and 1844 the Edinburgh magistrates closed upwards of 100 "superfluous" dram shops. Even so, there remained over 550 licensed premises – spirit shops, grocers, wine merchants, pie shops, eating houses, taverns, inns and hotels. In one street alone – the Cowgate – there were 53 shops licensed to sell exciseable liquors, and for the most part they were of a markedly inferior character. By the nineteenth century much of the venerable Old Town of Edinburgh had degenerated into a spectacular conglomeration of slums; the citizens of means had largely abandoned it, and their decaying mansions had been farmed out to the poorest classes. The New Town, to the "draughty parallelograms" of which the patrician class had flitted, was a world away from Blackfriars Wynd and other unsalubrious spots where the dram shops harboured pickpockets, fences, pimps, whores and beggars. But the New Town was not entirely devoid of public houses; there, however, they were relegated to minor thoroughfares such as Rose Street, which had no fewer than 32 pubs in 1846.

Until the passing of the Forbes Mackenzie Act in 1853 most grocers also sold spirits and frequently allowed them to be consumed on the premises. In the view of temperance reformers, this arrangement exposed virtually everyone to "the solicitations and to the temptations of a public house." It was held to be the cause of a considerable amount of surreptitious tippling among women, the whisky they obtained being entered in the weekly accounts as oatmeal or potatoes.

In a class by themselves were the early Victorian licensed houses known as singing saloons. These were rudimentary music halls, except that admission was secured by purchasing drink. Some singing saloons, resorts of business and professional men and representatives of the jeunesse doree, were expensively fitted up, but most were unpretentious establishments frequented by artisans, labourers and shopkeepers. With their pewter mugs of ale or porter conveniently to hand, the patrons sat on rough wooden benches, listened to the popular ballads of the day (rendered in stentorian fashion by resident vocalists), and joined in the choruses. The main singing saloons in Glasgow were situated in closes leading off the Saltmarket. They included the Shakespeare in Shakespeare Close, and the Jupiter in Jupiter Close. Such places did not meet with the wholehearted approval of the puritanical Scottish licensing authorities; by the turn of the century they had almost wholly succeeded in suppressing the toper's natural inclination to burst into song.

One of the most popular places of amusement in mid-Victorian Glasgow was the Whitebait, a licensed music hall, the entrance to which was in St. Enoch's Wynd, off Argyle Street. The prices of admission – sixpence and a shilling – also purchased a pint mug of beer or stout, a glass of spirits, or a cigar. John Muir, the worthy chairman of the Whitebait, was quite unlike the jovial, wise-cracking music hall chairman of nostalgic fiction. He had been a Free Church precentor in early life, and in the role of the Whitebait's master of ceremonies he carried out his duties with the utmost decorum. He did not speak much in his official capacity, seldom smiled, and hardly ever laughed. Whenever there was a particularly warm encore for some favourite turn, Muir would rise to his feet and exclaim, in sepulchral tones, "the lady will appear again, gentlemen!"

From the 1850s onwards many old-established Glasgow taverns were swept away in the course of redevelopment. Tom Hannah's in Gordon Street vanished in 1872 when a flamboyant glass and iron warehouse, modelled on the Venetian Casa d'Oro, replaced earlier buildings. Internally, Hannah's Tavern had been divided up into a number of small booths, each favoured by a coterie of boon companions; the habitues had included William "Crimean" Simpson the painter and sculptor John Mossman.

The gin "palace," a glorified gin shop, made its debut in London about 1828 and soon became tremendously popular. For the price of a dram, the starveling from the slum tenement gained admittance to a novel type of pub which, with its expensive fittings and bright lights, made him feel like a millionaire. It was not without its disagreeable aspects, however, and these were lovingly portrayed by George Cruikshank; in one of his most outrageously biased cartoons the gin palace was transformed into a place of nightmarish horror, with barrels resembling coffins, cadaverous customers, and hobgoblins capering in the spirit vaults. A zealous teetotaler, Cruikshank was a hostile witness. For a more impartial impression of the metropolitan gin palace we must consult Charles Dickens and "Sketches by Boz" (1835):

> A bar of French-polished mahogany, elegantly-carved, extends the whole width of the place, and there are two side-aisles of great casks, painted green and gold, enclosed within a light brass rail, and bearing such inscriptions as "Old Tom, 548," "Young Tom, 360," "Samson, 1421" – the figures agreeing, we presume with "gallons," understand. Beyond the bar is a lofty and spacious saloon, full of the same enticing vessels, with a gallery running round it, equally well furnished.

Sweetened gin had long been known as "Old Tom," and some of the distillers used the device of a cat, or a cat sitting on a barrel, on their labels and advertisements.

Throughout the 1830s and 1840s hundreds of gin palaces sprang up in London and other English cities, and by the 1850s the same phenomenon was also in evidence in Scotland. The Scottish equivalent of the gin palace was especially prevalent in Glasgow. "Midnight Scenes and Social Photographs" (1858), published under the pseudonym "Shadow" (the author was Alexander Brown, a jobbing printer with a well-developed social conscience), with a frontispiece by the irrepressible George Cruikshank, contains a reference to pubs with "flaring gas lights in frosted globes, and brightly gilded spirit casks, lettered by the number of gallons, under the cognomen of "Old Tom" or "Young Tom," as the case may be, with the occasional mirror at the extreme end of the shop." The "palatial" gin shop was mainly devoted to perpendicular drinking, although some provision was usually made for those who were too old, too tired, or too drunk to stand.

The Highland clearances and the Irish potato famine had brought many thousands of penniless immigrants to Glasgow, Edinburgh and other Lowland towns. The drinking habits of these newcomers – particularly their fondness for spirits – together with their poverty, no doubt helped to establish the popularity of the new-style dram shops. In spite of brilliant illumination and a certain amount of meretricious ornament the mid-Victorian gin "palaces" of Glasgow were evidently rather sordid places. They were resorts of the wretchedly poor, and the proprietors were not the sort of men to be disturbed by the spectacle of human degradation. Well nourished and exquisitely dressed (according to "Shadow,") they had a nod of welcome for every customer, no matter how emaciated and ragged.

The self-respecting artisan or trader not surprisingly preferred to drink in a tavern, or in a tavern and chop-house combined. Unlike the garish gin shops, these establishments retained some of the characteristics of the eighteenth century hostelries. The ordinary tavern had a small bar at which the casual customer could have a quick refreshment, and a range of sitting rooms (several of which were small enough to be termed "boxes,") which afforded privacy to those who had time to linger over their cups. The tavern and chop-house also had a bar, but instead of "boxes" it had stalls fitted up with bench seats and tables. The days of both taverns and taverns-cum-chop-houses were numbered, however. From the 1880s onwards there rapidly evolved the full-blown late Victorian pub with its intriguing blend of functional and decorative features. At first it was strikingly similar in design to the earlier gin shop. The interior was dominated by a long serving counter (with plenty of space in front of it for perpendicular drinkers to muster). Behind the counter there were the familiar spirit casks – though by this time they held whisky instead of gin.

A detailed inventory, taken in April 1879 in the premises of George Eunson, a deceased Glasgow publican, helps us to envisage the appearance of the more traditional sort of Scottish urban pub in the years preceding the innovations of the last quarter of the century. Eunson, formerly a wool, rag and rope merchant, entered the licensed trade in the mid 1860s. His premises were in Spreull's Court (182 Trongate) and consisted, at the time the inventory was made, of a public bar, two rooms, and six "boxes" – the latter being self-contained snugs. The bar was mainly intended for standing customers and was equipped with "counter and fittings," eight wooden stock casks, four china barrels, a "crystal rack with shelving and mirrors," a cigar case, two stools, an eight day clock, and two gas pendants. One of the rooms contained "waxcloth" (linoleum), a table, thirteen chairs, a register grate and fender, a mantelpiece mirror, a gasalier, and a barometer. The furniture, fittings and utensils in one of the "boxes" were itemised as "waxcloth," a mahogany table, seats and cushions, a grate and fender, a mantelpiece mirror, a gasalier, a water carafe and tumbler, and six spittoons. In the cellar of the pub there were beer cranes, a block and tackle, a bottling stool, a rack for bottles, and a "copper pump," together with a stock of beers, wines and spirits in casks, flasks and bottles, including English bitter beer, Dublin stout, Reid's London stout, porter, Campbeltown and Irish "aqua" (whisky), rum, brandy, gin, port, claret, sherry, and champagne. Eunson's douce establishment, tucked away in Spreull's Court, was a cut above the low dram shops of nearby Saltmarket – it would doubtlessly have been patronised by "white-collar" workers such as tradesmen, shopkeepers and clerks.

The Scottish taverns of the eighteenth and early nineteenth centuries had been frequented by all classes and types, aristocrats, merchants, artisans, labourers, beggars, and thieves, but in the Victorian period the well-to-do increasingly abandoned the pubs, preferring to drink in the privacy of their homes and clubs. The patrons of the late Victorian licensed houses were drawn almost exclusively from the working and lower middle classes. Regrettably, as the Scottish pub became more opulent, it also shed some of its humanity. This was mainly the fault of the licensing authorities, who seemed determined to prevent the Scots drinker from enjoying himself.

For many years after the advent of the late Victorian palace pub, hostelries of the old quasi-domestic sort continued to survive in the back streets of the towns and cities, in the suburbs, and in the country. In the early 1890s one of the oldest Glasgow taverns, the Institution (11 Old Wynd and 21 King Street) – reputed to have been patronised at one time by Sir Walter Scott – was still going strong, and serving the habitues with ale and stout in silver tankards as of yore. It had been the favourite resort of students and masters of the Old College in the High Street, in the days when a professor was just as likely to call for a quart of porter as the most thirsty of undergraduates. The Waverley Bar was another Glasgow pub which preserved the internal arrangement of the pre-Victorian tavern well into the 1890s – snugly located in the Old Wynd in the Trongate, it was chock-full of "curiosities" such as skeletons, stuffed animals and old weapons. The Old Burnt Barns, at the junction of South Saint Mungo Street and Great Hamilton Street, considerably older than the Institution and the Waverley, was demolished in 1903. At the turn of the century many old-established taverns were condemned by the inflexible policies of the licensing authorities. In 1902, for example, the magistrates of Dundee "recommended" that the city's public houses should be removed from back streets and lanes to the principal thoroughfares; this "recommendation" of the bailies was tantamount to an order.

With the extension and electrification of the Glasgow tramways, villages on the periphery of the city were rapidly transformed into suburbs, and flatted tenements of four or more storeys rose on the sites of the village pubs with their cosy bar-parlours and their adjoining gardens or bowling greens. The names of the vanished village hostelries were sometimes perpetuated by the handsome Art Nouveau pubs that were conspicuous features of the new red sandstone tenements in Barrachnie, Pollokshaws, Yoker, and elsewhere. In the late 1890s the Old Drum in Shettleston was a long, low, one-storey tavern with a thatched roof – not unlike Burns' Cottage in Alloway. A few years later Henry Mair, the proprietor, commissioned architect George F. Boyd to erect a four-storey tenement on the site, with a ground-floor pub which, when completed, consisted of "a large and spacious bar . . . of horseshoe form, with neat and airy sitting rooms all round, well lit and handsomely furnished." (The Victualling Trades' Review, September 1902).

* change-house = tavern

1 James Boswell: Journal, 1774-76; entry for Friday, November 4, 1774.
2 Burt's Letters from the North of Scotland, 1754; volume 2, letter XXIV.

[3] Burt's Letters from the North of Scotland, 1754; volume 1, letter VIII.

[4] Edward Topham: Letters from Edinburgh in 1774 and 1775; letter XVI, January 15, 1775.

[5] The Glasgow Journal, number 743 (October 27-November 3, 1755).

[6] James Boswell: Journal of a Tour to the Hebrides with Samuel Johnson; entry for Thursday, October 28, 1773.

Part One

2　Background

The substantial late Victorian public house was principally an urban phenomenon, closely linked to the ambitious scale of contemporary urban renewal. Prosperous towns and cities were investing in prestige architecture, and in Scotland the favourite building material was not brick, but fine quality sandstone or granite. There were severe but dignified blocks of flats for people of modest means, stately villas and terraced houses for the wealthy, and a plethora of civic and commercial monuments such as town halls, museums, libraries, exchanges and banks. The pubs, like the new buildings of which they formed a part, were solidly constructed of good quality materials. Highly skilled labour was readily available, and it was cheap. Every self-respecting licensee wanted to preside over a large and exceptionally handsome establishment, and pubs were occasionally torn apart several times, to emerge after each refitting more palatial than before. The monthly journal of the Scottish licensed trade tried to keep track of alterations which, towards the end of the period, sometimes became positively esoteric.

> The alteration in the meantime only affects the sitting-room, but this apartment has been transformed into a veritable marble salon, a view of which inspires thoughts of the glories of ancient Greece. As you enter the room there arise walls of marble set off in panels by handsome mahogany beadings, each wall being centred with a handsome diamond-shaped slab. . .

> Besides being highly decorative, this patent serves also a utilitarian purpose, being everlasting, and last, but not least, possesses the special virtue of being always clean.[1]

"Everlasting" the marble may have been; but the architect reckoned without twentieth century vandalism, and the Metropolitan Bar has since disappeared from Glasgow's Sauchiehall Street. To be sure, the Victorians did not only lavish ornament on public houses, but on thousands of objects, large and small. Our remaining Victorian pubs have survived the destruction of much of their complementary environment and have themselves been mellowed and modified by the passage of time. It might therefore be worthwhile to try to envisage the late Victorian pub in its pristine state and original surroundings. To do so we have to travel back in imagination, to the Glasgow of 1897.

The city presents some remarkable contrasts. By far the majority of Glaswegians are flat-dwellers; there are many thousands of tall ashlar-fronted tenements, interminable canyons of soot-darkened stone. The grand mansions and terraced houses of the exclusive residential suburbs and the splendid ornamental piles of the business and commercial centre testify to high prosperity based on world trade and heavy industries such as iron-founding, shipbuilding and engineering. To the east of the Cathedral there is a majestic rocky necropolis, the mausoleums and temples of which show where deceased Victorian entrepreneurs have gone to ground while awaiting the last trump.

Glasgow, in this year of 1897, is an exceedingly enterprising city with barely concealed megalopolitan ambitions. It held its first great international exhibition in 1888, and will stage another two such exhibitions before the outbreak of war in 1914. Its impressive self-confidence has been expressed in practical concerns such as the new Glasgow District Subway – the first underground cable railway in the world – and in prestigious buildings such as the municipal chambers, a neo-Renaissance palace on a scale commensurate with the aspirations of "the workshop and second city of the British Empire." Emblematical figures of Truth, Riches and Honour are set on the apex of the pediment, presumably to spur the citizens on to still greater efforts.

Neither the motor-car nor the electric tram-car has yet usurped the streets of the city centre, which are filled instead with horse traffic, pedestrians and a small army of sandwich-men, newsboys, Italian organ-grinders, sellers of "sweet Seville oranges, three a penny," English flower girls, ragged urchins selling "Vespers, a penny a box," street artists, fiddle-scrapers, harpists and flautists. Sandwiched between lofty shop-fronts of iron and plate-glass or advantageously situated at street corners are the pubs, more flamboyant than the neighbouring shops, with engraved or stained glass windows and ornate lanterns suspended from brackets. The older type of pub has an interior which conforms to an established pattern, with a long straight counter, behind which are ranged polished casks containing the most popular brands of whisky. There are many licensed houses of this sort, but they are yielding pride of place to newer and more fashionable pubs – pubs such as the Stag Vaults, Candleriggs, in which the stock platform with its row of spirit casks is enclosed by an oval serving counter.

Let us now proceed to view the interior of just one of Glasgow's 1426 public houses. As it happens the pub we have ventured into is neither one of the most opulent nor one of the meanest. It is, however, very narrow, with a straight counter of considerable length, and the linoleum-covered floor is generously strewn with sawdust. Behind the counter there are six casks – three on either side of the middle section of the back-fitment. The barrels sit in niches, and the names and prices of the various whiskies are inscribed on their highly polished bellies. The central portion of the fitment, surmounted by a segmental pediment, consists of shelving backed by panels of brilliant cut mirror glass. Wood panelling constitutes a dado, above which the walls are covered with a heavy paper, patterned in crimson and gold. Gasaliers are suspended from the Lincrusta ceiling and attached to the upper halves of slender cast-iron pillars. There are two fireplaces with carved oak surrounds, tiled hearths, and mirrored overmantels. All the woodwork, including

26

the cooperwork, is dark-stained. There is a spacious sitting room, located at the rear of the premises, and built-in seats with dimpled upholstery of dark brown morocco are also provided in the bar-room proper. The walls are adorned with brewers' mirrors in heavy carved frames – these advertise Adamson's Stout, George Younger and Son's India Pale Ale, and Tennent's Lager Beer. There are also several framed sketches of picturesque Glaswegians of former days, among them Old Hawkie, beggar, street orator and wit, and Rab Haw the notorious glutton. On the customer's side of the bar counter there is a shallow marble trough for spitting into, and opposite the counter, brass spittoons stand against the wall.

There are no female customers in this pub, and we notice, rather to our surprise, that there are no bare-headed patrons either. Curly-brimmed pot hats are much in evidence, and one frock-coated individual, who is sipping his "Lord of the Isles" with evident relish, is sporting a silk topper. The barmen, stout mustachioed specimens, are uniformly garbed in white shirts, dark waistcoats and long white aprons. With a last lingering look at this pristine Victorian hostelry, we leave it to several generations of topers and ultimately, to the tender mercies of the mid twentieth-century "improvers."

Many Scottish pubs of the late Victorian and Edwardian periods celebrated broadly patriotic themes. There were numerous Union Jack, Empire, and Victoria bars. Two distinguished survivors, the Abbotsford and the Kenilworth in Edinburgh, allude to the life and work of Sir Walter Scott. The long since vanished Rob Roy in Glasgow's Gorbals was decorated with oil paintings and stained glass panels, depicting episodes from the career of that resourceful outlaw. The Rabbie Burns, also in Glasgow, was a shrine to the national bard; it too has disappeared, but we at least possess a description.

There is probably no licensed house in Scotland, not even in the town of Ayr, which perpetuates more effectively the immortal memory of the national bard than the "Rabbie Burns" in Trongate. . . Mr. Gilmour* has recently further enhanced the appearance of the interior with twelve rare plates of Gustave Dore's famous pictures of the Wandering Jew. The "Rabbie Burns" is one of the most comfortable houses in the city. The bar is large and the sitting-rooms models of comfort and ease. From day-light till eleven at night there is a continuous custom. Mine host is a gentleman of indefatigable energy, one who looks after the smaller details as well as the greater interests. He keeps an excellent staff of assistants, and of the high tone of the various drinks vended it would be invidious to speak[2]

The publicans of late Victorian Scotland were among the most ardent admirers of Burns, who, in "Willie brew'd a peck o maut" and other poems and songs, had written gloriously in praise of strong drink. The Rabbie Burns consisted of a public bar and six sitting rooms – one at the front of the pub and five at the back. Seats and tables were also placed opposite the long bar counter. Behind the bar, the stock fitment, ornately carved and enriched with ornamental ironwork, encased twelve spirit barrels. There was much stained and etched glass, the windows being decorated with scenes from the poet's works.

Most Scottish pubs at this time were commissioned by individual publicans rather than by brewers, and house-proud licence holders such as the proprietor of the Rabbie Burns created pubs of character, many of which strongly reflected the personalities and interests of their owners. James Macmillan travelled some 900 miles by covered wagon, from Cape Town to the Kimberley diamond fields. There he "struck a lucky seam" – not a very important one, it is true, but large enough to enable him to return to Scotland and set himself up in the licensed trade. In 1889 he acquired the Tivoli Bar in Glasgow's Bath Street, renamed it the Kimberley Bar, and decorated it with photographs and mementoes of mining camp life at the diamond diggings. Comedian and ex-music hall manager Richie Thom's Comedy Bar, also in Glasgow, was a gallery of music hall celebrities. George Ward, veteran of the Indian Mutiny and the Crimean War, adorned the walls of his pub in Partick with paintings and engravings of an appropriately martial character. Tuck's Bar in Paisley Road boasted a fine series of stained glass windows depicting various sporting pursuits; the proprietor, James "Tuck" McIntyre, had been a professional footballer with the Rangers Club.

Some of the most prominent wine and spirit merchants of the late Victorian and Edwardian periods were featured in the weekly or monthly publications of the licensed trade, as examples to the rising generation. In Scotland, the National Guardian and the Victualling Trades' Review provided portraits and potted biographies of well-known publicans. Some liked to be depicted in full Freemasonic regalia, others preferred to strike heroic attitudes in Highland dress or Volunteer uniform. The hirsute embellishments, virtually obligatory, ranged from luxuriant beards to waxed and spiked moustaches. The Guardian and the Review were both published in Glasgow, and being strongly imbued with local patriotism, gave precedence to articles about Glasgow-based publicans. Archibald Lauder of the Royal Lochnager Vaults, Sauchiehall Street, "besides being a wine merchant," was "an author as well," having "published a book entitled The Family of Lauder," which had been "very favourably reviewed by the press of Great Britain." (The Victualling Trades' Review, July 13, 1891). Alexander Vallance of the Red Lion Vaults, West Nile Street, had been "elected captain of the Rangers Football Club in the year 1881, but, before that, had performed the difficult duty of selecting the players for many years, a delicate position which he filled with rare tact and sound judgement." (The Victualling Trades' Review, August 15, 1898). George Shields Peat of the Pavilion Bar, Hope Street, originally hailed from Strathaven, but "his rambling ambition began to fret at the quiet and confinement of his native village; so, earnest and energetic, determined to push his way in the world if possible, he left for America and duly arrived in Illinois." Peat worked on a cattle and grain farm for several years, "and having become acclimatised to the country and learned something of the ways of the people," he then proceeded to Chicago. There "he took the first opportunity which offered and entered the service of the Tramway Company as a conductor, where he remained till the great fire of 1872 in which seven square miles of a populous city were laid in ruins." In the aftermath of the disaster "robbery, violence, pillage, and lawlessness" were rife, calling for "special protective measures" such as "Pinkerton's Preventive Staff," which Peat joined. He subsequently "went into commercial life, travelling for Singers amongst others." (The Victualling Trades' Review, October 1896).

In the late Victorian period there were two main employment opportunities for unskilled women workers – the factories and domestic service. In view of the limited number of occupations which were open to women, it is not surprising that quite often, a female thrown on her own resources – perhaps by the death of the family breadwinner – preferred to work as a barmaid, even though the Victorian barmaid's lot was an unenviable one. In 1903 the publicans of Glasgow were sternly forbidden, on pain of forfeiture of their licences, to employ barmaids. The licensing magistrates' ultimatum was not, as one might suppose, delivered because of their concern for exploited female labour – at least some of the barmaids, deprived of their livelihoods, would have found work of an even more gruelling nature in factories. The magistrates felt that the barmaids were in great moral danger, and were resolved, in consequence, to save them from "a fate worse than death." The Glasgow bailies had previously made themselves objectionable by proposing to suppress the public exhibition of paintings which they considered to be indecent. Some Glasgow barmaids, averse to being abolished, made their way to London, Liverpool, and other places where the Glasgow magistrates' puritanism seemed merely comical.

There is much amusement in London over the determination of the Glasgow magistrates to abolish the barmaid, and their campaign is looked upon in much the same light as their notorious campaign against the "Slave Market" picture. London does not, however, fully understand the Glasgow position, being unaware that barmaids in public-houses, that are public-houses and nothing else, are practically unknown, and that the total number of barmaids in Glasgow is only about a hundred. The action of the Bailies, who are looked upon as terrible fellows – dour, Calvinistic, suspicious – has a tendency to puzzle the Cockneys, who can't understand how such people can be in a city that in many respects even the Cockneys regard as highly enlightened. In London the barmaids are numbered by thousands, and the likelihood of their abolition is practically nil. The Metropolis does not see the hand of the devil in the sale of a half-pint of beer.[3]

The late Victorian toper frequently had his enjoyment marred by the supplicants of all ages who importuned him for a few coppers, or insisted on telling him their personal tales of woe.

While enjoying a glass of ale at a well-known bar the other evening I was accosted by an Italian organ-grinder for a penny, by three boys to buy the latest edition of the Evening News, two girls to buy flowers, an old baker who had walked all the way from Leith and wanted 2d to help to pay a bed, an old woman selling Orr's Almanack, a boy selling puzzles, and three or four mixed ages and sexes selling matches. Would it not be to the interest of proprietors to keep these people out and not have their customers molested?[4]

As if it was not enough to be continuously assailed by the hapless casualties of laissez-faire, the long-suffering customer had also to endure such grotesque bar-room specimens as the Masher.

He surveys the world over his collar with that air of melancholy contemplation with which a donkey stretches his head on a gate; nor is this expression improved when he smiles the broad smile of idiocy, or when he laughs the vacant maniacal laugh which is peculiar to his kind. The laugh of the "masher" is as distinctive as the laugh of the hyena, and just as unpleasant; it is as characteristic of the "masher" as his collar. . .[5]

The Masher was a suburban dandy — lower middle class and impecunious, but full of affectations. He generally wore boots with pointed toes, "excruciatingly tight" trousers, a very short coat, a "stupendously high" collar, and a bowler hat with a brim "like a pig's tail." Mashers considered barmaids to be their natural prey, but in Glasgow at any rate, their fell designs had been anticipated by the ever-vigilant magistrates.

At the turn of the century it was customary for the young aspirant to public house ownership to enter the employment of an established licence holder in order to become thoroughly familiar with every aspect of the retail licensed trade. In due course, if hard-working and trustworthy, he graduated from bar-hand to charge-hand (manager). Having completed his "education," his next move was to start up in business on his own account, and since his savings were usually insufficient to allow him to take this step unaided, he was generally obliged to obtain financial backing. Comparatively few Scottish pubs were "tied houses" in the English meaning of the expression, but it was certainly not an unusual occurrence for a Scottish brewer or whisky merchant to advance money to a prospective licence holder, thereby enabling him to acquire suitable premises. In return, the publican was expected to take at least some of his stock from his creditor. To that extent the house was "tied," but the Scottish publican, unlike the tenant of an English "tied house," was the actual licence holder, and when he paid off the loan — as sooner or later he often contrived to do — he became a free agent and was able to take his stock from anyone he pleased.

In the early 1900s Messrs. G. & J. MacLachlan controlled a large network of pubs in Glasgow and the neighbouring counties of Lanarkshire and Renfrewshire. Brothers George and John MacLachlan originally hailed from the Perthshire village of Strathallan. They migrated to Glasgow as young men; George opened licensed premises in 1869, and John followed suit, in an independent capacity, in 1876. George, the elder and more enterprising of the pair, acquired the prestigious Grand Hotel at Charing Cross, subsequently sold it at a healthy profit, then purchased the old-established firm of Messrs. J. & J. McCulloch, spirit brokers. In 1888 the brothers went into partnership, and having adopted a castle as their trademark, along with the motto "Fortes et Fides," they proceeded to acquire a chain of retail outlets. "Their Castle licensed houses increased in number. These took the place of establishments which had not the best repute, and were so well managed by Messrs. MacLachlan as to be regarded by the authorities and even by strong temperance advocates as models in their line. Only the best liquors were sold in them, anything of the "kill the carter" character* being rigidly excluded." (The Grocer's Monthly, May 1, 1905). In 1889 a disused mill at Maryhill was transformed into the Castle Brewery for the production of ales and stouts, and in 1900 a second Castle Brewery was established at Duddingston, Edinburgh. The following year the brothers MacLachlan purchased the Auchentoshan distillery at Duntocher. In the Edwardian period the firm's "Castle Brand" ales and stouts and

"Five Castle," "Iona," and "Auchentoshan" brands of whisky were being exported to South Africa, Australia, and India. The nerve-centre of the brothers' operations was Castle Chambers, an imposing office block, erected in central Glasgow in 1899-1902.

An enthusiast of horseracing, George MacLachlan maintained "a fairly numerous stud," and was "the possessor of many cups and other trophies." (The Bailie, November 27, 1895). He helped to establish Hamilton Park Racecourse, which was opened, in 1888, on the Duke of Hamilton's grounds at Hamilton Palace. Hamilton Park became the favourite venue of sporting publicans and their cronies.

Mr. and Mrs. George MacLachlan and family resided at 8 Park Terrace, in the most exclusive part of Glasgow's West End. Like any other prosperous individual in late Victorian or Edwardian Scotland, the successful publican was able to live exceedingly well. If he could not afford to rent or buy a house in the most fashionable part of town he was at least able to build one in a newly emerging residential suburb. He dressed as nattily as any professional man, and occasionally even kept a carriage. Of the most prominent Glasgow publicans, David Ross, Philip MacSorley and John MacLachlan lived in the West End, at Carlton Terrace, Queen Margaret Crescent and St. James Terrace respectively. Gray Edmiston had a villa in Shawlands, John Scouller occupied "The Moss," Pollokshields, and Samuel Dow stayed at "Brae-Rannoch," Bellahouston.

Samuel Dow was a famous name in connection with the licensed trade in Glasgow. There had been a Samuel Dow in the Glasgow trade since at least 1807, and the tradition was carried on through three generations, until 1895. In that year the last Samuel Dow died, aged 48 – as a boy of 15 he had migrated from Lochaber to Glasgow in order to enter the wine and spirit establishment of his uncle and cousin; in due course he became one of the partners, and in 1881 sole partner. He increased and extended the business considerably, transferring the headquarters from Mitchell Street to Great Clyde Street where he had offices, sample rooms and vats. "Samuel Dow's Special Blend" of "old Highland whisky" was exported to Australia, India, China, the United States and the Continent. On the death of the proprietor the business was carried out by a general manager, John C. Barratt; in 1899 it was converted into a limited company with Barratt as managing director.

Before the First World War houses for rent were generally provided by private landlords and speculative builders rather than by local authorities, and an appreciable number of Scottish publicans took advantage of this situation to invest in property, the rents of which, collected by factors, provided them with a steady and sure return. Glasgow, the industrial heart of Scotland, saw a prodigious amount of tenement building in the Victorian and Edwardian periods. There were handsome terraced tenements for the middle classes, with flats containing many generously proportioned rooms, and more utilitarian tenements for the working classes in which the flats were much smaller. All the tenements were imposing in scale and immensely solid in construction. Due to the tenement mode of housing, the density of population was extremely high, and by 1914 there were no fewer than 700,000 people living in three square miles – the most heavily populated central area in Europe. The working class family with a very low income usually occupied a "single-end" (Anglice, single-apartment flat), which was kitchen, living-room and bedroom, all in one. In spite of gross overcrowding there were a considerable number of empty flats, since quite a lot of people economised by taking lodgings instead of renting a flat of their own. In some of the working class tenements metal labels (known as "tickets") were affixed to the door frames of the flats, indicating the number of adults and children permitted to sleep there; sanitary inspectors occasionally made nocturnal spot-checks to ensure that the number was not being exceeded.

In view of the city's exploding population (it was over three quarters of a million by 1891, and reached the million mark shortly before the Great War) and the overcrowding which prevailed, it is not surprising that many people, publicans among them, considered tenement property to be a particularly safe investment – "as safe as houses" in fact. Thus, in 1893, a Glasgow publican by the name of John Meikle acquired a tenement in Sandyfaulds Street for the sum of £5,300, and in 1898 a similar property in Rutherglen Road for £2,450. At the time of Meikle's death, in 1905, the Sandyfaulds Street tenement was realising £219. 17s per annum in rents; the yearly rent for a room and kitchen flat was £9. 18s. Glasgow publicans did not only purchase existing tenements; they also financed the building of new ones. Typical in this respect was George Honeyman Farmer, one of the best known licence holders in the East End of Glasgow. He erected a five-storey tenement on the site of his old place of business at Parkhead Cross, one of the tramcar termini. Designed by the firm of Burnet, Boston and Carruthers and completed in 1902, it was constructed of red sandstone ashlar and polished granite. Spacious licensed premises were provided for Mr. Farmer on the ground floor. The building, with its distinctive corner tower, is still standing, but the pub, alas, is no more. David Ross of the Waterloo Bar, Wellington Street, and the Gordon Bar, Mitchell Street, was a friend and business associate of architect Frank Burnet. In 1900 he commissioned Burnet to erect a range of tenements, replete with shops, in Battlefield Road, Sinclair Drive, and Battlefield Gardens. When the Glasgow publican built a tenement he frequently incorporated shops, along with a pub which, if it happened to be his second or third such establishment, would probably have been placed in the hands of a close relation , a business associate or a manager.

Lloyd George's budget of 1909-10, which put a twenty per cent tax on the increment value of all heritable property, made it uneconomical for private enterprise to continue to erect tenement houses to rent, while the Rent Restrictions Act of 1915 further limited the profitability of tenement properties.

Glasgow publicans occasionally also built warehouses and offices, utilising some of the space themselves and letting or leasing the remainder. David Ross's greatest property venture was Gordon Chambers, designed by Frank Burnet and completed in 1907 – a large block of buildings comprising offices, warehouses and shops, situated in Mitchell Street, Mitchell Lane, and Gordon Lane. Several flats of George and John MacLachlan's Castle Chambers (West Regent Street and Renfield Street) were occupied by the General Post Office and the Board of Trade. Above the Vale of Leven Spirit Vaults in Dundas Street there were an additional four storeys. William Campbell, the spirit merchant who had erected the building, envisaged that the two flats immediately above the bar would be "let as offices or warehouses," while the upper storeys would be "used as a Masonic hall, with adjuncts of committee and side rooms." (The Victualling Trades' Review, November 12, 1891).

Surprisingly, only a small minority of Glasgow's licence holders owned the actual properties in which they plied their trade – the rest leased their "shops," paying rents which, in 1897, varied from £15 to £1000 per annum (the average annual rental was £96. 18. 6d). Glasgow publicans frequently complained bitterly about "rack-renting" landlords – landlords, that is, who demanded excessively high rents – and blamed the licensing magistrates for their unsympathetic attitude to licence holders who wished to move from one set of premises to another. It is noteworthy that in the early 1900s, when the temperance movement was particularly strong in Glasgow, the owners of public house properties in the city included a fair sprinkling of "pillars of society" – Members of Parliament, magistrates, councillors, doctors and clergymen, as well as such reputable institutions as the Bank of Scotland, the Clyde Trust, the Glasgow District Subway Company and the Faculty of Procurators.

In October 1910 the Scottish Licensed Trade drew its subscribers' attention to a lot consisting of nine public houses in Glasgow which were up for sale. The pubs were respectively situated at 126 Trongate, 21 Candleriggs, 315 Port Dundas Road, 203 Wallace Street, 253 St. Vincent Street, 112 King Street, 273-5 Buchanan Street, 128 Piccadilly Street, and 540 Dobbie's Loan. The rents of these premises ranged from £30 to £280 per annum, while the weekly drawings averaged from £11 to £47. The average yearly turnover of spirits "for the last three years" was stated to run from 348.5 to 815.9 proof gallons, while that of the beer and stout totalled from 70 to 286 barrels, "entirely exclusive of bottled beer and stout."

Since late Victorian Glasgow lacked sprawling suburbs, heavily populated districts such as Cowcaddens, Maryhill and Gorbals were within easy walking range of the city centre, while the "distant" suburbs were easily accessible by tram or Subway. At night, therefore, central Glasgow did not quieten down, it livened up, and on Saturday night in particular it was full of noise and bustle: the pubs were chock-a-block, and so were the theatres and music halls. The Victualling Trades' Review (December 12, 1891) thought that the "wild hurly-burly" in the city centre on a Saturday night was "even more pronounced" than in central London or New York. Live entertainment was the great attraction in the days before radio and television, and there was, apparently, something for almost everybody; serious drama at the Theatre Royal, melodrama at the Metropole or the Royal Princess, or variety turns at the Britannia, Tivoli, or Queen's. And what turns! Hector Wright, "patriotic character and descriptive vocalist;" Peter and Minnie Lee, "black and white burlesque and speciality artistes;" J. H. Anthony, "the Scottish Dan Leno;" Miss Tina Crawford, "the Scottish Jenny Lind;" Nellie Hughes, "serio comedienne and top boot dancer;" Miss Polly Heath, "refined vocalist and coon songstress." The pubs in the immediate vicinity of the theatres and music halls gloried in their proximity to the "temples of Bacchus," proudly announced that they were "favourite resorts of the artistes," displayed posters advertising forthcoming attractions, and kept theatrical newspapers such as Music Hall, Era, and Stage.

In late Victorian Scotland the licensing authorities were generally reluctant to increase the number of public houses as towns and cities grew more populous. At the same time they were extremely anxious to do away with "low-class drinking dens" in run-down areas, hangovers from the bad old days when the licensing magistrates had been notoriously easy going. In 1876 the eight principal cities and towns of Scotland—Glasgow, Edinburgh, Dundee, Aberdeen, Greenock, Leith, Paisley, and Perth – had 2867 licensed premises between them, but by 1897, in spite of the overall increase in population, this figure had been reduced to 2523. In counties the proportion of licences to population varied from 1 to 2,251 in Nairn, to 1 to 202 in Kinross, and in burghs from 1 to 833 in Dumbarton, to 1 to 60 in Auchtermuchty.

Inevitably, the authorities' policy of restriction increased the value of public houses of the better sort, in the smaller towns as well as in the cities; for example, a pub in Inverness which had sold for £2,000 in 1869 fetched £7,000 in 1896. This was the equivalent of £70,000 in our debased modern currency.

In the Scotland of the 1880s £1,500 was considered to be a tidy sum to pay for a pub, and even in the late 1890s, when the value of licensed premises rose considerably, a pub of sorts could occasionally be purchased for as little as £700. Thriving concerns were fetching £6,000 to £10,000, however, and much larger sums were sometimes paid for pubs in central Glasgow – in Sauchiehall Street for instance.

These prices were paid largely on the strength of "goodwill" – that is, in consideration of factors such as the location of the pub, the duration of the lease, and the net annual trading profits over a number of years. In terms of "goodwill," a pub situated in a congested, over-licensed area (such as the Gorbals district of Glasgow) was likely to be worth considerably less than a pub situated in an area that could justly be described as under-licensed (such as the Mount Florida district of the same city). The Scottish Licensed Trade (December 1911) referred to a rule-of-thumb method of arriving at the "goodwill" value of a licence, which had been in vogue during the "boom" period in the licensed trade (i.e. – in the late 1890s). This was to allow £100 for every £1 of drawings, irrespective of what the rent or other charges were, so that if the average weekly drawings of a licensed business were £20, the value of the business in terms of "goodwill" was considered to be £2,000. Where the licensee was also the owner of the property in which his place of business was situated, the heritable property and the "goodwill" of the licensed business were usually valued separately.

Scottish pubs seldom changed hands for astronomical sums, akin to those that were being paid for pubs in some parts of England, and particularly for pubs in the Greater London area. This was mainly because the Scottish retail trade was relatively free – the brewers were not jostling each other to buy up pubs, pushing up prices to a fantastic level in the process.

Regarding the late Victorian public houses of London, Mark Girouard has argued that they were "largely the creation of tough, flashy men who were out to make money quick and had a sharp eye for new gimmicks to keep their customers from succumbing to Temperance propaganda or counter attractions, who exploited and over-worked their staff and sold their pubs as soon as they could make a good profit on them." (Victorian Pubs; Studio Vista, 1977). North of the border there was little scope for raffish and mercenary individuals who rapidly bought up pubs at grossly inflated prices, did them up in high style, then disposed of them as soon as possible at even more ridiculous prices. In Scotland, indeed, the licensing authorities were on the look-out for such speculators, since they considered "trafficking in licences" to be a particularly heinous crime. In some parts of Scotland the magistrates or justices even objected to more than one licence being granted to the same person; in 1897 the Chief Constable of Dundee told the Royal Commission on the Liquor Licensing Laws that there was only one instance in the city of a person holding more than one certificate.

In Glasgow in 1871 the proportion of licensed establishments of all kinds had been 1 to every 281 of the population, but by the end of the century the ratio was 1 licence to every 424 citizens. Some Glasgow magistrates, ardent teetotalers, regarded pubs solely as resorts of "the dissipated and dissolute classes" and publicans as enemies of society, but others seem to have been genuinely concerned about the preponderance of pubs in what would nowadays be termed deprived areas. In 1898 a disproportionate number of Glasgow's 1425 pubs were concentrated in heavily populated and predominantly working class districts such as Cowcaddens (population 40,700; 116 pubs) and Gorbals (population 36,000; 102 pubs). In these districts there was a pub at almost every street corner. Several of the best residential districts were practically devoid of pubs. Working class Calton had 120 pubs and only 4 licensed grocers, while middle class Kelvinside had 14 licensed grocers and only 1 pub.

In some of Glasgow's most congested and least salubrious areas a high proportion of the pubs had been squalid and disreputable places. These unsavoury establishments, resorts of "dissolute men and women of easy virtue," the licensing magistrates had marked down for extinction: some ceased to exist because the proprietors were deprived of their licences, and others were swept away in the urban renewal schemes of the late nineteenth and early twentieth centuries. In 1890 the Corporation of Glasgow owned 34 licensed houses, having obtained them, along with a number of slum properties, under special powers embodied in the City Improvement Acts. The Corporation continued to let some of these pubs from year to year, but gradually the licences were withdrawn, as the Corporation, under the auspices of the City Improvement Trust, demolished the condemned buildings and erected model tenements suitable for "mechanics, labourers and other persons of the working and poorer classes." Provision could also have been made at the same time for fewer, but better, pubs. But the Trustees resolutely refused to let any of their property as licensed premises.

In the course of the Victorian and Edwardian periods, Scotland acquired a substantial body of licensing laws. The simple provisions of the 1828 Home Drummond Act had been enough (and possibly more than enough) for the pleasure-loving subjects of George the Fourth, but the strong-minded Victorians were less disposed to tolerate the more objectionable features of the licensed trade.

In 1846 a Select Committee of the House of Commons reported that there was an excess of licensed premises in Scotland; licences were being granted indiscriminately and the licence holders were ill-qualified, and the combination of the grocer's trade with that of the spirit dealer was "productive of evil consequences to the working classes." These and other conclusions of the Select Committee led to the controversial Forbes Mackenzie Act of 1853 (16 and 17 Vict. c.67), called after its sponsor the M.P. for Peebleshire. The Act introduced three forms of licensing certificate – for innkeepers and hoteliers, publicans, and grocers – and separated the food and drink trades. Licensed grocers were henceforth only to be permitted to sell liquor for consumption "off the premises," and the publican was to be prohibited from selling groceries. There were also modified forms of publican's and grocer's certificates restricting the sale of exciseable liquors to wine and beer. Publicans had now to observe statutory hours – the hours of closing on weekdays were fixed from 11 p.m. to 8 a.m., subject to certain discretionary powers of the authorities – and they were forbidden to open their premises on Sundays, but innkeepers and hoteliers were allowed to supply drink on the Sabbath to residents, residents' guests, and bona fide travellers. It became an offence to supply liquor to children apparently under fourteen years of age, or to intoxicated persons.

As an immediate result of the Forbes Mackenzie Act, there was an appreciable drop in the number of cases of public drunkenness; Sunday drunkenness decreased considerably. In the last year of the "old law," 1853, there were 1218 cases of Sunday drunkenness in Glasgow; the following year, a mere 464. Temperance enthusiasts hailed Sunday closing as an important staging post on the road to the New Jerusalem and looked forward to the time (not too far distant, they felt sure) when the pubs of Scotland would be closed on all seven days of the week. But rather than endure the desolation of the Scottish Sabbath without the consolation of strong drink, people who were not temperance enthusiasts began to travel several miles from their own localities on Sundays, ending up in the taproom of an hotel. The less energetic took to frequenting the shebeens – illegal public houses where the whisky was "a fearful and wonderful compound, in which genuine Scotch whisky was the least prominent ingredient." The poorer districts of Glasgow had long been honeycombed with shebeens of a particularly low and repulsive character, part brothels, part thieves' kitchens, but Sunday closing gave rise to a number of "superior" shebeens, some of which were located in the West End of the city.

The Public House Amendment Act of 1862 (25 and 26 Vict. c.35) provided penalties for the owners of irregularly conducted licensed houses, persons found drinking in shebeens, people who got drunk and incapable in public, and those unscrupulous individuals who falsely represented themselves to be Sunday travellers for the purpose of obtaining drink. On a more permissive note, the Act authorised the magistrates or justices to extend the opening hours of licensed premises at their discretion.

Under the provisions of the Publicans' Certificates Act, 1876 (39 and 40 Vict. c.26), the licensing authorities' refusal of new applications for certificates was held to be final, and the right of appeal to Quarter Sessions, which had existed in such cases, was taken away. The Act also required the grant of new certificates to be confirmed by a joint committee appointed for that purpose.

The 1887 Hours of Closing Act (50 and 51 Vict. c.38) permitted the licensing authorities to impose ten o'clock closing, towns of 50,000 or more inhabitants being exempted, while the Intoxicating Liquors (Sale to Children) Act of 1901 (1

Edw. VII. c.27) prohibited the sale of alcoholic beverages to children under fourteen, except in quantities of not less than one reputed pint, and in corked and sealed vessels.

Largely as the outcome of the deliberations of the 24-strong Royal Commission on the Liquor Licensing Laws (1896-98), the Licensing (Scotland) Act (3 Edw. VII. c.25) was passed in 1903, consolidating into one Act the various licensing statutes and incorporating a number of new provisions. One of the principal objects of the Act was to prevent, or at any rate lessen, public drunkenness; it permitted all licensing authorities to fix the hour of closing at ten o'clock, prohibited the sale of spirits to children under sixteen, and made it an offence to be drunk and incapable on licensed premises or in any other place to which the public had access, whether on payment or otherwise. It also became an offence to be drunk in charge of a carriage, horse, or steam engine, or while in possession of loaded firearms. The Act set up a licensing court in every town with a population of 7,000 or over, and also authorised county councils to divide the counties into licensing districts of not less than 7,000 population. This brought to an end the curious state of affairs whereby a small royal burgh like Culross (population 348) had its own licensing tribunal, while a large police burgh like Govan (population 82,000) had no licensing tribunal of its own – the justices of the peace for the counties had been the licensing authorities for these burghs. In future the magistrates in royal and parliamentary burghs with a population of less than 4,000 were to be deprived of their licensing powers, while the police burghs, if their populations exceeded 7,000, were to have licensing courts of their own. Hitherto no certificate for the sale of exciseable liquors had been granted unless an absolute majority of the licensing magistrates or justices had voted in favour of it; this was altered to a majority of the bench voting in favour. The licensing courts were also empowered to make by-laws under which licensed premises could be wholly or partially closed on New Year's Day and four other days in the year.

The establishment of bogus clubs had been one way of evading the provisions of the Forbes Mackenzie Act. Many a literary and social institution had enjoyed exceptional popularity from eleven o'clock on Saturday night until the early hours of Monday morning. Under the Act of 1903, however, only the club which had been granted a certificate of registration, valid for twelve months, could supply liquor to its members. Registration entailed lodging with the Sheriff-Clerk the constitution and rules of the club, together with a list of the officials and members. The decision of the Sheriff in dealing with an application for an original certificate or for the renewal of a certificate was final, and not subject to review. Registration was conditional on the evident bona fide character of the club, and a club could be struck off the register if its members permitted irregularities such as the sale of liquor to non-members, or the admittance of new members within less than forty-eight hours of nomination. Among the competent grounds of objection to registration were that the club was mainly used for the supply of exciseable liquors, that the rules were habitually broken, that drunkenness on the premises was permitted, and that persons in a state of intoxication were frequently seen leaving the premises. In 1904, the year in which Glasgow adopted ten o'clock closing, there were 49 registered clubs in the city. A year later the number was 60, and there was a steady increase until 1908, when the total was 71. In spite of registration many clubs were little more than drinking dens and gambling hells, and they continued as such until the officials, sooner or later, fell foul of the authorities.

Publicans quite naturally resented the existence of the so-called "working men's clubs" and complained of unfair competition; clubs, they argued, had all the privileges of licensed premises as regards the sale of liquor, with none of the attendant disadvantages such as Sunday closing, early closing, licence duty and close police supervision (it was only when evidence was forthcoming that an offence had been committed that the police could obtain a search warrant to enter club premises). Whereas the Chief Constable and the Corporation alone could object to the registration of clubs, the residents in any locality could object to the granting of public house certificates. Club proprietors, unlike publicans, did not have to convince the licensing authorities that they were of sterling character, nor did they have to obtain the consent of the authorities before making alterations to their premises.

In February of 1910 the town council of Glasgow called for a return of clubs against the conduct of which objections by the Chief Constable had been lodged; these numbered 35, and the complaints were practically the same in every case – "drunkenness on premises, and persons in a state of intoxication frequently seen to leave the club."

The Scottish Licensed Trade (December 1910) – admittedly not the least prejudiced of publications where registered clubs were concerned – observed that the Glasgow "working men's clubs" were a very mixed bag. Many were "shut all day and open all night." Some had "alluring names, borrowed from the old clubland of Glasgow, or associated with different forms of sport." Several professed "to cater for commercial men, others for sporting men, a few for artisans, and one or two for night workers." At the bottom of the scale was the most disreputable type of club, "the haunt of more or less broken-looking men, idle young men, and fast young men," all of whom shared a passion for gambling.

Town councils throughout Scotland made use of their powers under the 1887 Hours of Closing Act and the 1903 Licensing (Scotland) Act to close licensed premises at ten instead of eleven, and by 1909 Dunoon was "in the unique position of being the only town in Scotland" where the pubs were "open in the summer months after ten o'clock." (The Scottish Licensed Trade, May 1909). This was because the magistrates of Dunoon had granted an extension of business hours to the licence holders of the town, allowing them to keep their premises open until 10.30 p.m. during the peak holiday months of July and August.

The Temperance (Scotland) Act, 1913 (3 and 4 Geo. V. c.33), introduced a democratic scheme of local option, putting into the hands of the voters the power of controlling the numbers of licensed premises in their own area by carrying, at three year intervals, resolutions for no change, no licence, or the limitation of licences. The local option power under the Act did not come into operation until 1920.

Unlike Johnnie Dowie and other old-time landlords, the late Victorian or Edwardian publican had usually been granted a certificate only after he had succeeded in convincing a punctilious licensing board that he was a "fit and proper person" to be in charge of licensed premises. When considering an application for a new certificate, the authorities were duty bound to give careful thought to the needs of the locality, the fitness of the applicant, and the suitability of the premises. They had by and large declared war on the old-fashioned tavern with its huddle of dark and secluded box rooms where "questionable practices" could be carried on without the licence holder being any the wiser. The more open a pub was, the better the magistrates or justices liked it. They frequently recommended structural modifications of the sort conducive to easier supervision by the men behind the bar, and the promise to carry out such alterations was very often a condition of the grant of a licence. Some licensing magistrates exhorted the publicans to equip their premises with family, or "jug and bottle," departments, so that women or children acting as messengers would not have to enter the pub proper. Other magistrates took the opposite view; being under the impression that women (who were not always welcome in Scottish pubs) obtained a surreptitious dram in those same family departments, they recommended that the appendages be removed. By providing for the deposit of plans, the Licensing (Scotland) Act of 1903 empowered licensing courts to control the building or reconstruction of licensing premises.

In November 1891, as an example of the fickle nature of licensing authorities in general, the Victualling Trades' Review cited the sad case of Thomas Downie, who had paid £700 "as the price of the goodwill of a licensed house in the neighbourhood of Cessnock Dock, Govan." Due to demolition work in connection with the new dock, Downie was subsequently obliged to quit his premises, without compensation. He "naturally expected that when not compensated for the old shop, he would have no difficulty in getting a new licence." No such luck, for "the Justices for some inexplicable reason refused his application," and Downie "lost not only his £700 but his business." This was bad enough, but "a few minutes before he was refused, the Court granted a licence to a man in the same district who had already a public-house in Govan."

The cast-iron right of magistrates or justices to refuse the renewal of a licence was upheld by a whole series of pronouncements in the famous case of Sharpe versus Wakefield. In 1887 an innkeeper by the name of William Redding applied to the Kendall, Westmoreland, licensing bench (of which a Mr. Wakefield was chairman) for the renewal of the licence of the Low Bridge Inn, Kentmere. Although the licence had been in existence for about thirty years, the application was refused on the grounds that the inn was remote from police jurisdiction and was not required for the wants of the neighbourhood. Against this decision Susannah Sharpe, the owner of the inn, appealed to the Court of Quarter Sessions. The decision of the magistrates was sustained, but Miss Sharpe was not one to give in without a fight; there followed unsuccessful appeals to the Court of Queen's Bench, the Court of Appeal, and as a last resort, the House of Lords. In 1891, after four years of litigation, the Lord Chancellor administered the coup de grace by affirming that the grant of a licence was "expressly within the discretion of the magistrates."

In the early 1900s sober pursuits such as ice skating, roller skating, cycling, and animated picture shows were "crazes" which tended to diminish the profits of Scottish publicans who were already feeling the pinch, due to the effects of a general trade depression. The ice rink at Crossmyloof, Glasgow, opened in 1907 and described at the time as "the largest frozen area under cover in Europe," incorporated dining, tea, and smoking rooms. Football matches, while they boosted the takings of publicans whose premises were situated in the vicinity of stadiums, had an averse effect on the profits of other licence holders, since they provided an alternative to the traditional Saturday afternoon pub crawl.

The antithesis of the handsome urban pub was the squalid tippling shop, of which there were many in the poorest districts of Scottish towns and cities, in spite of magisterial moves to suppress them.

There is at least one public-house within a stonethrow of the Tron clock where the licence holder, in order to lure customers, supplies beer and porter at a penny a glass. The quality of the liquor is guaranteed, and for a very small sum the denizens of this thickly-populated locality can purchase a few hours of oblivion. In this grog shop there is no sitting accommodation, and sometimes in the space in front of the bar there is a dead wall of human beings four deep, drinking, cursing, and indulging in the coarsest ribald talk.

Not in the worst dens of New York can a more brutalised crowd be witnessed. Bareheaded and barefooted women with infants in their arms, uncouth Magdalenes scarred with the leprosy of sin, men on the borderland of delirium tremens, whose slumbers will be disturbed by weird spectral sights that will make the blood run cold in their veins are there, and no matter how intoxicated they are served without the least reluctance. . .[6]

A scene reminiscent of Cruikshank's most uncomplimentary pictures of the London gin-shops in the 1830s, but the place was Glasgow and the year 1892. Here indeed was the sleazy side of life in a great Victorian city: a twilight world of farmed-out tenements and model lodging houses, inhabited by tens of thousands of social derelicts, many of them engaged in prostitution, shebeening and petty crime. But only the most naive adherent of the temperance movement could insist in all seriousness that drink, and drink alone, was the primary cause of such poverty and misery.

If Glasgow's late Victorian liquor palaces provided the toper with an impressive and (in spite of temperance propaganda to the contrary) congenial ambience, the interiors of the city's famous tea-rooms did much the same thing for the teetotaler. Perhaps the strength of the anti-drink party had something to do with the proliferation of tea-rooms; at any rate they were a characteristic Glasgow amenity, their charms unrivalled even in London, as "James Hamilton Muir" pointed out in "Glasgow in 1901."

It is not the accent of the people, nor the painted houses, nor yet the absence of Highland policemen that makes the Glasgow man in London feel that he is in a foreign town and far from home. It is a simpler matter. It is the lack of tea shops. . .[7]

Temperance enthusiasts of both sexes no doubt hailed the advent of the tea-room and helped to boost its popularity. For women, it was indeed a godsend, a place in which to recuperate after a day's sight-seeing and shopping. The Glasgow pubs were bastions of male supremacy, and women – "respectable" women at any rate – were largely excluded from them (as late as the 1960s there were still a fair number of Glasgow pubs to which women were not admitted, and in some pubs, until recently, they were still not encouraged to use the public bar). Glasgow women were also unwelcome in popular licensed luncheon rooms such as William Lang's and John Forrester's. Significantly, perhaps, it was a woman – Miss Catherine Cranston – who was responsible for some of the most stylish tea-rooms in the city. She employed decorators of outstanding talent—George Walton, Messrs. Scott Morton of Edinburgh, and Charles Rennie Mackintosh. The elegant and sophisticated Glasgow tea-rooms became justifiably celebrated, but ultimately they were dismantled, mutilated or destroyed, sharing the fate of so many of their aggressively masculine rivals, the palace pubs.

* The proprietor, David Gilmour.
* i.e. raw fiery whisky.

[1] The Victualling Trades' Review; Volume XVI, 1902, page 98. The Metropolitan Bar was situated at 164 Sauchiehall Street.
[2] The Victualling Trades' Review, March 1, 1893. The Rabbie Burns was situated at 153 Trongate.
[3] The Victualling Trades' Review; volume XVI, 1902, page 119.
[4] The Scottish Wine, Spirit and Beer Trades' Review, December 12, 1888.
[5] The Scottish Wine, Spirit and Beer Trades' Review, June 7, 1887.
[6] North British Daily Mail, November 7, 1892.
[7] James Hamilton Muir (pseudonym for James Bone, Archibald Hamilton Charteris and Muirhead Bone): Glasgow in 1901, part III, chapter II.

Part Two

1   Drink

The Scottish pub underwent a remarkable transformation in the latter half of the nineteenth century. The small howff with its private sitting rooms, genial landlord and flexible opening and closing times had become, by the 1880s, the liquor palace with its open plan, punctilious bar staff and statutory hours. There were considerable changes too, in the pub's principal commodities – beer and whisky. Pale ales had become increasingly popular, gaining ascendancy over old favourites such as dark strong ale, porter and stout.

> Many brewers complain of difficulty in securing any considerable sale for black beers, and there is no doubt that the whole tendency of the brewing trade is to develop itself in the direction of light bitter ales of low alcoholic strength and of that delicate flavour, imparted by careful hopping with high-class materials. We think, however, that there is still a fair demand for, and business to be done in stouts, if of satisfactory quality. By far too much of the stout brewed in ale brewings might well be described as coloured mild ale; indeed, we know of a case where porter is made from the same mash as mild ale by adding to the last copper a large quantity of sugar to raise the gravity, and enough black malt to impart the requisite colour. Little surprise can be felt that the article thus produced did not give satisfaction to the customer.[1]

For centuries beer had been brewed from malted barley, hops, water and yeast. Hop substitutes had occasionally been used from 1862 onwards and the use of sugar was authorised by Act of Parliament in 1847. In 1880 the brewers were given much greater freedom, for by the substitution of beer duty for the old malt tax, Gladstone's Liberal government inaugurated the "free mash tun" system. The brewer, said Gladstone, "will brew from what he pleases, and he will have a perfect choice both of his materials and his methods." Excise duty was levied on original gravity – the specific gravity of the unfermented beer (wort) – and was payable at the rate of 6s 3d per 36 gallon barrel at the standard gravity of 1,057 (1,055 from April 1889, when the duty on beer was increased by reduction of the standard gravity).

In addition to barley malt and hops, the fully emancipated brewers were at liberty to use malt substitutes (adjuncts) such as flaked maize, flaked rice, unmalted barley, invert sugar and glucose. "Saccharine" was prohibited in 1888, not because it was considered to be injurious to health but because it was a "chemical or artificial extract likely to prejudicially affect the interests of the Revenue."

As late as 1895 there were still 4,893 all-malt brewers for sale in the British Isles (55.1%), as against 3,981 brewers for sale using malt adjuncts of various kinds (44.9%). However, the majority of all-malt brewers were small fry, and they only accounted for about one-eighth of the malt used; approximately seven million bushels. Within the United Kingdom the average percentage of malt used in the brewing industry varied considerably from place to place. In 1897, for instance, the brewers of England and Wales used 75.6%; Scotland's brewers used 90.6%, while those of Ireland (where Arthur Guinness and Son brewed from malt and hops only) used 98.03%.

Not everyone approved of the "free mash tun" and of its presiding genie, the brewer's chemist. The use of brewing sugars and other substitutes for malted barley certainly did not please the farmers, while all-malt brewers complained that rivals who used cheaper materials made larger profits from inferior products. Other people went so far as to suggest that beer made with malt substitutes was not really beer at all, and that it ought, in all fairness to the consumer, to be called by some other name. Several Members of Parliament campaigned for a pure beer law similar to Bavaria's famous Reinheitsgebot (pledge of purity), in force since 1516. Sir Cuthbert Quilter's Pure Beer Bill was first introduced in 1885 and was periodically revived. As defined by Quilter and his supporters, the expression "beer" meant a beverage made exclusively from barley malt, hops, water, and yeast, "with or without such adjuncts approved by the commissioners of Inland Revenue, as may be necessary in the preparation of water for brewing purposes, or for colouring or fining, and with or without sugar to an amount not exceeding three per cent in volume for priming purposes." In 1896 the Bill was withdrawn by its promoters on the understanding that a Parliamentary Committee would be appointed to inquire into its desireability. The resultant Committee on Beer Materials was perhaps unduly influenced by the representatives of a vast and powerful section of the brewing industry; at any rate its report, issued in 1899, was strongly in favour of the status quo.

The British public had long had a penchant for old heavy beers, brewed purely from malt and hops (except when, as sometimes happened, unscrupulous brewers added adulterants such as liquorice, tobacco, wormwood, or coculus indicus), and stored in wooden vats for long periods before being racked into casks and sold. These were heavily hopped beers, sometimes acid or sub-acid in flavour and highly intoxicating. Lighter bodied and more subtle beers made their appearance in the course of the nineteenth century – mild: a lightly hopped beer, usually dark in colour, and bitter: a well hopped pale beer. India Pale Ale, a high quality bitter, originally produced by London brewers Abbot & Hodgson, was brewed in increasingly large quantities in centres such as Burton-on-Trent and Edinburgh where the water, hard, and highly charged with gypsum, was pre-eminently suitable. The new types of beer were of relatively low gravity and so less duty was paid on them. Unlike the dark, strong, vatted ales and porters they were ready for consumption in a matter of weeks, enabling the brewers to turn over their capital far more rapidly than formerly. Owing to these commercial advantages, mild and bitter ales were vigorously promoted by the brewers and their agents, and by the turn of the century they had become the British beers par excellence. They were certainly more refreshing than old ale or porter, and the sparkling, light coloured variants looked particularly inviting when served up in the glass tumblers which had largely replaced pewter tankards. Although late Victorian bitter and mild ales were of lower alcoholic strength than the vatted ales and stouts they were potent beers just the same; mild ales with an original gravity of 1,042 and bitter ales with an o.g. of 1,060 were fairly common.

As weaker beers became more popular so too did German and Scandinavian lager beers, which were imported by agents such as A. Bischoff and Company of Glasgow, and the Gamle Carlsberg Lager Beer Import Company of Leith. Served ice-cold, lager proved to be a very acceptable summer tipple; an ideal lunchtime drink, it was more digestible than pale ale and less intoxicating.

> It is undoubtedly a fact that a taste for lighter, and less heady beverages is rapidly gaining ground in Scotland. This is evidenced in the establishment of an agency in Scotland for the Kaiser Lager Beer Company Limited. The brewery is situated at Niedermendig, on the Rhine, and is fortunate in being in the immediate vicinity of a lake, the waters of which are peculiarly adapted for brewing purposes.[2]

Continental lager differed from traditional British beers in being produced by the bottom fermentation system, at a considerably lower temperature than British top fermentation, and placed in cold storage for long periods before being sold, "lagerbier" being German for store beer. In 1887 the Scottish Wine, Spirit and Beer Trades' Review commented on the growing popularity of imported lager, and called for a national brew of a similar nature.

> Go into any restaurant and see the conspicuous notice, "lager beer," on the walls, and note the comparative number of drinkers of this and of English (sic) beers – all in favour of the lager. Yet lager is dearer than our high-priced pale ales and is inferior to them in palate and quality. In the semi-tropical weather we have lately experienced, however, human nature cries out loudly for something light, refreshing, and cool – especially cool – these conditions are supplied by lager beer. We trust that before another summer, arrangements will be made to induce licensed victuallers to pay a little more attention to the condition in which beer is delivered to their customers, and upon brewers we would again urge the necessity of producing a beer for summer consumption akin to lager.[3]

A lager beer brewery had been established by a syndicate of Manchester businessmen at Wrexham (North Wales) in 1882. A few years later the Wrexham Company established an agency in Glasgow, and so did another pioneer company, the Tottenham Lager Beer Brewery, London. These firms failed to set the heather on fire; when inclined to drink lager, the Scotsman of that period seems to have preferred the imported German or Danish varieties. In the late 1880s, however, J. and R. Tennent of Glasgow, brewers of ales and stouts at the Wellpark Brewery since 1745, started to produce small quantities of lager; the beer had an encouraging reception, being hailed as an admirable summer drink, and the company proceeded to brew it on a larger scale.

Messrs J & R Tennent, of Wellpark Brewery, having discovered that there is a really good field for lager beer in Scotland, are we hear, to erect a German Lager Beer Brewery in Glasgow. This is what, on former occasions, we advised some of our local brewers to do, and we believe it will be a prosperous undertaking.[4]

Tennent's lager, initially brewed by specially imported Germans, was of the pale, dry Pilsner type. The bottled version was labelled "J & R Tennent's Munich beer". It was apparently brewed entirely from malt and hops, no adjuncts being used. Commenting on the success of the first lager to be brewed in Scotland, the Victualling Trades' Review patriotically declared it to be superior to the authentic product of the Fatherland.

There is literally no comparison between the two, and yet Tennent's is sold at a price which compares favourably with that of the foreign-made article. It is a beer that not only drinks well, but will keep well in any climate. No matter how much the bottle may be shaken or what the temperature may be, this lager will remain clear and bright, a pleasure to drink, pure and wholesome.[5]

Tennent's even experimented with "lager stout," said to be "specially adapted for the winter season." In 1899 the famous firm of Allsopp and Son established a lager brewery at Burton-on-Trent; Allsopp's used American plant and their lager, "made from the highest class of malt and hops," was "matured, perfected, aged and ready for the market" in just three weeks. Lager was also brewed in Edinburgh, under German supervision, by John Jeffrey and Company from 1903 onwards. For home consumption, Jeffrey's lager was stored for three months, and for the overseas markets nine or ten months. The beer barrels were lined with pitch resin so that the heavily carbonated lager did not come in contact with the wood. Another Scottish lager was the "Pioneer" brand, brewed by M. J. Cameron and Company, Canongate, Edinburgh, and first introduced in 1906.

It was a time of intense and ill-fated rivalry between the British Empire and the German Reich, and the lager enthusiast in this country was doubtlessly eager to drink Tennent's or Allsopp's in preference to Munich spatenbrau. Many a patriotic toper, returning from the pub swollen with all-British lager, and full too of indignation at the thought of German dreadnoughts, would have given vent to his feelings by bawling out the most popular jingoistic ballad of the day.

Sons of the Sea, all British born,
Sailing every ocean, laughing foes to scorn,
They may build their ships, my lads, and think they
know the game,
But they can't build the boys of the bulldog breed
who made Old England's name!

In the late nineteenth century most people associated Scotland with whisky rather than beer. Of the 34,456,345 barrels of beer produced in the United Kingdom in 1895, only 1,845,703 were brewed north of the Tweed (5.7%). It was in the last quarter of the century that Scotch whisky began to have a much wider appeal. As early as 1578, however, Raphael Holinshed had lauded its virtues in his Chronicles.

Beying moderatelie taken, it sloweth age; it strengtheneth youthe; it helpeth digestion; it cutteth fleume; it abandoneth melancholie; it relisheth the harte; it lighteneth the mynde; it quickeneth the spirites; it cureth the hydropsis; it healeth the strangury; it pounceth the stone; it repelleth grauel; it puffeth awaie ventositie; it kepyth and preserveth the head from whyrling – the eyes from dazelyng – the tongue from lispyng – the mouth from snafflyng – the teethe from chatteryng – the throte from ratlyng – the weasan from stieflyng – the stomach from wamblyng – the harte from swellyng – the bellie from wirthchyng – the guts from rumblyng – the hands from shiueryng – the sinowes from shrinkyng – the veynes from crumplyng – the bones from soakyng . . .trulie it is a soueraigne liquor.

"If it be orderlie taken," Holinshed prudently added. The publication of such a splendid testimony ought to have led to a considerable demand for the wonderful Caledonian elixir, especially from those afflicted with wamblyng stomachs or stieflyng weasans. But three centuries were to elapse before Scotch whisky came into its own. The vine pest phylloxera (American grape louse) was instrumental in boosting the popularity of Scotch in the 1880s and 1890s, for it devastated the Cognac district of France, forcing the brandy drinker to seek an alternative stimulant. In a relatively short time, Scots were able to take pride in the fact that their national spirit had at last been accorded international recognition.

A generation ago, nay, a score of years ago – the taste for Scotch Whisky was very well confined within the borders of Scotland. Today, it is the popular liquor – today, it is popular North, South, East and West. It is a familiar spirit in Piccadilly clubs and in Cheapside restaurants. You can get it in Broadway in New York; you can get it on the Prater in Vienna; it is vended unter den linden in Berlin; you can get it, and of an excellent brand, in L'Avenue de l'Opera in Paris.[6]

Throughout the nineteenth century, Scotland was widely regarded as an exceedingly romantic prospect. The world – and especially the English-speaking part of it – was as ready to appreciate Scotch whisky as it had been to devour the Waverley novels or Queen Victoria's Highland journal.

The traditional Scotch was a potent and pungent spirit, produced by two separate distillations in two different pot stills. At one time it had been made from both malted and unmalted grain, but by the early nineteenth century malted barley – often strongly impregnated with aromatic peat smoke – was used almost exclusively. Since the fifteenth century, pot still whisky had been uisge beatha* – water of life – to the Gaelic-speaking Highlander and by the eighteenth century its admirable properties were also well known to the Lowlander, who called it aqua vitae, or aqua for short.

The patent or continuous still, invented in 1826 by Robert Stein and vastly improved in 1830 by Aeneas Coffey, was destined to transform the whisky trade into a major industry and in so doing alter the character of whisky itself. Malt whisky was occasionally made in the patent still, but the apparatus was mainly used for the production of spirits made largely from unmalted grain such as maize or rye. The patent still produced spirits more quickly, more cheaply, and in much greater quantities than the traditional pot still, and the invention was soon being exploited by Lowland capitalists who built distilleries in or near populous towns. Grain whisky, being almost pure alcohol, took less time to mature than pot still malt whisky but was comparatively characterless, lacking the oils and aromatic substances (congerics) that gave pot still whisky its body and flavour; for this reason it was sometimes called "silent" or "neutral" spirit.

The old Highland, Islay, and Campbeltown malts possessed strong, even aggressive characteristics, and before the advent of blends, the insignificant amount of Scotch whisky consumed by English people mainly consisted of Lowland malt whisky, either "silent" malt, which was lightly peated, or "plain" malt, which was not peated at all. In the mid-nineteenth century whisky could not be imported into England in casks of smaller capacity than eighty gallons. Gladstone's Excise on Spirits Act (1860) removed this restriction and also allowed whisky merchants to blend whiskies from various distilleries in bond. In the years that followed there grew the practice of blending together pot still and patent still spirits to produce a variety of mild, cheap and light bodied whiskies, more suited to the palates, pockets and constitutions of townsfolk than the noble malt liquor of the north.

In the 1880s, due in no small measure to the swashbuckling methods of whisky entrepreneurs such as James Buchanan and Thomas Dewar, blended Scotch whiskies became – in the parlance of the times—"all the rage." Brilliant advertising and salesmanship prompted many thousands of people to taste whisky for the first time in their lives. By the turn of the century blended Scotch whiskies were also being exported in appreciable quantities to Australia, New Zealand, India, South Africa, Canada and the United States. Doctors helped to popularise Scotch whisky by recommending it as a pick-me-up in place of brandy. Robert McNish and Company, whisky merchants of Glasgow, actually marketed a proprietary blend called the Doctor's Special, advertised as "the medical whisky of the world."

"The nearly extinct effigy of the Highlander of the snuff-shop still dwells in the mind's eye of the Englishman as he drinks his four of Scotch," remarked the Victualling Trades' Review (August 1904), "and though the brand hail from Dundee, Kilmarnock, or Leith, the average consumer feels sure that the shelter of a Highland glen, mountain stream and kilted native have had something to do with the favourite stimulant." The more discriminating whisky drinkers, the Review added, were "demanding their drink from the bottle of a Highland chieftain, whose temporary abiding place in the Lowlands of Glasgow fails to awaken any misgiving."

When brandy consumption declined, Irish whiskey, unlike Scotch, failed to rise spectacularly in the popular estimation; the art or science of blending had been neglected in Ireland and as people became accustomed to whisky of a less pronounced flavour, through the activities of the Scottish blenders, the market for Irish malts diminished.

Merchandisers of blended Scotch whiskies supplied pubs and licensed restaurants with handsome advertisement mirrors depicting stags at bay or ferocious claymore-wielding Highlanders, and they made sure that the names of their proprietary blends conjured up romantic images of "Caledonia, stern and wild." By 1895 there were upwards of a thousand registered blends and brands of Scotch in existence, together with an untold number of unregistered "specials." The works of Robert Burns and Sir Walter Scott furnished names for many of these blends. Messrs. Wright and Greig, a Glasgow firm of distillers and blenders, were proprietors of the popular "Roderick Dhu" brand (inspired by the outlawed Highland chieftain in Scott's poem "The Lady of the Lake"). In 1898, when they erected stores and offices in Waterloo Street, the ornate red sandstone ediface was decorated with statues of the principal characters in the poem (the building is now the property of the Distillers Company Limited).

To be sure, some blenders preferred to eulogise Highland malt whisky in their advertisements rather than put a fair proportion of it into their bottles. A considerable quantity of execrable blended whisky was marketed by speculators who were anxious only to cash in on the growing popularity of Scotch. Their activities led the Scottish licensed trade's National Guardian to publish a mild rebuke.

> If cheap blends must be made up in order to secure orders and bigger profits than legitimate business should require, demand will die away, and something else will come in to take the place which Scottish whiskies, especially Northern malts, have been making for themselves so rapidly in every part of the world within the last ten or twelve years.[7]

Whisky destined for the cellars of the well-to-do was frequently matured in bond for an appreciable length of time, but until the nineteenth century was drawing to a close ordinary public house whisky was not usually well-matured. Much of the whisky dispensed in English pubs was of deplorable quality; sometimes it consisted of English grain spirit, flavoured with a dash of malt whisky. One "Scotch" whisky of mainly English origin was sold under the initials N.S.S. These stood for Nicholson's Scotch Whisky, but some wags preferred to interpret them as "Never Saw Scotland."

The characteristic smoky flavour of heavily peated malt whisky was used by some blenders to cloak a multitude of sins. "The blending of whiskies," remarked the Victualling Trades' Review (May 1896) was "a scientific operation" which was "achieved with conspicious success in the case of several well-known brands." But at the same time, the practice of blending was "the opportunity of the unscrupulous manufacturer of cheap and semi-poisonous rubbish." Raw grain spirit was "so much less costly than the malt that the temptation to raise it to a chief position in the blend, instead of making it a mere qualifying agent," was "in some cases irresistable." The result was a considerable number of "cheap, nasty, and unwholesome whiskies, made for the most part of new raw grain or German potato spirit, with a mere qualification of malt," which found a ready sale in the poorer districts of the industrial towns and cities, where people were "credulous enough to believe that whisky worthy of the name" could be obtained for 1s 9d or 2s a bottle.

Blending in bond for home consumption of either "German potato spirit" or any other foreign spirit with Scotch whisky was forbidden, but there was nothing to prevent an unscrupulous dealer from mixing German spirit and Scotch malt or grain whisky together in his private store and calling the admixture "Scotch whisky." He would have been obliged to pay a differential duty of 5d per gallon for the foreign product, in addition to the ordinary rate of duty on whisky (11s per gallon in the 1890s), but assuming that the imported spirit was sufficiently cheap and nasty, it would still have been worth his while to do so.

In some parts of Scotland the ordinary public house whisky consisted of grain whisky a few months old, blended with very small amounts of malt whisky several years old. Blends were sold at from 6d to 8d per gill. Pure grain whisky was also consumed, particularly in Clackmannanshire and Fifeshire where many of the inhabitants seem to have preferred it to pot still or blended whisky; if relatively new it was cheaper than blended whisky by a penny or so per gill, but well-matured grain whisky sometimes cost as much, if not more, than a blend.

It was customary for the Scottish publican to make up a special blend of his own – Joseph Muir of the Royalty Bar in Glasgow's New City Road created one such blend in 1900 and named it the "Baden Powell Rare Old Highland Whisky" in honour of the defender of Mafeking. One rather suspects that many publicans' "specials" would have been crude mixtures rather than carefully balanced blends of malt and grain. In some pubs the ordinary whisky was pure grain, such as Cambus or Cameron Bridge. In others the special whisky was pure grain whisky several years old and the ordinary whisky was the same spirit, only younger. Sometimes, indeed, the only difference between a publican's special whisky and his ordinary whisky was that the former contained less added water than the latter.

Raw, fiery whisky was "a torchlight procession down the throat," and sometimes drove the imbiber berserk. Malt whisky was considered to be "fit for a king's table at five years of age," and it was feared that those who sold spirits of greater age "might be accused of selling whisky which was too mild." Undoubtedly the average whisky drinker of those days was accustomed to the fiery taste and toxic effect of immature spirits, and it is a moot point whether he would have appreciated the more mellow whiskies of today.

Prolonged storage in sherry casks mellowed the whisky and imbued it with an attractive golden colour. At least that was the theory – for the bulk of the whisky produced did not receive prolonged storage, and a good deal of it certainly never saw the insides of genuine sherry casks, since the demand for these greatly exceeded the supply. John McQueen, whose cooperage and cask stores were situated in Brown Street, Glasgow, was described by the Victualling Trades' Review (September 1896) as "the largest cask importer in the world." McQueen's sherry casks, imported direct from Spain, were "all so thoroughly permeated with the best juices of the wine" that "ten months in bond" were "sufficient to mellow and add bouquet to the spirits with which they were re-filled." Certain Spanish firms met the demand for seasoned casks by doctoring new casks in various ways, and in this country too, "patent wine-prepared casks" were offered for sale. Another Glasgow firm, W. P. Lowrie and Company, distillers and whisky blenders as well as cask merchants, sold casks guaranteed to have been seasoned with "high-class expensive sherry," but were also prepared to supply casks seasoned "by steam, under pressure, in conjunction with suitable re-agents." In a letter to the Victualling Trades' Review (October 15, 1898) a correspondent who described himself as "a Highland malt distiller" referred in scathing terms to the spurious sherry casks in which some speculative bonders chose to store his whisky. Such casks were, he averred, "doctored inwardly with an abominable black sweet decoction," which converted fine malt whisky "into a coarse, cheap-like rum."

Patent colouring and maturing agents were frequently brought to the notice of blenders and whisky merchants through the medium of the licensed trade press. "I find that new spirits treated with Melline leave no bad after-effect on the system," declared one satisfied user, adding that Melline gave the spirits "a clean and palatable style," unlike "the ordinary sweet and sickening agents used by some inexperienced blenders." The product was advertised by the Melline Company Limited as being "largely used by blenders, rectifiers, and whisky dealers in all parts of the world for ageing and mellowing whiskies, brandies, rums, and sherries. When added to the new spirits, it has the effect of neutralising the Fusel Oil, and making them mellow and more palatable." Maturite was another patent preparation for modulating the unpleasant characteristics of raw spirits. "It was simply marvellous" enthused the Victualling Trades' Review (December 1898) "to find immature whisky aged in the space of about a minute to that of a three or four years old." A few drops of Maturite had worked the transformation, imparting to the raw grain spirit "such mellow and palatable properties that, while its potency and strength were retained, it was pleasant to the taste, and smelt as old malt." The boast of the London-based Mechanical Spirit Maturing Syndicate (Limited) was that they could make new whisky equal to whisky that had been kept in wood for seven to ten years, "in the course of a few hours and at a very small cost." Peter McDonald and Company, a Glasgow firm of rectifiers, distillers and blenders, could supply spirit merchants with "an exquisite damson wine," which was "unrivalled for ageing, mellowing and improving whisky, rum, wine, gin and brandy," and which was "rapidly superceding prune wine and pineapple wine for blending and maturing whiskies." The temptation to "mature" whisky artificially was very strong, as not only did storage tie down capital, but when whisky was left to mature in the normal way it suffered losses in volume and strength. It must have been patently obvious that whisky "matured" by artificial means was not quite the same thing as whisky mellowed by age, but the merchants who made use of Melline or Maturite no doubt did not hesitate to describe their products as "old Highland whiskies." The Lancet (January 11, 1902) pertinently remarked that artificial maturation certainly did "not leave old whisky or old brandy behind and such extracted spirit would probably never be the better or more wholesome for maturing in the absence of those ingredients which make old spirit acceptable to the palate and the economy." Artificially matured spirit could "never be looked upon as fit to replace the spirit mellowed by age, and any attempt to substitute it" was "to be deplored and certainly on medical grounds to be discountenanced strongly."

The proprietors of large urban pubs retailed a wide selection of whiskies, dispensed from numbered barrels, and the customer was able to make his choice from grain and blended whiskies of different ages and strengths, sometimes also from single malts and vatted malts (malt whiskies from the same distillery, but of different ages, blended together). Most publicans also stocked bottles of proprietary whiskies from the leading blending houses. As sold from the barrel, late Victorian public house whisky varied greatly in alcoholic strength. It could be obtained at more than 110 proof, or less than 80 proof. The minimum strength allowed by schedule 6 of the Sale of Food and Drugs Amendment Act, 1879, was 25 degrees under proof for whisky, brandy, or rum, and 35 degrees under proof for gin. The courts dealt with many cases in which spirit dealers were accused of selling whisky that was drastically under proof (they could have escaped prosecution by displaying notices in their premises to the effect that their whisky was so many degrees under proof). The proprietary blends were usually bottled at 75 or 80 proof. Not until the First World War, when cereals became scarce, did bottling at 70 proof become the general rule. Whisky sold for consumption "off the premises" mainly came in bottles with cork stoppers, but c.1913 William Teacher and Sons issued their Highland Cream blend and several other blends in bottles with patent "self-opening" tops. White Horse Distillers were the first to introduce screw caps for their bottles, but that was not until the 1920s.

In the late 1890s the finest proprietary blends of Scotch, containing a reasonable amount of malt whisky, sold at 3s 6d to 4s per bottle. A bottle of well-matured malt whisky or liqueur whisky (superior blended whisky) would have cost an extra sixpence or so. Cheaper whisky, containing a very much higher proportion of patent still spirit, was also available – Lipton Limited, of tea trade and family grocery fame, were selling whisky at 1s 10d per bottle in 1899.

In 1897 – an unusually "sober" year in Scotland insofar as relatively few people appeared before the courts on drunk and disorderly charges – the Scots consumed nearly seven million pounds' worth of whisky. They also spent nearly a million pounds on other spirits, close on four million pounds on beer, and another one-and-a-half million pounds on wine.

The whisky boom gathered momentum in the late 1880s, and by the mid 1890s the distillers were hard pressed to meet the insatiable demands of blenders, brokers and wholesale merchants. The number of distilleries increased from 130 in 1892 to 161 in 1899, and in the same period the annual production of whisky rose from 20,127,077 gallons to 35,769,114 gallons. The stocks of whisky in bond increased proportionately as the denouement approached – over 61 million gallons in March 1894; over 77 million gallons in March 1897; over 89 million gallons in March 1898. In March 1899 there were over 103 million gallons in bond. By then, however, the boom was over, having come to a sudden end with the collapse of Pattison's Limited in December 1898. The firm was controlled by two brothers, Robert and Walter Pattison, whose flair for self-publicity far outweighed their moral integrity. At the height of their success, the Pattisons were brewers as well as whisky blenders; they were ahead of their time in their fondness for extravagant promotional gimmicks: on one occasion they supplied selected licensed grocers throughout Scotland with grey parrots which were trained to cry out "drink Pattison's whisky." The brothers were wont to refer to their premises in Breadalbane Street, Leith, as "the largest bonded warehouse in the world," but the building's impressive exterior concealed blending methods that were most inferior. During the subsequent trial of the Pattisons on charges of fraud it was revealed that their

80,000 gallon stock of "fine old Glenlivet" consisted mainly of raw Irish grain whiskey.

After the demise of Pattison's Limited a large number of financially embarrassed speculators and investors were obliged to throw their stocks of whisky on the market and dispose of them at rock bottom prices. There ensued several very lean years for many of those engaged in the production, blending and merchandising of whisky, and especially for the Highland malt distillers. Recovery was impeded by a general trade recession following the end of the Boer War, and also by Lloyd George's Budget of April 29, 1909, which raised the duty on whisky from 11s per proof gallon to 14s 9d; purchasers of proprietary brands were called upon to pay 6d extra per bottle, while the price of ordinary public house whisky rose by 1d per glass. Eventually the output of whisky was substantially reduced as distilleries either closed down or severely curtailed production. The Distillers Company Limited, a powerful combination of Lowland grain distillers formed in 1877, were better placed than most to weather the storm, and indeed, they even managed to consolidate their position in the interim. The consumer at any rate derived some benefit from a slump caused not by a marked decline in the popularity of Scotch whisky, but by reckless speculation and over-production, for the stock pile of whisky was so large that relatively well-matured spirits soon became more readily available. In the early 1900s even the cheapest public house whisky had, as a rule, been at least twelve months (!) in bond.

By their foresight and enterprise the leading blenders had created the nucleus of a world market for their products, but their activities had not met with universal approval. The Highland malt distillers had every reason to deplore the popularity of "old Highland whiskies" composed largely of Lowland patent still grain spirits, and they had the moral support (for what it was worth) of a small section of the whisky drinking public – people who ignored the ubiquitous advertisements for blended whiskies and continued to drink the unadulterated "barley bree" of the north. They did not always have the opportunity to do so, for the blending houses, then as now, laid claim to the bulk of the supplies of malt whisky.

New grain whisky cost only about one-third of the price of new malt whisky. The cheapest (raw) malt whisky from Campbeltown cost about 2s 6d per gallon, while the cheapest (raw) grain whisky cost about 10d per gallon. As sold by the butt or hogshead, matured patent still whisky was also appreciably cheaper than matured pot still whisky. For example: in 1890, at a whisky sale in Glasgow, Highland Park 1885, matured in sherry wood, realised 5s 5d per (bulk) gallon, while Cameron Bridge 1885, matured in sherry wood, realised 2s 7½d per (proof) gallon. Bruichladdich 1882, matured in plain wood, fetched 5s 1d per (bulk) gallon, while Cambus 1882, matured in plain wood, fetched 3s 6d per (proof) gallon (the Victualling Trades' Review, March 12, 1890).

The Select Committee of 1890-91, appointed to inquire "inter alia" whether it was desireable that certain classes of spirits should be kept in bond for a definite period, and also to inquire into the question of blending of spirits and the application of the Sale of Food and Drugs Act and the Merchandise Act to spirits, presented a report which was entirely of a negative nature; no definition of "whisky" was attempted, and the cavalier activities of the less reputable whisky merchants escaped censure. While it conceded that "there was evidence that much whisky entered into consumption within six months of its distillation," the Select Committee nevertheless concluded "that compulsory bonding of all spirits for a certain period" was "unnecessary, and would harass trade." When replying to their critics, the wholesale blenders argued that they rather than the malt distillers had made Scotch whisky known all over the world; they also pointed out that if legislative restrictions were placed on the blending trade, there would be serious economic repercussions, since most people at home and abroad preferred blends to pure malt.

Oddly enough, it was from London that the challenge to the grain distillers and wholesale blenders eventually came. It happened in 1905, when Thomas Samuel Wells, a publican, and James Davidge, the holder of an off-licence, were prosecuted by the Islington Borough Council under the Sale of Food and Drugs Act, 1875, for selling spirits alleged to be wrongly described as Scotch and Irish whisky. Wells' "Irish" and Davidge's "Scotch" consisted mainly of raw spirits from the patent still. When the magistrate of the North London Police Court before whom the case was heard gave judgement against the defendants, the proprietors of patent still and blended whiskies were understandably dismayed (the defence in the Islington prosecution had been arranged by the giant Distillers Company Limited), but worse was in store for them, for an appeal to Clerkenwell Quarter Sessions failed to reverse the earlier judgement. The "what is whisky?" controversy led in due course to the appointment, in February 1908, of the Royal Commission on Whisky and other Potable Spirits; it was composed of English chemists and officials whose aquaintance with the subject of whisky was apparently of the slightest. The result was a decisive victory for the Lowland whisky magnates and for the laissez-faire spirit of the age.

In its final report, published on July 28, 1909, the Commission made no distinction between pot still and patent still spirits, defining whisky as "a spirit obtained by distillation from a mash of cereal grains saccharified by the diastase of malt." This put patent still whisky, made largely from unmalted grain "saccharified" (turned into sugar) by "the diastase of malt" (i.e. through the addition of a relatively small amount of malted barley), on the same footing as pot still whisky made wholly from malted barley. Scotch whisky, the Commission had decided, was whisky "as above defined distilled in Scotland," and Irish whiskey was whisky "as above defined distilled in Ireland." The Commissioners absolved the blenders from any obligation to reveal the various proportions of malt and grain in their products, and also failed to recommend that whisky (and other spirits) should be matured in bond for a minimum period prior to consumption.

Giving evidence before the Royal Commission in April 1908, a Glasgow publican who had been twenty-five years in the trade – George Thomson by name – threw interesting light on the nature of public house whisky as sold in Glasgow at that time. Thomson retailed Cambus grain whisky, Glenburgie malt whisky, and a blend of the two, which he blended himself. He also sold Dewar's, Walker's, and Mitchell's – proprietary blends in bottles. His cheapest whisky was Cambus at sixpence a gill. His own blend, sold at 7d a gill, contained 80 per cent grain and 20 per cent malt. He charged 8d and 10d a gill for proprietary blends, and

10d a gill for Glenburgie. In an average week, Thomson sold half-a-gallon of pure malt, roughly the same quantity of the proprietary blends, and fourteen gallons of Cambus. He used the label "fine old Scotch whisky" indiscriminately for pure grain, pure malt, and blended whisky, and he sold no whisky under three years old.

In the late Victorian period those Scotsmen who preferred beer to whisky could be extremely fastidious if they so desired. The nineteenth century saw a great increase in the production of beer in Scotland. In 1835-6 there were 640 licensed brewers in the country, and probably many more who were not licensed, but by 1866 their numbers had fallen to 217, of whom 98 were selling wholesale. Wholesale breweries, producing (relatively) large quantities of beer of consistent quality, were supplanting home and public house breweries producing very small quantities of beer of variable quality. In the late nineteenth century many new brewery companies came on the scene, and by 1898 there were 135 "brewers for sale" in Scotland, compared with 8022 in England and Wales.

Between them, the Scottish "brewers for sale" produced an extraordinary array of bitter and mild ales, old ales, sweet ales, porters and stouts. By present-day reckoning, production was often on a very modest scale; in 1898, for example, the average weekly output of Turner's Brewery at Newton-on-Ayr was 100 barrels – and that was an increase of more than 500 per cent on the same brewery's output in 1881.

Edinburgh was "the Burton of Scotland," with 35 breweries in the early 1900s. The city's brewers exploited abundant supplies of excellent water to produce sparkling pale ales of superior quality. Breweries had long been established in the historic Canongate, and at Holyrood and Abbeyhill, and in the late nineteenth century brewing operations were extended to the suburbs of Craigmillar and Duddingston. Among the leading Edinburgh brewers at the turn of the century were Lorimer and Clark (Caledonian Brewery), Alexander Melvin (Boroughloch Brewery), John Jeffrey (Heriot and Roseburn Breweries), Archibald Campbell, Hope and King (Argyle Brewery), Thomas Usher (Park Brewery), and William Younger (Abbey and Holyrood Breweries). The golden age of Edinburgh's brewing industry is enshrined in the imposing architecture of the McEwan Hall and the Usher Hall, both of which were presented to the city by munificent brewers. Brewery combines were not unknown even in those days; in 1890 six of the smaller Edinburgh breweries merged to form the Edinburgh United Breweries Company.

Alloa, in Clackmannanshire, was also celebrated for sparkling and delicious pale ales. In 1889 eight breweries were in operation in the town (population approximately 11,000), among them being Archibald Arrol and Sons (Alloa Brewery), James Blair (Townhead Brewery), and John Thomson (Caponcroft Brewery). The leading Alloa brewers were George Younger and Son (Candleriggs Brewery) who had been among the pioneers of India Pale Ale. Younger's of Alloa was the largest brewing concern in Scotland outside Edinburgh, and their bottled "Revolver Brand" export enjoyed a world-wide reputation. The independent brewers elsewhere included James Aitken (Falkirk), Hugh Ballingall and Son (Dundee), John Fowler (Prestonpans), William Whitelaw and Son (Musselburgh), and Thomas Marshall (Aberdeen). The products of Scottish brewers found their way to places as far apart as Malta and Mexico. In the financial year ending

September 30, 1897, Scotland exported 140,373 barrels of beer; the smallest amount (2 barrels) went to Russia; the largest (66,296 barrels) to the British East Indies.

It was possible to drink Glenlivet ales and stouts, brewed at Craigellachie on Speyside (apart from the Craigellachie Brewery there were another two breweries in Banffshire, which in 1903 boasted 24 distilleries). English and Irish beers were readily available too, and the thirsty cosmopolitan could sample lager from Denmark, Norway, Germany, Austria and Russia, not to mention spruce beer, imported from Danzig.

Edinburgh, Alloa, English and Continental beers were all popular in Glasgow, and so too were the products of local brewers such as Gillespie and Sons (Crown Brewery), Steel and Coulson (Greenhead Brewery), George Dalrymple (Home Brewery), and William Adamson (Barrowfield Brewery). There were ten breweries in Glasgow in 1902. The soft water supplies of Glasgow and neighbouring Paisley were highly suitable for the brewing of porter and stout.

The teetotaler was also catered for; several non-intoxicating "beers" were produced, one of which, Tonbur (Burton with the syllables reversed), was said to be "superior in many respects to the finest Burton beer, and more sustaining than the finest London stout." Tonbur was the invention of John Cummock, a manufacturing chemist whose other products included perfumes, cosmetics, hair restorers, and coffee and chicory essence; it was brewed (if that is the word) in Glasgow at the former Clydesdale Brewery, Victoria Road, which had been rebuilt and enlarged in 1896 for the Tonbur Brewery Company Limited.

A great many late Victorian and Edwardian beers had to be treated with considerable respect – McEwan's 126 shilling sweet ale, for instance, or William Younger's 90 shilling ale, either of which would be the undoing of many of today's effete beer drinkers. In Archibald Lauder's Royal Lochnagar Vaults, Sauchiehall Street, Glasgow, they dispensed a strong ale of fearsome potency.

By the bye, have you tasted Lauder's ten-guinea ale? You may venture on a glass of it, but if you wish to repeat the dose, get a hansom in readiness to convey you home.[8]

The independent brewers and their distinguished products have almost totally disappeared, victims of the modern mania for "rationalisation," but Maclay of Alloa and Belhaven of Dunbar still maintain the finest traditions of Scottish brewing. Many other famous names now survive only in terms of ornamental lettering on embossed advertisement mirrors. In the heyday of the independents the consumer, whether he preferred his favourite tipple to be fairly weak or formidably strong, was sure to find something to his taste among the hundreds of available brews. In ascending order of strength there were the Light 40 shilling, 50 shilling and 60 shilling ales (the equivalents of English mild beers), then there were the Heavy 70 shilling, 80 shilling and 90 shilling ales (corresponding to English bitter beers). Stronger beers were also produced, including such heroic brews as William Younger's Twelve Guinea Ale. The terms "shilling" and "guinea" originally referred to the prices which the brewers charged for different strengths and qualities of beer; made obsolete by the passage of time and the inflationary spiral, they survive as useful indications of the strength of particular brews: to this day several Scottish brewers produce 60 shilling, 70 shilling, 80 shilling and 90 shilling ales.

Scottish brewers, as John Bickerdyke observed (The Curiosities of Ale and Beer, 1889) were "great believers in malt and hops." This attitude stood them in good stead in 1900, when there were many cases of illness and several deaths in northern England through the consumption of poisoned beer – beer made partly from glucose (used as a malt substitute) which had been contaminated with arsenic. Scotch ales enjoyed a reputation for purity, and until the scandal was forgotten, there was an appreciable increase in the demand for the products of the leading Scottish brewers.

Then as now, a considerable number of Scottish pubs were "free houses" – that is to say they were not tied to breweries, and the proprietors were at liberty to stock a good range of ales and stouts. A remarkable amount of beer was consumed in some of the larger pubs. In 1891 a Glasgow publican by the name of Alexander Stewart actually purchased a complete March brewing of McEwan's 90 shilling Edinburgh ale – 125 hogsheads. In Stewart's Vaults, at 733 New City Road, some ten to twelve barrels were constantly on tap, including Salt's, Bass's, Allsopp's and McEwan's ales, and Guinness's, Reid's and Barclay Perkins' stouts.

The draught beer came in wooden barrels, the phenomenon of filtered beer in pressurised metal containers (kegs) being as yet unheard of. A brewery dray, hauled by hefty draught horses, delivered the sturdy oak casks to the pub, and there the beer was matured and conditioned before being sold.

For centuries beer had been dispensed direct from the casks, which had been set up in a cool back room or a cellar. The introduction in the early nineteenth century of the beer engine – a suction pump consisting of a piston inside a cylinder – saved the publican a great deal of trouble. He no longer had to commute between the beer store and the bar; instead, all he had to do was manipulate a lever handle and the ale was drawn from a barrel in the cellar through a pipe to the serving counter.

In the late nineteenth century many Scottish pubs (and some English ones) changed to an alternative beer dispensing system – hydraulic compression (a combination of air and water pressure). A compact little engine converted mains water pressure into air pressure, which was then used to push the beer on its way from the cellar to the service point. The bar staff filled the glasses by turning on a tap, not by pulling a handle as in the case of the manual beer engine. The water engine (as it was generally called) could also be employed to raise whisky and other spirits from the cellar to the bar.

The "McCallum and Harris automatic beer and liquor raising engine" was invented by Robert Harris (works: 17 West Street, Glasgow) and manufactured by him until his death in 1896, when Thomas Sim (works: 81 Govan Road, Glasgow) took over the manufacturing rights, modified the design, and changed the name of the product to "Sim's improved automatic beer and liquor raising engine."

In the 1880s Archibald Bruce, a Glasgow plumber and gasfitter whose premises were located in Cathedral Street, patented the "Bruce, Challenge, and Waste Not" hydraulic beer and spirit raising engines. He also anticipated modern practice by marketing a patent aerator, the function of which was to "improve" draught beer by infusing it with extraneous carbon dioxide gas. Referring to Bruce's engines, the Victualling Trades' Review (May 12, 1892) observed that their "utility and usefulness" had been "demonstrated by over a thousand proprietors of licensed houses scattered over Great Britain and Ireland," adding that in Glasgow they were "almost in universal" use. Bruce later transferred his operations to Clyde Street in the Calton district of Glasgow.

Allan and Bogle and McGlashan water engines were also made in Glasgow where the publicans, like the rest of the citizenry, were enamoured of all things modern, and needed little prompting to scrap their "old-fashioned" handpumps. The counter fount was invariably placed below the level of the bar top, an arrangement which allowed the publican, if sufficiently unscrupulous, to make use of "slops" or waste beer without the customer being any the wiser. The tall founts which required glasses to be filled above the bar top in full view were a much later introduction (they are still operational in some Scottish pubs). Hydraulic compression was held by its sponsors to improve the appearance and palatable qualities of beer. This was somewhat of a debatable point; at any rate the beer emerged from the fount slightly aerated, and usually with a tight creamy head. One of the indisputable advantages of the water engine was its ability to raise beer to a much greater height than was possible with the handpump. The proprietary water engines were made in several sizes to suit various water pressures and were capable of being worked direct from the water main or through a cistern.

South of the border there was a tendency to regard the air pressure system with suspicion. In the late 1890s the Water Motor and Automatic Liquid Elevator Company of London tried to induce the English publican to get rid of his "obsolete" beer pump and substitute a water engine invented by Scotsman James Keith, a hydraulic engineer, and manufactured in Arbroath, but the response was not encouraging. Many of the older barrels in use in England were not sufficiently sound to withstand the pressure used to push the beer from cellar to serving counter: these were liable to spring leaks. As a rule, Scottish brewers used casks that were sufficiently strong to withstand such pressure.

As the nineteenth century advanced, brewing became an increasingly scientific pursuit. The introduction of the thermometer and the saccharometer allowed precise measurements of temperature and specific gravity to be made, while temperature control by means of cold water (circulated through pipes immersed in the beer) made it possible to brew throughout the year, not just from autumn to spring as formerly. Brewers still occasionally incurred heavy losses through the use of impure yeast, however. Louis Pasteur was the first to discover the full functioning of yeast in relation to alcoholic fermentation. In 1871, on being shown round Whitbread's London brewery, he used his own microscope to examine a small quantity of yeast from a brew of porter and immediately pronounced it to be infected with a trouble-causing micro-organism. On visiting the same brewery a week later, he found that all the yeast had been changed, and a microscope had been purchased. The publication, in 1876, of Pasteur's book "Etudes sur la Biere" was a seminal event which led to the rapid proliferation of brewery laboratories, both in this country and on the Continent. The microscope joined the thermometer and saccharometer among the brewer's indispensable instruments, enabling him to make his product more stable and consistent.

Pasteur had previously shown that the life of wine in bottles could be greatly prolonged if the bottles were once subjected to a certain temperature, and in due course the technique of "Pasteurisation" was applied to some British bottled beers, lagers and stouts in particular.

It had long been the practice of brewers to send their beers out in casks, along with a supply of labels, to the bottling agents, who then put the liquor into bottles, wired down the corks, and stuck on the labels. The late nineteenth century saw an enormous increase in the demand for bottled beers, and in order to ensure that their products reached the consumer in the best possible condition, the leading brewers erected extensive bottling halls, replete with appliances for washing, filling and corking bottles. Beer was still being bottled by individual publicans, and also by licensed bottlers such as Messrs. Mair and Dougall, whose Annfield Bottling Works in Glasgow were described by the Victualling Trades' Review (November 12, 1891) as "the largest of the kind in Scotland." Mair and Dougall bottled the products of the great Burton brewers; they did not, however, "confine themselves to Bass, Allsopp and Salt," but "also dealt in Scotch beers." Like many bottling merchants, they were also aerated water manufacturers.

Before being run into bottles, the beer was first stored in butts and hogsheads until mature. Export ale and strong winter ale, porter and stout, were allowed to mature over a prolonged period. Once they had been filled, corked, and wired, the bottles were labelled, stacked, and left for a number of weeks (longer in winter than in summer) until the contents were in prime condition and ready for use. William Younger's export ale was brewed from October to March. When brewed it was racked into butts and conveyed to the export stores in the Queen's Park, adjoining the Abbey and Holyrood Breweries. It then lay undisturbed until it reached maturity and was ready for bottling – usually in about a year.

Storage in casks and bottles involved a slow turnover of capital and took up a considerable amount of space. These factors led some brewers to introduce artificial conditioning which allowed their products to be sent out for immediate consumption. The beer was bottled in bright condition (having been clarified by filtration beforehand) and charged with carbonic acid gas after the fashion of mineral waters. The absence of deposit in the artificially conditioned bottled beer made for ease of pouring, but the product was generally acknowledged to be inferior in palate to properly matured and naturally conditioned beer, and for a long time some firms continued to ensure that their beers were bottled under normal conditions only.

At the turn of the century the "schooner of beer" was a popular refreshment in Scotland. The tumbler known as the schooner was of transatlantic origin and held 2d worth of beer – two-thirds of an imperial pint (bitter beer cost 3d per pint). In 1902 a Glasgow publican was prosecuted and convicted for selling beer by the schooner, a measure which was not of the legal imperial standard, and thereafter its popularity waned, but in 1904 it was reinstated by the new Licensing Act, Clause 52 of which excepted measures containing quantities less than a pint from the imperial standard. The pony, another American-style beer measure, held nine-tenths of an imperial gill and sold for a penny. Beer bottles were often secured by wired corks, although metal crown tops and ebonite screw stoppers with vulcanised rubber rings were coming into use in the 1890s. Lager and stout frequently came in attractive stoneware bottles – Glasgow brewers J. and R. Tennent had their own pottery in which they manufactured stoneware containers for their lager and stout. A large number of Scottish publicans supplied porter, stout, and even whisky in stone bottles and jars, emblazoned with their names and trademarks. The glass-lined whisky jars were particularly handsome, being decorated with scenes of old-time convivialia. These containers were manufactured locally by firms such as the Barrowfield Potteries (Henry Kennedy and Sons), Glasgow.

Wines from the wood were obtained in bodega bars such as those of Rogano Limited. This firm had its central premises in Glasgow's South Exchange Square; it was founded by James Henry Roger who had formerly been in the employment of the Bodega Company Limited of London. Red wine of a sort not to be met with in bodega bars was sold in pubs of the lowest class – cheap and potent, it was almost as deleterious as raw whisky.

The Glasgow man was inordinately fond of a "hauf an' a hauf pint," a half glass of whisky and a half pint of beer – the latter being known in this context as a "chaser." Mulled ale and whisky toddy were popular winter tipples, and at least one Glasgow publican offered his customers hot spiced stout, which must have been something of an acquired taste.

To dispense the immensely varied (and sometimes fearfully potent) products of the late Victorian and Edwardian brewers, distillers and whisky merchants, there were the barmen, whose working day began shortly before eight o'clock in the morning and did not end until after eleven o'clock at night. The larger pubs employed a host of these functionaries – all uniformly garbed in long white aprons and white shirts. Sometimes the barman had to be a jack of all trades; there were barrels to be set up and tapped, or taken off, spirits to be reduced to the correct proof and transferred from the cellar to the row of casks behind the bar counter, and English beers such as Bass, Salt, or Worthington to be bottled. In 1903 the average Glasgow barman worked a 65-hour week, with two or three hours per day for meals and one afternoon and evening off per week, and in that year the magistrates recommended to the city's licence holders that no employee be employed for more than 60 hours in any one week.

Apart from alcoholic beverages, Bovril and soft drinks such as Mackay's Sparkling Kola and Clydesdale's Imperial Champagne Ginger were also stocked by publicans. Bovril, the brainchild of Scotsman John L. Johnson, was accredited with great revitalising properties in the 1890s. The Victualling Trades' Review (November 12, 1891) roundly declared that every man who desired "the race to march on unimpeded to the goal of its high destiny" was "bound to encourage the use of a stimulant so far-reaching in its effects." According to the Review, Bovril had been found to be "a certain remedy against melancholia and influenza." Iced Bovril was recommended as a particularly efficacious pick-me-up.

To accompany the liquid refreshments there were often comestibles of one sort or another – oatcakes and cheese, twopenny mutton pies, sardines on toast, sausages, or Welsh rarebit. After the Licensing (Scotland) Act of 1903 came into force, licensing authorities in various parts of Scotland passed by-laws obliging licence holders to provide a fresh and sufficient supply of bar-snacks. The free lunch system, popular in the north of England, was also a feature of many Scottish pubs, and in these the customer could purchase a twopenny glass of ale and proceed to attack the free bread, cheese and cake with gusto. Some publicans also supplied free morning coffee or afternoon tea to their customers. The ever-vigilant Glasgow magistrates strongly disapproved of the free lunch system, viewing it as an insidious method of persuading casual customers to become regular patrons, and on several occasions they issued stern warnings to the city's publicans, bidding them to refrain from the practice.

In 1899, according to the Royal Statistical Society's Journal (January 1912), the British people, per head of population, downed 32.53 gallons of beer and 8.72 pints of spirits. In 1900 beer consumption had fallen slightly to 31.56 gallons, while spirit consumption had risen to 8.86 pints. By 1910 beer consumption had fallen to 26.32 gallons while the decline in spirit drinking was even more marked – 5.20 pints (in 1909, to be sure, the duty on spirits had been raised from 11s per proof gallon to 14s 9d; in contrast, the duty on beer had stood at 7s 9d per 36 gallon barrel since March 1900).

Bearing in mind that "respectable" women did not drink much in those days, while teetotalers did not, in theory at any rate, imbibe at all, it is clear that some people were drinking much more than was good for them. Drinking to excess was indeed a very common human failing in late Victorian and Edwardian Britain. It was a failing which took a heavy toll in terms of broken lives and early deaths, and it not surprisingly served to fuel the fires of militant teetotalism. Drunks and teetotal militants were alike ubiquitous at the turn of the century.

*uisge was in time corrupted into usky and finally into whisky.

[1] The Scottish Wine, Spirit and Beer Trades' Review, September 6, 1887.
[2] The Scottish Wine, Spirit and Beer Trades' Review, May 10, 1887.
[3] The Scottish Wine, Spirit and Beer Trades' Review, August 9, 1887.
[4] The Victualling Trades' Review, December 12, 1889.
[5] The Victualling Trades' Review, January 1908, page 3.
[6] The Bailie, number 1225, April 8, 1896.
[7] The National Guardian, March 19, 1897.
[8] The Scottish Wine, Spirit and Beer Trades' Review, May 10, 1887.

Part Two

2   Demon Drink

When Doctor Johnson firmly asserted that "there is nothing which has yet been contrived by man, by which so much happiness is produced as by a good tavern or inn," he was merely putting into words the heartfelt belief of a substantial number of his contemporaries of all classes. In the nineteenth century, however, the widespread abuse of liquor led growing numbers of people to recoil in horror from the taverns and all that they ostensibly stood for. The first temperance societies were in favour of moderation in the use of intoxicants, venting their ire on spirits and blaming cheap whisky, gin and rum for the appalling condition of the slum dwellers and the destitute. As the societies grew influential they became less tolerant, and it was not long before spirits, wine and beer were being impartially denounced as Demon Drink. What had begun as a plea for temperance duly became a total abstinence movement embracing millions of men, women and children.

In Scotland the first shots in the war against Demon Drink were fired by John Dunlop (1789-1868), a Greenock lawyer and philanthropist who established moderation societies in Greenock and Maryhill in October 1829. At his first public meeting in Glasgow Dunlop was fortunate enough to enlist the support of William Collins, founder of the great publishing house; Collins started to produce large quantities of temperance tracts, and both men travelled extensively, lecturing forcefully on the evils of drunkenness, with the result that temperance societies were soon flourishing in other parts of the country.

Demon Drink was far from being a mere bogy; on the contrary, the problem was a formidable one, due in no small measure to the ready availability of cheap raw spirits. In 1822 the duty on spirits had been lowered from 7s. to 2s. 6d. per gallon, and in Scotland, where "freedom an' whisky" had long been considered to "gang thegither," this led, predictably, to a dramatic increase in spirit consumption – from 2,079,000 gallons in 1822 to 5,777,000 gallons in 1829. Chronic drunkenness was rife, resulting in scenes of indescribable misery which provided ample fuel for fiery temperance speeches and tracts.

The temperance movement was international. It was particularly strong in the United States (where it originated), but Ireland was the country in which it scored its first, spectacular, success. When Father Theobald Matthew, a parish priest well known for relief work among the slum dwellers of Cork, signed the pledge in 1838, he was soon besieged by thousands of people eager to follow him in renouncing alcohol. He lectured on total abstinence to audiences all over Ireland, and by 1840 his following was estimated at two million. A year later it was being claimed that there were at least five million on the teetotal role, in a population of eight million. Breweries and distilleries went out of business, and the consumption of spirits dropped from over twelve million gallons in 1838 to less than six million gallons four years later. Some Irishmen, unwilling to revoke their pledges, but craving a stimulant of sorts, took to drinking a heady mixture of methylated ether and water. "The Irish apostle of temperance" received many invitations to lecture in Scotland and England. He visited Glasgow in August 1842; special trains brought supporters from Edinburgh, Ayrshire, Lanarkshire, Dunbartonshire and Stirling; a procession of 50,000 people marched to Glasgow Green to hear him preach, and in the course of three days an estimated total of 40,000 people signed the pledge. His triumphal progress continued all the way to London, where he met Prime Minister Sir Robert Peel and the Duke of Wellington.

Other remarkable personalities emerged to lead the growing army of total abstainers, among them barn-storming orators who appealed to the heart rather than to the head and were not averse to backing up their blistering attacks on alcohol with imaginative but scarcely credible statements. Some of them informed their audiences that the habitual drunkard was liable to undergo spontaneous combustion.

John Bartholomew Gough, the temperance evangelist par excellence, had emigrated from England to America at the tender age of 12. After experiencing a considerable degree of hardship he became a minor music hall turn, in which capacity he increasingly took to the bottle. In 1842, however, he signed the pledge and was soon in demand as a redeemed alcoholic with a salutory tale to tell; indeed, he was such a success in this role that he decided to become a professional redeemed alcoholic. His "lectures" were really histrionic performances, redolent of the atmosphere of contemporary melodrama, and they made him a fairly wealthy man. Gough revisited the land of his birth in 1853 and his tour was a temperance triumph reminiscent of that enjoyed by Father Matthew ten years before. His oft-repeated peroration in praise of water earned him the journalistic appellation of "the American high priest of the water pump."

Coloured ribbons – blue, white or red – were the emblems of various pledge-signing temperance organisations that spread to this country from the United States. The blue ribbon in particular became the badge of militant teetotalism and figured in many temperance poems, of which "The Blue on the Shroud" was probably not the worst:

> God speed the triumphs of Temperance,
>   May the ribbon still deck the brave;
> You'll wear it in life's rough path, mother,
>   And I in my silent grave.

The International Order of Good Templars, scorning to advertise its presence by means of a mere ribbon, devised a colourful regalia, secret signs and an accompanying ritual. Good Templary was introduced to Scotland by an exiled Scot who had settled in the United States. The first Scottish Lodge was established in Glasgow, in August 1869, and by 1876 there were no fewer than 1,131 Lodges, with a total membership of 83,717.

Temperance friendly societies such as the Independent Order of Rechab, and the Sons of Temperance, also adopted complex rituals and distinctive regalia; their success was mainly due to the sickness benefit and life insurance schemes which they operated.

Perhaps the most stirring manifestation of temperance militancy was the Salvation Army. In 1879, for the first time, Salvationists were on the march in Scotland, and they soon became a familiar sight, parading in their smart uniforms through drab working class streets, with banners flying and bands playing.

Among the most idiosyncratic of the teetotal groups were the Temperance Lifeboat Crews, who wore red shirts in imitation of Garibaldi, and were "ready, aye ready" to cast a metaphorical lifeline to the nearest drunk.

> Throw out the Life-line across the dark wave!
> There is a brother whom someone should save;
> Somebody's brother! Oh, who then will dare
> To throw out the Life-line his peril to share?
>
> Throw out the Life-line!
> Throw out the Life-line!
> Someone is drifting away!
> Throw out the Life-line!
> Throw out the Life-line!
> Someone is sinking today.

It would possibly take more than the battle hymns of abstainers to disturb the composure of the modern publican, but in the late nineteenth century there was a mighty upsurge of temperance sentiments, and talk of total prohibition was in the air, notwithstanding the fact that at that time, the drinker was burdened with a hugely disproportionate share of the national finances (no wonder he was sinking). In 1890, for example, the National Revenue was £89,304,000, of which £29,798,910 – more than a quarter – was derived from the abhorred "drink traffic." William McGonagall, poet and tragedian, was greatly in favour of the temperance reformation, and, as usual, he expressed his sentiments in imperishable verse.

> Oh, thou demon Drink, thou fell destroyer;
> Thou curse of society, and its greatest annoyer.
> What hast thou done to society, let me think?
> I answer thou hast caused the most of ills, thou
>   demon Drink.
>
> Thou causeth the mother to neglect her child,
> Also the father to act as he were wild,
> So that he neglects his loving wife and family dear,
> By spending his earnings foolishly on whisky, rum,
>   and beer.

And after spending his earnings foolishly he beats
his wife –
The man that promised to protect her during life –
And so the man would if there was no drink in
society,
For seldom a man beats his wife in a state of
sobriety.

Scottish publicans took the threat to their livelihoods more seriously than most people took McGonagall's poetry. By 1896 nearly 10,000 of the country's 11,006 licence holders supported the Scottish Licensed Trade Defence Association, while the trade's own journals, the weekly National Guardian and the monthly Victualling Trades' Review, devoted a great deal of space and much editorial ingenuity to counter-propaganda. From the 1890s onwards the Liberals were closely identified with the cause of temperance reform, and so were the embryo Socialists; the prohibition of the "liquor traffic" was part of the programme of the Scottish Labour Party, founded in 1888. The Conservatives, on the other hand, were largely representative of the liquor interests. In Scotland – traditionally Liberal and prospectively Socialist in its voting habits – the holder of a public house licence could not afford to be complacent.

When temperance campaigners plastered towns with posters illustrating the evils of drink, their opponents retaliated in kind with posters bearing testimonials in favour of alcoholic beverages. One such poster depicted an extremely robust-looking beer-drinking centenarian whose father before him (the accompanying text made perfectly clear) had also been a beer-drinking centenarian.

The anti-drink movement, like other radical movements before and since, was particularly anxious to recruit the young. The first juvenile temperance association was founded in Paisley in 1830. The Band of Hope, the most successful temperance youth movement, originated in Leeds in 1847. It grew rapidly and the first Scottish branches came into being a few years later. The organisation had more than three million members by the late 1890s. The Band of Hope offered children recreational facilities at a time when these were almost non-existent. A variety of innocent amusements were provided, not the least popular of which was the magic lantern lecture – with a temperance punchline, naturally. Youthful adherents of the Band of Hope were expected to shun the Demon Drink for life. The adult membership sanguinely looked forward to the time when this indoctrination would bear fruit in a 100% teetotal Britain; in the 1900s, however, the organisation began to lose ground to Baden-Powell's adventurous new youth movement.

The abstemious hero was one of the stock characters in late Victorian melodrama. The heroine could generally be relied on to marry the staunch teetotaler (leaving the drink-sodden and brutish alternative suitor to go to the devil in his own way), but occasionally a good woman managed to redeem a habitual drunkard; when this happened it was usually because the teetotaler – in this case the alternative suitor – sacrificed his own chance of happiness in order to throw out the lifeline to his sinking brother.

In the Glasgow of the early 1900s, between the hours of nine and eleven at

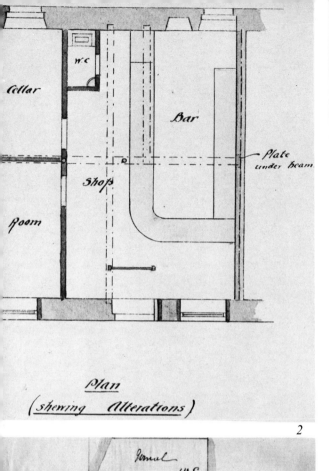

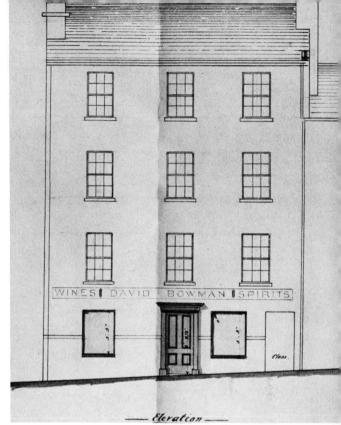

2

4

Suburban pub layout of 1879 – Stevenson's Bar, Dumbarton Road, Partick (top left).

Elevation of Bowman's Bar, Weaver Street, Partick (1886).

Plan of pub at 55–57 Candleriggs, Glasgow, before alterations of 1887 (bottom left).

Plan of Bowman's Bar, Weaver Street, Partick (1886).

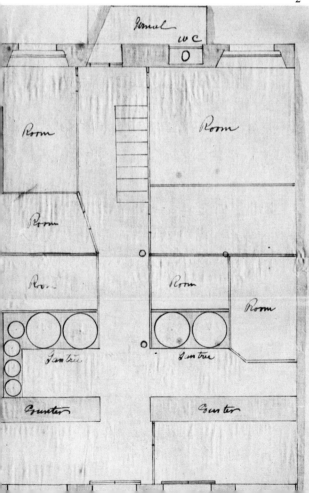

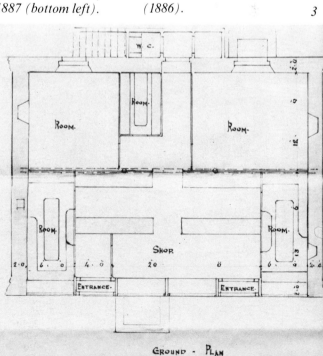

3

5

The well-preserved
exterior of the
Horseshoe Bar, Drury
Street, Glasgow
(above).

A corner of the immense
public bar (left).

Farrier at work
(below).

6

8

The island bar; note rear extension to original oval-shaped counter (below).

Detail of capital in public bar showing characteristic horseshoe decoration (right).

ELEVATION TO CLASSFORD STREET

ELEVATION TO GARTHLAND STREET.

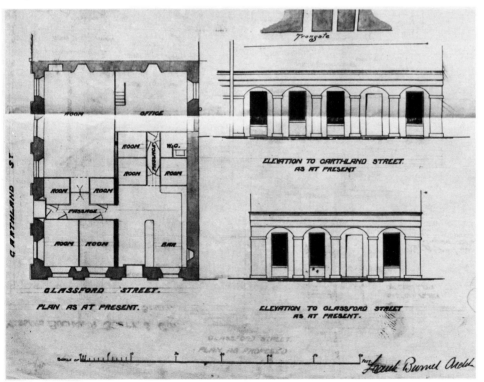

Trongate

ELEVATION TO GARTHLAND STREET.
AS AT PRESENT

ELEVATION TO CLASSFORD STREET
AS AT PRESENT

GARTHLAND ST.

GLASSFORD STREET.

PLAN AS AT PRESENT.

Elevation of the Blane Valley (Change House) as remodelled by Frank Burnet in 1887 (above).

Plan and elevation of the Blane Valley (Change House), Glasgow, as it appeared before alterations of 1887 (left).

The Blane Valley (Change House) as it is today (below).

11

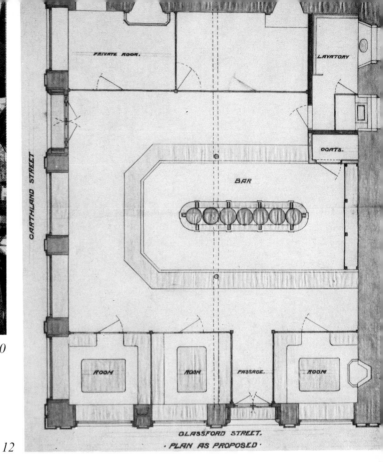

Wall of mirrors in the Horseshoe Bar (above left).

Plan of the Blane Valley (Change House) (right).

10

12

14

The Gordon Bar,
Mitchell Street,
Glasgow (Frank Burnet,
1906) (opposite page).

The Old Toll Bar,
Paisley Road West,
Glasgow (1892-93);
view of the bar counter
and gantry (right).

Mirror advertisements
by Forrest and Son
(above).

Ornate lettering on a Forrest and Son mirror (left).
The Old Toll Bar's inner glass doors are richly decorated (above).

Clock set with elaborate cornicing in the public bar (below).
Elevation for MacSorley's Bar, Glasgow (opposite). 18, 19, 20, 21

ELEVATION to ANN ST.

23

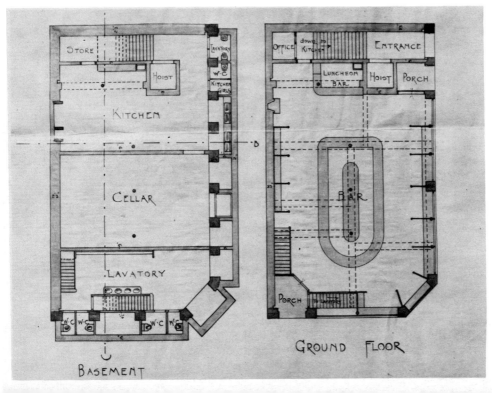

George Bell's plans for MacSorley's Bar and Restaurant (left).

MacSorley's, Jamaica Street, Glasgow; detail (above).

STORE

LAVATORY

HOIST

W·C

KITCHEN GIRLS

KITCHEN

D

CELLAR

LAVATORY

W·C W·C   W·C W·C

BASEMENT

OFFICE down to Kitchen

ENTRANCE

LUNCHEON BAR

HOIST

PORCH

BAR

PORCH to LAVATORY

GROUND FLOOR

22

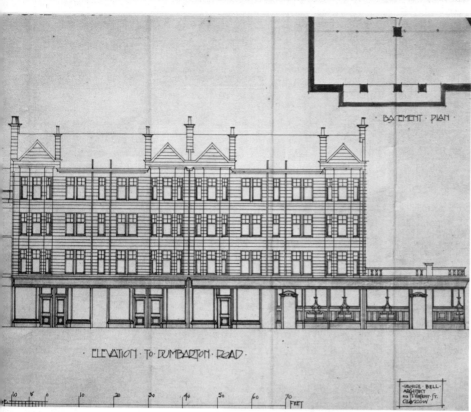

BASEMENT PLAN

ELEVATION TO DUMBARTON ROAD

GEORGE BELL
ARCHITECT
au S.Vincent St.
GLASGOW

Design for tenements, incorporating shops and pub (Hayburn Vaults), Dumbarton Road, Partick (George Bell, 1904) (left).

The well-preserved frontage of the Hayburn Vaults (below).

VINES · HAYBURN VAULTS · SPIRITS · R. ANDE

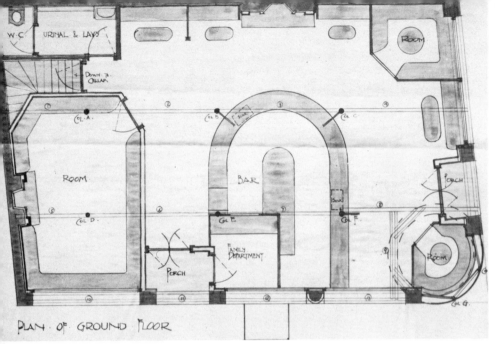

PLAN OF GROUND FLOOR

The Roost Bar, now known as the Exchequer Bar, Dumbarton Road, Partick (J. H. Craigie, 1900) (below).

The Corona Bar, Shawlands Cross, Glasgow (Clarke and Bell, 1912–13); ground floor plan (left).

The exterior of the Corona Bar; note Palm and Passion-Cross motif above the entrance to the public bar (left).

View of the spacious public bar (above).

Island stock fitment in the Corona Bar (left).

The King's Arms (Griffin), Bath Street, Glasgow (William Reid, 1903–04); detail (below).

Wilson's Bar, Byres Road, Partick (William Reid, 1904) (above).

Plan of St. Mungo Vintners' pub, Queen Street, Glasgow, before alterations of 1904 (below).

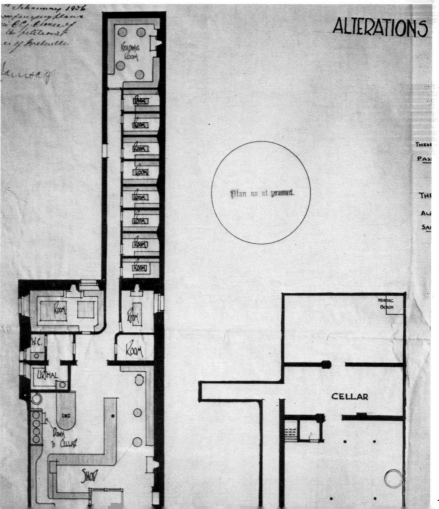

ALTERATIONS

Plan as at present.

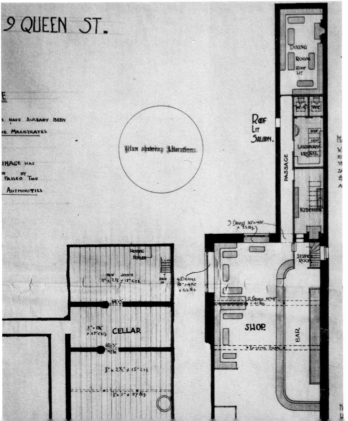

Plan of St. Mungo Vintners' pub as remodelled by MacWhannel and Rogerson (left).

Interior of the St. Mungo Vintners' as it appeared before the fittings were dismantled for shipment to the U.S.A. in 1974 (Glasgow Herald) (above).

night, teetotal activists could occasionally be espied lurking outside public houses. The advocates of early closing (for such they were) belonged to organisations such as the Citizen's Vigilance Association and the Glasgow United Young Men's Christian Association. Each vigilante was equipped with a box of sweets bearing the name of the publican whose premises were under surveillance. When a man or woman passed through the portals of the establishment the vigilante took a sweet out of the box and transferred it to his pocket: this was a discreet way of keeping tally of the number of drinkers.

Several decades before the suffragette movement got under way, disgruntled females were able to make their presence felt in the British Women's Temperance Association, which adopted a white ribbon as its symbol. It was formed in 1878, two years after Mrs. Elizabeth "Mother" Stewart, a formidable American lady militant, had toured Britain. The teetotal women of this country, through inhibitions or good breeding, fought shy of the methods of such picturesque American groups as the praying women, who knelt outside saloons, calling down Divine wrath on the proprietors' heads, or the axe women who, operating on the principle that "God helps those who help themselves," stormed the saloons with hatchets (Mrs. Carry Nation was one of the most efficient members of the latter group). But they were nonetheless to the fore in the struggle against the Demon, and when Frances Willard, doyenne of the American Women's Christian Temperance Union spoke at the Royal Albert Hall in 1895, they turned out in strength to hear and cheer the "uncrowned queen of American womanhood." The Scotsman's correspondent was somewhat less enthusiastic.

For the mere male creature, the proceedings of the body that calls itself the World's Women's Christian Temperance Union is doleful reading. He perceives that the time has come for him to walk the plank, or at least take his seat on the lower steps of the platform from which Aroused Woman demonstrates and harangues the world. Since Wednesday the mighty floods of the eloquence of the "White Ribbon Pilgrims," who have congregated in London, have been pouring forth from that centre towards the ends of the earth whence they came; and the emptying of these vials of wrath will not be complete until tomorrow. It may seem presumptuous to say a word on behalf of the inferior sex about the display, especially before it is finished. But one can at least pay a tribute to the fine eye for broad effects of colour and theatric grouping that has been displayed by the organisers of the New Crusade. Nothing in the shape of a raree-show has been seen to equal the exhibition of Thursday in the Royal Albert Hall. There was an effort to give "picturesque representation of the far-reaching ramifications" of a movement which boasts that it has got a footing in all the countries of the world, including (so at least Miss Willard assures us) the "Antarctic Continent," which ignorant man has hitherto imagined was uninhabited and uninhabitable. There were "teetotal sailors, soldiers, policemen, firemen, postmen, railwaymen," all fastened to the triumphal car of that New Woman whom Lady Henry Somerset* describes as terrible as an army with banners. There were great beds of brilliant colour, made up of "Sons of Phoenix, Rechabites, Catholics, League of Cross, Good

Templars," dressed in their robes and paraphernalia. But these were quite eclipsed by the splendour of the group costumed to represent the countries of the world which the Union has invaded and annexed, including all lands from Iceland to Tasmania, and from Mexico round the circumference of the globe by Madeira, Madagascar, Ceylon, the Straits Settlements, China, and Japan, to the Hawaii Islands. Round the hall was draped the great Polyglot Petition, reputed to be eight miles long and to weigh 13 cwt., on which a trusty White Ribboner has spent two years of work, averaging eight hours a day, in counting the eight millions of names – according to other accounts, only two millions – and in classifying, trimming, pasting, and sewing the monstrous document to its present form. Polyglot talk was as much in evidence as the Polyglot Petition, and in the interludes an "action song was sung by genuine slum children," and Miss Agnes Weston** marched past with her sailor bodyguard, each of them decorated with a medal attesting that the wearer is not one of those vulgar and unregenerate tars who can swig off their glass of grog.[1]

The Polyglot Petition, signed by women in fifty different languages, asked for the prohibition of alcohol and opium (!) in the territory over which British rule extended.

The United Kingdom Alliance, or to give it its full resounding title, the United Kingdom Alliance for the Suppression of the Traffic in all Intoxicating Liquors, was an out and out prohibitionist body. Founded in 1853, it was strongly influenced by the example of the American state of Maine – the "banner state of prohibition," which had forbidden the general sale of intoxicants in 1846. Evasion of the Maine Law was a way of life for many of the inhabitants of the state, and not least for the bootleggers and the proprietors of "blind pigs" (illegal saloons). Like the United Kingdom Alliance, the Scottish Prohibition Party, formed in Dundee in 1901, was totally uncompromising in its attitude to the drink question. The Party's leading personality, Edwin Scrymgeour, was elected to Dundee town council in 1905; in 1922 he unseated Winston Churchill from his Dundee constituency to become Britain's first (and last) Prohibitionist M.P.

The British prohibitionists were never to know the heady delights of total victory, as experienced by their American counterparts when the Eighteenth Amendment to the Constitution enforced prohibition on the entire United States from 16th January 1920. But they were indefatigable campaigners, and it was undoubtedly a red letter day for them when the Forbes Mackenzie Act (1853) became law, forbidding Scotland's pubs to open on Sundays. In theory, this should have put a stop to "drink trafficking" on the Sabbath, but in practice it certainly did not – as the Scottish Wine, Spirit and Beer Trades' Review, with some irony, observed.

Thanks to that glorious piece of monumental legislature (sic), the Forbes Mackenzie Act, nobody can get anything to drink in Glasgow on the Sabbath. Just walk along Argyle Street on Sunday evening, and you will see from the "walk, talk, and conversation" of the passers by how true this is. You never see a drunken man, do you? Nor does the presiding genius at the Central* ever

66

have any "drunks" to deal with arising from Sunday drinking! Bah! what a farce the whole thing is! A respectable man has no difficulty in getting good whisky on the seventh day, and as for the non-respectable portion of the community there are plenty of shebeens where poison can be obtained at fourpence a glass.[2]

The Forbes Mackenzie Act enabled a small army of people who were accustomed to living on their wits to gain a lucrative livelihood. There were hundreds of unlicensed liquor purveyors in Glasgow alone, ranging from those right at the murky bottom of the Victorian social scale, whose special blends of whisky owed much to methylated spirits, to shebeen proprietors whose West End establishments were quite genteel.

It was on a Sunday afternoon that I made my first call at a house in Garnethill. Of course I cannot give the exact address; it must suffice to say that the house is in a quiet thoroughfare, and, from the exterior, presents a highly respectable appearance. I was accompanied by a friend, who, to use an expressive term, "knew the ropes;" and as soon as the door was opened in response to our ring, we were ushered into a very comfortable parlour – one of the three reception rooms, which, as I afterwards ascertained, were devoted to business purposes. There were seven or eight men in the room, and three young women – daughters, nieces, or friends of the landlady of the house; and I thought the assembled company looked rather uneasy as I entered, my features being unknown to the habitues of the place. But my friend's presence reassured them, and the conversation, which our arrival had interrupted, was resumed.[3]

A far cry from the typical American speak-easy of the Roaring Twenties! Entrance to the superior type of shebeen was restricted to "respectable" inbibers. Each establishment had its regular clientele, composed of people who took care not to abuse the privilege of late-night or Sunday drinking. White-collar workers such as shop assistants were frequently kept busy until late on a Saturday night; they were, of course, at leisure on Sunday, but unluckily for them, all places of entertainment were locked and shuttered on the Sabbath. In the better class of shebeen, however, they were able to enjoy a drink in pleasant surroundings. The West End shebeen, situated in a detached villa or a terraced tenement, consisted of several comfortably furnished apartments. Customers, obstensibly "guests," were attended to by individuals who, whether or not they were actually related, gave every indication of being members of a prosperous bourgeois family. When obtaining supplies of liquor, the proprietor of the West End shebeen had to exercise great caution.

Several very clever ruses are resorted to. Of course, the "family" take in their own supplies openly; and as they receive a good deal of company, this legitimate consumption is extensive. They get through a good deal of bottled beer; and the licensed grocer whom they patronise sends his "six dozen" at a time openly, and frequently. But six dozen of beer does not go very far; so orders are given to various grocers in the district for "single" dozens, which, being delivered by message boys, can cause no suspicion among the neighbours. As to the stock of whisky or brandy, that is easy enough. Once a month, or oftener, one of the "family" takes a trip to the coast – at least she departs in a cab, with plenty of luggage, and drives to the Central. There, however, she places her luggage in the waiting-room, and sallies forth into the city. She buys a gallon here, a gallon there, and it is duly sent to the station. Here, as it arrives, it is deftly placed in the big boxes with which the young lady finds it advisable to travel; and if the cabman who finally conveys her and her belongings back to Kelvingrove fancies the luggage is somewhat heavy, a good douceur silences his tongue, if not his suspicions. Thus, by drawing her supplies from various quarters, and bringing them in by a constantly flowing but hardly susceptible stream, all the trouble and danger of unloading a big cargo at once is avoided.[4]

The West End shebeen was conducted on decorous lines; when the customers were leaving, "papa" accompanied them to the door, wished them a hearty "good night, dear boys," and urged them to "look round again soon."

The whisky dispensed at sixpence a glass in the douce shebeens of Garnethill or Kelvinside may not have been Old Glenlivet, but neither was it likely to have been positively harmful, at least when taken in moderation. The most unscrupulous shebeeners of all were the itinerant pedlars of near-lethal hooch.

Sunday shebeening may be said to commence when the public-houses have closed. Then the peripatetic shebeener appears on the scene. This person may be a male or a female, very often the latter. But whether man or woman, they are ghouls of the night, and move about the streets as silently as the silken flight of the owl. Their prey is invariably drunken men. The peripatetic carries concealed about his or her person a bottle containing a vile concoction of methylated spirits and vitriol. They entice their victim up some dark close and there dose him with the stuff. He is, if the methylated spirits act as expected, relieved of any valuables he may possess, very often his shoes and his coat are removed. . .[5]

The shebeen proprietors of Glasgow had to be ingenious in order to stay in "business," and on the whole, they rose to the challenge.

The ways of the shebeener are like those of the serpent on the rock – past finding out. Some of the most extraordinary tricks are resorted to, to elude the vigilance of the police. A house in King Street (City) was suspected by the police and it was placed under espionage. Every Sunday a raid was made on it, but no liquor of any description could be found in the premises, although the police were satisfied that a large trade was being done. Eventually, however, one of the patrons was bribed, and the secret of how the shebeener baffled the police leaked out. An inspector and a couple of constables invaded the house on a Sunday. The inspector went to the gas pipe, turned it full on, and the liquid came pouring out. The spirits were concealed in the wall and the gas pipe attached to the jar. The man was arrested, but he paid the fine without the least difficulty, and is busy at the old game in another part of the city.[6]

Anyone could become a shebeener for the modest outlay of a few shillings, and so there was little prospect of the illicit liquor trade vanishing altogether.

Nevertheless, there was some suspicion that the police were not doing their utmost to harass the culprits.

Are you aware, my good sir, that there is scarcely a billiard saloon in Glasgow which is open after eleven o'clock that is not also a good-going shebeen. Within a radius of half a mile from where I write I can count up at least a score of billiard rooms where I can get a glass of execrable whisky at two or three o'clock in the morning. This sort of thing, too, goes on under the very noses of the police. They are bound to know of the illicit liquor traffic in these "dens," for though I have no very high opinion of the common intelligence of our constabulary, I will not insult the little intelligence that they have by imagining that a flagrant system of shebeening can exist on their beats without their knowledge. How is it, then, that we never hear of the proprietors of these places being brought into court? Is it that they "square" the police?[7]

Evidently the shebeens did very well, not only on Sundays, but whenever the orthodox public houses were closed. The Victorian Glaswegian's thirst for whisky seems to have been matched only by his passion for the game of billiards. The proprietors of ice-cream shops occasionally offered their patrons something more stimulating than the delicious but innocuous "Macallum" (a concoction of ice-cream and raspberry juice). The Scottish Licensed Trade (February 1910) reported that "Many enterprising Italians, not content with the legitimate profits of the ice-cream trade," were "suspected of hastening the day of their return to a villa in sunny Italy, by doing a little shebeening."

Bona fide publicans, forbidden to sell liquor on Sundays (or "after hours" on weekdays for that matter) loathed the thought of shebeeners waxing rich on the sale of dubious substitutes, and their monthly journal returned regularly to the attack.

Let the prohibitionists beware, lest in their Quixotic attempt to stamp out one evil they do but create another and a greater. If a man wants good whisky or beer, and is willing to pay for it, why should he be forced to break the law in order to obtain a villainous substitute that never saw the bond or the Customs officer.[8]

*　　　　*　　　　*　　　　*　　　　*

As a sequel to the shebeen raids in Glasgow last month, the Trade Association resolved, on the motion of Mr. Duncan Walker, "that a representation be made to the Magistrates to allow Dr. Clark and Mr. Tatlock, the city analysts, to select six samples of the whisky from the forfeitures by the police of the shebeens, so as to give the public an idea of the mysteries of Glasgow shebeen whisky." Along with every right-thinking member of the trade, we will look forward with interest to the result of this investigation, as calculated to bring to light some of the baleful results of excessive prohibition. . .[9]

Travellers, being entitled to a legitimate refreshment on the Sabbath, multiplied prodigiously. It was rumoured that the drinking classes of certain neighbouring towns changed places on Sundays. Glaswegians, journeying to Paisley in search of something more stimulating than Dandelion and Burdock Stout, passed on the road Paisley folk heading for Glasgow with the same object in view. The spokesmen for the licensed trade lost few opportunities to hit out at what they considered to be the manifest absurdities of the Sunday closing law.

> If there is one thing that this Sunday drinking shows more than another it is the absolute uselessness of the Forbes Mackenzie Act. If people want to drink on Sunday they will do so in spite of all the laws enacted under heaven. Experience has shown more than once that it is impossible to make people sober by legislation. On the first day of the week the rich man dips into his cellar. The poor man has no cellar, but he knows the nearest shebeens, and if he is too respectable to consume fire-water amid questionable surroundings, then he becomes a bona fide traveller and patronises some hotel.[10]

One very enjoyable way of avoiding the worst implications of the Forbes Mackenzie Act was to take a leisurely trip "doon the watter". On board a pleasure steamer, sailing from Glasgow's Broomielaw to Arran and the Kyles of Bute, the citizenry could partake of alcoholic refreshments with impunity – at least until 1882, when Gladstone's Government passed an Act (45 and 46 Vict. c.66) prohibiting the sale of liquor on Sundays on board passenger vessels in Scotland. In the mid-Victorian period excursions by Clyde steamer frequently led to drunken excess; to this day Glasgow folk are familiar with the slang expressions "steaming" and "steamboats," denoting intoxication. On some passenger boats alcoholic drinks were not supplied, but day-trippers made up for this deficiency by bringing their own; at one time hip flasks were called "Ivanhoe flasks," after the S.S. Ivanhoe, a "teetotal" paddle steamer of the 1880s.

The enforcement of the law pertaining to Sunday drinking was sometimes carried to extravagant lengths – occasionally with droll results. In order to enjoy the privileges usually reserved for hotel residents and bona fide travellers, a Glasgow man by the name of Edward Stewart went one evening from his home in Watt Street to an hotel in Bridge Street and secured a bed for the night. As he relaxed in the hotel lounge with a drink conveniently to hand, Stewart caught the attention of two plain-clothes policemen, on the look-out, as usual, for mala fides. Stewart was asked for his name and address – information which he rapidly supplied, adding that he was staying at the hotel overnight. Suspecting that he would not in fact do so, the officers decided to keep him under surveillance. When he left the premises late on the Sunday evening they followed at a discreet distance and when he reached home they materialised and solemnly charged him; whereupon Stewart wisely retraced his steps to the hotel and stayed the night after all. Hardly surprising under the circumstances, the case was dismissed when it came before the court.

As early as 1690 the town councillors of Glasgow took rather a jaundiced view of the liquor trade, for in that year they ordained that in all time coming, no person should be chosen to occupy high civic office who kept a change-house or tavern. Two hundred years later the temperance party in Glasgow claimed to have a large majority in the Corporation; 50 of the 75 members were believed to be favourably disposed to temperance reform; 32 of the 50 were said to be total abstainers, and of the 14 magistrates 11 were abstainers. In 1890 the town council passed a resolution that no more licensed premises would be allowed on Corporation property.

The leader of the teetotal group in the Corporation was the autocratic Samuel Chisholm, an implacable opponent of the licensed trade; from 1887 when he first entered the town council he aired his views on "the temperance question" at every opportunity, and with a considerable degree of vehemence. Throughout the 1890s the licensing magistrates laid down the law with exceptional severity. The large number of appeals against the decisions of the Glasgow magistrates sustained at the court of Quarter Sessions pointed to the excessive zeal with which the Glasgow bailies discharged their duties. In 1899 Chisholm was elected Lord Provost, his three years' tenure of office being something of a "McCarthy era" in terms of temperance militancy and intolerance.

In the late nineteenth century, when the radical teetotalers were clamouring for prohibition, other more moderate campaigners were pressing for "reformed" pubs. They reasoned that the typical pub, with its extrovert character, was designed to ensnare the unsophisticated and impressionable artisan; the towering display stand, creaking with barrels and bottles, the mirrors advertising pale ales, stout, and whisky, were strong incitements to recklessness and over-indulgence. They envisaged a plain pub with an inobtrusive counter and back-fitment, plenty of chairs and tables, and a supply of alternative, non-intoxicating beverages such as tea and coffee. But were these beverages really non-intoxicating? The Scottish Wine, Spirit and Beer Trades' Review, no friend of the temperance public house, professed to believe otherwise.

Coffee drunkenness is the last discovery of our medical friends. Working-class women of the great industrial centre of Essen are said to suffer from it very considerably. According to the British Medical Journal the cure includes "small doses of brandy." Promoters of the "public house of the future" will do well to make a note of this. As they propose to abolish brandy and encourage the consumption of coffee, the future victims of the latter stimulant have a bad look-out.[11]

Advocates of "reformed" pubs were influenced by the example of Gothenburg, in Sweden, where the spirit trade was in the hands of a trust company or bolag and the town treasury received the bulk of the profits. Under the so-called "Gothenburg system" drinking to excess was supposed to be discouraged, and food or coffee was dispensed as readily as the fiery native brandy – or rather more readily, since those in charge of the public houses were encouraged, by means of incentives, to push the sale of non-intoxicating drinks and edibles of one kind or another. In 1895 British critics of the system unkindly pointed out that Gothenburg, with a population considerably smaller than that of Dundee, had four times as many drunkards as the Scottish city.

The Public House Trust (Glasgow District) Limited was modelled on Earl Grey's Public House Trust Company in Northumberland, and came into being in 1901 with a capital of £25,000 in £1 shares. In the same year trusts of a similar nature were launched elsewhere in Scotland. The directors were well-known citizens or country gentlemen, and the return to shareholders was restricted to interest on capital – in the Glasgow Public House Trust the maximum rate was 4 per cent. Promoters of public house trusts argued that ever since the licensing authorities had set about reducing the number of pubs the grant of a new licence had "become equivalent to the gift of thousands of pounds." One of the principal objects of the trusts, therefore, was to "secure for the community the monopoly value of new licences." The managers of trust pubs were paid fixed salaries with no commission on sales of liquor, but with special inducements to sell food and soft drinks. The surplus profits were made over to trustees independent of the directors and shareholders, to be expended on "rational recreation and entertainment" for the public. It was envisaged that through the trust system, every local community would be able to eat and drink its way to the ownership of bowling greens, workmen's clubs, allotment gardens and other amenities. Trust pubs had relatively sober interiors, and the sponsors hoped that the average customer would take his cue from his surroundings and remain fairly sober. Draughts and dominoes were usually available to modify the tippler's behaviour.

In 1904 the Glasgow Public House Trust Company held four licences – two in Glasgow (one in Sauchiehall Street, the other in London Street, now London Road), one in Stirling, and one in the village of Newton, near Glasgow. The profits of all four establishments for the year 1903-04 amounted to a paltry £103. "Evidently four per cent philanthropy does not pay in Glasgow," was the Victualling Trades' Review's tart comment (December 1904).

Towards the end of the century temperance cafes, designed to keep people out of the pubs (whether "reformed" or not), were established in many towns. Such cafes were usually sited in provocative proximity to popular licensed hostelries. Sometimes, too, they were remarkably pub-like in character, with ornate joinery and stained glass windows; it was almost as though the teetotal sponsors had asked themselves (paraphrasing General Booth) why on earth the devil should have all the best refreshment houses. To confuse the unwary, some turn of the century pubs were also styled "cafes;" doubtlessly the proprietors of these establishments were trying to get away from the pub image which, after many years of temperance propaganda, was decidedly tarnished.

Licensed trade spokesmen were particularly anxious to draw attention to the "hypocrisy" of the temperance zealots. Some of the latter could well have been pious frauds, for in the excessively puritanical milieu of late Victorian Scotland it would have been to the advantage of many ambitious young men to pay lip service at least to the ideals of the temperance movement. When, as occasionally happened, grocers were prosecuted for selling "temperance" beverages containing a far from insignificant amount of alcohol, the cases were usually publicised in the columns of the licensed victuallers' monthly journal. Here was proof that the teetotaler, for all his airs of superiority, was human, all too human!

> Rigid teetotalers who have taken as their motto "Touch not, taste not, handle not," and a great many self-sufficient and very respectable people have doubtless been under the delusion that certain sparkling beverages had not the remotest connection with intoxicants. It is now, however, found that some temperance drinks are of greater strength than London porter, and that their

popularity has increased in proportion to the number of proof spirits they contained. Brewers of herb beer and other innocent refreshing draughts have, it seems, not hesitated to go beyond legality. Malicious persons will, in all likelihood, see in this fact a reason for the popularity of temperance drinks, and an explanation of the reckless geniality that has been observed now and then at Good Templar picnics.[12]

In May 1893, having received information to the effect that large quantities of liquor were being taken into an unlicensed hall on the south side of the town – a hall owned by a pillar of the Vigilance Society and used, theoretically at least, for teetotal functions – the Edinburgh Evening Dispatch sent a member of its staff to investigate. The Dispatch man duly reported that he had witnessed the beginnings of a bacchanalian orgy, with much "promiscuous" drinking and dancing. At one stage fighting broke out among the tipsy vigilantes, and in the early hours of the morning the hall echoed to choruses of "The Man Who Broke the Bank at Monte Carlo."

The boisterous Edinburgh vigilantes were obviously not total abstainers, and if they seem to have preferred popular songs to temperance hymns, then it is certainly true that the music halls occasionally returned the compliment – several lugubrious temperance ballads actually found their way into the standard music hall repertoire. "Don't Go Out Tonight, Dear Father" dates from 1889; sentimental Victorian audiences would have been able to offer little resistance to its devastating lyrics.

> Don't go out to-night, dear Father,
> Don't refuse this once, I pray;
> Tell your comrades Mother's dying,
> Soon her soul will pass away;
> Tell them, too, of darling Willie,
> Him we all so much do love,
> How his little form is drooping,
> Soon to bloom again above.
>
> Don't go out to-night, dear Father;
> Think, oh, think, how sad 'twill be
> When the angels come to take her,
> Papa won't be there to see.

Hardened cynics, alas, parodied this and similar songs with versions of their own:

> Don't go to the pub, Father;
> It's Mother's turn to-night.

With all his faults, the Victorian toper ought to be given credit for successfully resisting considerable pressure to reform. Besieged by enthusiastic teetotalers determined to "save" him, implored by his tearful daughter (in all probability an ardent member of the Band of Hope) not to go out to the pub, warned by the temperance redshirts that he was in grave danger of sinking or drifting away, he continued to accord Bacchus the devotion that was his due.

In 1888 the Conservatives, who were then in power, introduced their Local Government Bill in which they unexpectedly conceded the principle of local option (or local veto). The Bill, which created County Councils, empowered them to set up local licensing authorities with the power to suppress licences, and also provided for compensation (from the rates) for displaced licensees. The influential temperance lobby would have none of this – compensation for "drink traffickers" was an unspeakable proposition – and the whole licensing plan was therefore dropped. A further local option Bill, introduced by Lord Randolph Churchill in 1890, had no better luck, the teetotalers, under their irrepressible leader Wilfred Lawson M.P., resolutely opposing the payment of compensation. The alliance between Tories and teetotalers foundered on this issue, and local option found its way into the official party policy of the Liberals in the same year. Three years later they were in power and Sir William Harcourt duly introduced the Liquor Traffic (Local Control) Bill – which never received a second reading. In 1895 a second, modified Bill was also abandoned. In the subsequent General Election the Liberals were resoundingly defeated.

John Wilson, M.P. for Govan, proposed local control of the Scottish licensed trade in his Liquor Traffic Local Veto (Scotland) Bill of 1899. This was rejected by the House of Commons by a decisive majority of 74, but Wilson secured the votes of the majority of Scottish members.

The object of the local option Bills, both Tory and Liberal, was to give the electorate of a district the right to decide by majority vote such issues as the limitation of licences and local prohibition. The Liberals made no provision for compensating licensees affected by local prohibition or limitation, but they were to have time to "arrange their affairs." While the issue hung in the balance there was considerable apprehension within the licensed trade at the prospect of widespread compulsory closures. Some licence holders vowed that they would circumvent the imposition of local prohibition by establishing artisans' clubs. The idea was that the condemned public houses would be remodelled; billiard tables and other amenities would be installed, and books, magazines and newspapers would be available for reference. At the time when compensation was a burning issue for both the publican and his arch enemy the prohibitionist, the Scottish licensed trade's weekly and monthly publications played their part in boosting the sagging morale of their subscribers.

> We note a cartoon in the St. Stephen's Review, in which the confiscating teetotaler is hit off very neatly. The scene is the bar of an inn, to which a British artisan has resorted for his tankard of beer. A band of puritanic abstainers, with long hair and rueful countenances, has just entered, armed with formidable pamphlets which preach confiscation. But Mr. Ritchie* steps into the breach with a placard on which are written the words, "Vested interests and compensation."[13]

England and Wales continued to stand firm against local option, but the Temperance (Scotland) Act of 1913 eventually imposed it north of the border. The outbreak of war in 1914 turned the nation's attention to more pressing issues, and it was not until 1920 that the first veto polls were held. The long-term results of the polls fell far short of the expectations of ardent temperance campaigners, who had hoped that in time local veto would lead to total prohibition. Veto polls were abolished in 1976, but some areas of Scotland have remained "dry" since the 1920s.

The discretionary power of magistrates or justices to withdraw licences, upheld by the judgement of the House of Lords in the case of Sharpe versus Wakefield, gave birth to enterprises such as the Licences Insurance Corporation and Guarantee Fund Limited, which was established in 1891 – capital £1,000,000 – "to insure and guarantee compensation to licence-holders for losses incurred" in the event of non-renewal or confiscation.

If several generations of dedicated temperance reformers failed to vanquish the Demon, they at any rate managed to intimidate it with their rhetoric, slogans, banners and processions. On a more practical level, of course, they helped to mould public opinion and pave the way for the major licensing acts of the nineteenth and early twentieth centuries. At least as effective in curtailing the abuse of alcohol were the restrictions and shortages of the First World War. Afterwards the drinker had to contend with much higher prices – between 1914 and 1920 the duty on whisky rose from 14s. 9d. per proof gallon to 72s 6d. – while post-war society had lost a good deal of its old ebullient sociability. But if the tippler had reason to fear that his halycon days were behind him, so too had the teetotaler: American Prohibition had led, not to the New Jerusalem, but to the Chicago of Al Capone.

*One-time president of the British Women's Temperance Association and World's Women's Christian Temperance Union; died 1921.
**Miss Agnes Weston of Bath, "the sailor-boy's friend." She opened temperance institutes in many ports.
*Central Police Court.
*The Right Honourable Charles Thomson Ritchie, M.P., moderate temperance reformer. Chancellor of the Exchequer, 1902-03.

[1] The Scotsman, June 22, 1895.
[2] The Scottish Wine, Spirit and Beer Trades' Review, May 10, 1887.
[3] The Victualling Trades' Review, March 1, 1894.
[4] The National Guardian, September 27, 1893.
[5] The Victualling Trades' Review, June 1, 1893.
[6] The Victualling Trades' Review, June 1, 1893.
[7] The Scottish Wine, Spirit and Beer Trades' Review, October 11, 1887.
[8] The Victualling Trades' Review, May 12, 1890.
[9] The Victualling Trades' Review, April 12, 1890.
[10] The Scottish Wine, Spirit and Beer Trades' Review, September 27, 1887.
[11] The Victualling Trades' Review, March 12, 1890.
[12] The Scottish Wine, Spirit and Beer Trades' Review, May 3, 1887.
[13] The Scottish Wine, Spirit and Beer Trades' Review, June 12, 1888.

Part Two

3 Drunks

Captain Edward Topham, who has already been quoted at length on the subject of oyster cellars, also noticed the Scots' predilection for strong drink:

> They rather pay too much respect to the divinity of Bacchus, and offer too copious libations at the shrine of that jovial deity.[1]

No citizen of Georgian Edinburgh could have allayed his wife's suspicions by averring that he was "as sober as a judge" – judges were among the worst offenders. Witness the remarks of Lord Hermand (a celebrated toper as well as a distinguished judge) at a murder trial. "We are told," he said, "that there was no malice, and that the prisoner must have been in liquor. In liquor! Why, he was drunk! And yet he murdered the very man who had been drinking with him! They had been carousing the whole night; and yet he stabbed him; after drinking a whole bottle of rum with him; Good God, my Lords, if he will do this when he's drunk, what will he not do when he's sober?"

In the Victorian and Edwardian period this alarming national trait was mitigated to some extent by factors such as the puritanism of the increasingly influential middle class and the crusading zeal of the temperance movement, but it was still much in evidence. At Whitsun 1890, for example, Beatrice Potter and Sydney Webb attended the Glasgow Co-operative Congress and Miss Potter, who kept a diary, took note of an evening stroll "by glorious sunset through the crowded streets, knocking up against drunken Scots." (Beatrice Webb, My Apprenticeship, 1926). Eighteen years later Sir Andrew Reed, a former Inspector General of the Royal Irish Constabulary, recorded his impressions in a letter to the Times.

> In August 1906, I visited Scotland to inquire for myself into the allegations frequently made in the Irish Press as to the disgraceful scenes of drunkenness to be seen in Scotch towns. I visited Glasgow, walked about the principal streets at night, I talked to the police on beat duty, who seemed to me to be fine, intelligent, courteous men and well suited for their work. I found towards the closing hour of the public-houses some of the streets crowded with drunken men. In no city in Europe, the United States, or in Canada I have ever

76

visited did I see such a number of drunken persons. I thought the scene I witnessed was most disgraceful to any civilised place. I was told by the manager of a Trust public-house (who read from a register which he kept) that on the average 116 drunken persons daily were refused intoxicating liquor at his bar (700 for the six days). The police had no power whatever under the law to interfere with these drunkards, called in Scotland "tipsy people," and as regards the incapable drunkards, not able to grope their way home, or not having friends to carry them, I was told that when the police prosecuted them, the fines inflicted by the magistrates were often small, generally 2s. 6d, to 7s. 6; seldom even for repeated offences of drunkenness was the full penalty of 40s. inflicted. The question operating upon the minds of some of the magistrates appeared to be how much the offender could easily afford to pay. The people had plenty of money, as trade was good, and the fines were not deterrent in their effects. The publicans drove a roaring trade, as the law in its operation encourages open intemperance.[2]

1906 produced a vintage crop of inebriates. Ten o'clock closing had been introduced in Glasgow in May 1904, with the predictable result that liquor was consumed proportionately faster between the hours of nine and ten. In 1903 there had been 14,176 prosecutions for drunkenness (18 per thousand of the city's estimated population) and 9,298 convictions. Three years later there were 20,247 prosecutions (25.3 per thousand of the population) and 13,239 convictions. There was a large amount of drunkenness which was not reflected in the number of apprehensions since the law recognised drunkenness as an offence only when the drunken person was a danger to himself, or when he caused annoyance to others by disorderly conduct or by the use of obscene language. The more reckless or feckless elements of society undoubtedly swelled the statistics by getting drunk and being run in by the police with monotonous regularity. Much drunkenness, however, was a Saturday only affair. Comparatively little drinking was done on a Friday since most artisans and labourers worked a five-and-a-half day week and were not paid until Saturday. In the larger industrial concerns the men were paid fortnightly, and "pey Seterday" was duly celebrated in an appropriate fashion. The publican whose premises were situated in close proximity to a shipyard or an engineering works prepared for the rush which he knew would ensue shortly after the operatives had received their wages by filling a great many glasses with beer and whisky and arranging them, in serried ranks, in readiness on the bar counter.

For a few hours, the riveter or the boilermaker grew progressively euphoric as he swallowed beer by the "schooner" and whisky by the half-gill. By closing time he was, more often than not, dead drunk. If he had been swilling bad whisky, then he was fighting drunk. Either way, he was the bane of sober citizens.

On Saturday night Argyle Street holds Saturnalia – not the "Continental Saturnalia" we hear so much about, but a time of squalid license, when men stagger out of shuttered public-houses as out of a pit, and the street echoes to insane roaring and squabbles, to the nerve collapse that ends a day's debauch of drink and football.[3]

Before the afternoon was well advanced, those who had been drinking on empty stomachs were already half-seas-over. The seasoned toper took time off from the Saturday spree to go home for a meal and afterwards to go on to a football match, but the evening drinking bout occasionally proved too much even for him.

Men in steady employment who went on a weekly or fortnightly binge and ended up outrageously drunk were a public nuisance, though a minor one compared with the habitual drunkards who were deterred neither by fines nor imprisonment. In the late nineteenth century it was conceded that, since these individuals were indifferent to punishment, some other remedy ought to be tried. The Habitual Drunkards Act of 1879 (42 and 43 Vict. c.19) had set up a number of private retreats for the reception of voluntary patients who were addicted to alcohol. Once the chronic inebriate had formally agreed to undergo a course of treatment he was statutorily bound to remain at the retreat for the duration of the cure. In 1898 the Inebriates Act (61 and 62 Vict. c.60) gave magistrates the power to commit any person four times convicted of drunkenness to a reformatory for a term not exceeding three years. The following year Glasgow Corporation purchased the mansion house of Girgenti, in Ayrshire, for the sum of £7000 and had it equipped and licensed as a reformatory for "degraded drunken women." The house was situated 21 miles from the city, the nearest towns being Stewarton and Irvine; it stood in extensive grounds and provided accommodation for some sixty female drunkards, whose reformation was to be accomplished by means of "immunity from all bibulous temptation, pure air, and horticultural work of a light nature." Hopes were also entertained that a specific drug treatment might prove even more beneficial than a strict regime, and the management called for volunteers willing to submit to it. The drugs used were atropine, quinine, ammonium, sodium, and aloin mixture. The result in every case was failure, and the experiment with drugs was discontinued. One of the draw-backs of Girgenti was that "the grounds were not satisfactorily fenced," which rendered it "comparatively easy for the inmates to give their keepers the slip, notwithstanding all precautions." Indeed, there were so many escapes and escape attempts that the efficiency of the institution was seriously impaired.

In 1907 there were nine Scottish institutions for the treatment of inebriates. Of these, three were retreats, five were certified inebriate reformatories, and one was a State inebriate reformatory. The total accommodation provided by these institutions amounted to 214 beds, of which 66 were in retreats, 116 in certified inebriate reformatories, and 32 in the State reformatory at Perth General Prison. By far the majority of inmates in the certified reformatories were women.

By 1908 each inmate at Girgenti Reformatory was costing the ratepayers of Glasgow £68 per annum, and with little to show for this expenditure but relapsed female drunkards, the Corporation came to the conclusion that the institution had no future. In any case the Reformatory, relatively small, had proved "insufficient for the segregation of all the worst of the Glasgow drunken women." After the failure of the Girgenti venture, Glasgow seriously considered banishing its habitual drunkards of both sexes to the wild Hebridean islet of Shuna, which was Corporation property (the Corporation's Inebriates Act Committee went so far as to get a quotation from MacBrayne for shipping the people out there).

Other Scottish towns and cities besides Glasgow had their share of confirmed dipsomaniacs. In Edinburgh, out of 7,330 persons convicted of drunkenness in the local police courts in 1908, 90 men and 197 women had been convicted over 50 times; 16 men and 58 women over 100 times; 3 men and 34 women over 150 times, and 32 women over 200 times.

Under the provisions of the Licensing (Scotland) Act of 1903, anyone with more than three convictions of drunkenness within a twelve month period could be "black-listed" by the court to prevent him from obtaining exciseable liquors for a period of three years. Licence holders received a photograph and description of the proscribed individual along with an injunction not to supply him with alcoholic refreshments, and the publican who neglected to enforce the ban rendered himself liable to prosecution. The 1903 Act also made it an offence to be intoxicated on licensed premises. In order to keep in the licensing authorities' good books some publicans stationed a man at the entrance to their premises. This functionary, whose job it was to ward off drunks trying to gain admittance, was sometimes resplendently attired in a Ruritanian uniform with much gold frogging and braid. On Saturdays – especially Saturday nights – it was not always possible for the doorman or commissionaire to distinguish between the half drunk and the wholly drunk.

Dead drunk individuals could not, in all conscience, be permitted to litter the streets of a "model municipality" like Glasgow, and so they were conveyed to the nearest police station in the "drunk's barrow." An indispensible aid to policing until the 1920s, this was a long narrow hand-barrow fitted with a stretcher, to which the prostrate drunk was firmly attached by means of leather straps. It was said that small boys were paid 3d per trip for wheeling the barrow to the station. In the early 1900s Edinburgh, more decorous than its brash western rival, used a covered police van to transport its drunks to the lock-up.

In order to preserve the citizens as much as possible from temptation, the magistrates of Glasgow repeatedly urged the city's licence holders to close their premises early on public holidays. On New Year's Day, 1898, many Glasgow pubs were closed at four o'clock in the afternoon on the recommendation of the authorities. The magistrates promptly took advantage of the additional powers conferred on them by the 1903 Licensing Act and passed a by-law closing the city's pubs on New Year's Day and on the spring and autumn holidays. This form of prohibition was first imposed on Easter Monday, 1905, and led to a positive exodus of thirsty Glaswegians; in large numbers they descended on the pubs of Paisley, Cambuslang and other neighbouring towns and virtually drank them dry, to the distress of the indigenous topers. The consequences of all-day closing embarrassed the Glasgow bailies, and in 1906 they relented to the extent of passing another by-law allowing the pubs to open for a few hours on public holidays, New Year's Day excepted.

Temperance zealots considered that the Glasgow Saturnalia was a formidable indictment of "the nefarious traffic" and a powerful argument in favour of its total suppression, while their opponents saw it as the inevitable result of repressive legislation, particularly Sunday closing, which simply encouraged people to make the most of their opportunities on a Saturday night.

Nothing amazes the Londoner visiting Glasgow for the first time more than the disorderly half-drunk crowd of the Glasgow public-houses on a Saturday just before Forbes Mackenzie rings down the curtain. To the Londoner the thing is incomprehensible. In his native place, be he ever so thirsty or considerate for the morrow, he has no occasion or need to lay in half-mutchkins or other weird Caledonian fractions of the Imperial pint, because he knows that next day the Fox-under-the-Hill, the Spotted Cow, or whatever his house of call may be, will be open from one o'clock till three, and again from six till eleven. The Glasgow idea of purchasing "supplies" on the Saturday night may be good enough in theory, but London hears that the stock thus laid in is not kept for the first day of the week, but is consumed on the Saturday night, with the result that the purchaser, instead of being sound and fit on the Sunday, lies in bed the greater part of the day, reading Sunday papers from Manchester, and is thus lost to his duties as a citizen.[4]

Truly, Forbes Mackenzie had a lot to answer for! In late Victorian and Edwardian Glasgow the licensing authorities were reluctant to come to terms with the abhorred "drink traffic," particularly since an influential body of opinion was in favour of legislating it out of existence. Some well-meaning people felt that pubs, as "necessary evils," ought to be made as unattractive as possible – they would, one imagines, have thought highly of the dreary utilitarian pubs that are all too prevalent in the Glasgow of today. By discouraging music and other public house diversions, the Glasgow magistrates hoped to diminish the popularity of the city's pubs, but all they succeeded in doing was preventing Glasgow's hostelries from developing along the sociable and civilised lines of the pubs of London and other English cities. With their immense bar counters, ornate display stands and mirrored walls, the Glasgow liquor palaces did not lack character, but they were hedged round with restrictions.

They are purely shops for perpendicular drinking, for the Magistrates in the interests of the young, have succeeded in making them places in which no man, from the fatigue of standing, will linger long. And this is the main reason why the "sing-songs" and "cosies" which you hear of in Manchester are unknown in Glasgow. The Magistrates will not grant a music licence to a public-house. But, perhaps, there is something un-Scots in these random gatherings that would make them distasteful to Northerns. Smoking concerts, though dreary past words, seem not to be unpopular, when they are formally organised and announced. It is quite a different matter to meet unbidden and unacquainted in some one's public-house and spend a night of hilarity with song and smoke and beer. It offends one's sense of reserve, even one's self-respect, and perhaps it is incompatible with the drinking of whisky. That is the liquor which is, it seems, and end in itself – the spirit, as it were, that purges the mind of gross matters and passions, and leaves it aching for dialectics, for arguments, and conflict. Singing may go with beer, but not with whisky.[5]

Smoking concerts, highly popular in late Victorian and Edwardian Scotland, were a more formal variation of the "free and easies" – the impromptu public house concerts which had influenced the development of the Victorian music hall.

80

Unlike the "free and easy," in which anyone could participate, admission to the "smoker" was by invitation only.

In the view of a contributor to the Westminster Review, Scotland's pubs had been dehumanised by restrictive legislation framed by fanatical teetotalers, and he drew the comparison between Glasgow, tyrannised by temperance militants, and "free Sheffield:"

> Sheffield is governed, so far as the drink "traffic" is concerned, with very few restrictions – governed, broadly and generally speaking, on tolerant and commonsense lines. Glasgow is governed by the temperance party. Governed as this remarkably short-sighted party want English towns to be governed. Careful and impartial consideration of the case of Glasgow enables us to forecast, with some degree of accuracy, what will happen in England if we permit, through apathy, the temperance party to have the dominating and final voice in our licensing Legislation. Glasgow has submitted to the cast-iron rules and regulations of the temperance party – here we have an example of temperance party government in actual operation. The publican and the drinker in Glasgow are harassed, restricted, and interfered with at almost every turn. To begin with, Glasgow has Sunday closing. On the other days of the week the public-houses are not permitted to open until 8 a.m., and they are obliged to close at 10 p.m. In some parts of the city they are closed at nine. And on some of the popular holidays they are closed all day – like Sunday. Moreover, no music, singing, reciting, or games of any kind or description are permitted in Glasgow's public-houses. And there are now no barmaids'! You are not allowed even to look at a sporting paper, and if you laugh you are turned out. This is no fancy picture, but the absolute truth. The police are always prying, and spying, and scouting inside the public-houses in a manner understood by Englishmen to prevail only in Russia. The boast of the temperance party is that "drinking is not encouraged" in Glasgow, and, as a matter of fact, the "pubs" are not centres of social intercourse, but "drink shops" only.[6]

In Sheffield, on the other hand – "another typical working class city" – where the pubs were open twenty-four hours a week longer than in Glasgow, and where music, singing, and reciting were liberally indulged in, the citizens could spend their evenings "in recreation, freedom, and fun."

In Edwardian Glasgow policemen in plain-clothes could frequently be espied making rounds of the pubs with a view to detecting "irregularities" of one sort or another; they could also be found standing outside pubs in groups of two or three at ten o'clock, to ensure that the early closing regulation was punctually observed. Nor was police "spying" confined to public houses. The Licensing (Scotland) Act of 1903 had prohibited the consumption of alcoholic drinks in unlicensed refreshment houses such as tea-rooms and ice-cream saloons "during the hours that the said premises would have been closed had they been licensed." The Victualling Trades' Review (March, 1908) reported the case of one Bollini Ermet, an Italian immigrant, who had unwisely allowed three men to consume whisky, along with "soft" drinks, in his cafe in Glasgow after the closing hour of the pubs.

The proprietor was asked to have a drink, "but he refused, and at the same time warned the men to be careful." Too late, as it proved, for plain-clothes policemen had witnessed the incident.

From May, 1914, under the provisions of the Temperance (Scotland) Act, Scottish pubs opened at ten o'clock in the morning, instead of eight o'clock as previously. This measure was designed to prevent the workers in the Clyde shipyards and other large industrial concerns from obtaining drink during their morning break – which in almost all cases was usually from nine until nine forty-five or ten.

If Sunday closing and restricted opening hours on weekdays failed to diminish the popularity of Scotland's pubs, then some ardent spirits were prepared to go much further. The teetotal camp was divided into mensheviks and bolsheviks, the former being temperance reformers and the latter prohibitionists. On the last day of November, 1908, Mrs. Carry Nation, self-styled "Boadicea of Temperance," arrived in Scotland to tour the country in support of the Prohibition Party. Carry was the acknowledged champion bar-smasher of the United States, and at the age of sixty-two she was still capable of wielding a vengeful hatchet on occasion. She had not come to Scotland to demolish pubs, however, but to make inflammatory speeches. Councillor Edwin "Neddy" Scrymgeour of Dundee, organising secretary of the Scottish Prohibition Party (and a future prohibitionist M.P.) and Carry Nation took to each other at once. Speaking at one of her meetings, he declared that "if the women of the country would do away with five o'clock tea and fiddle-faddling and burst into the bars, as Mrs Nation had done, they would strike terror into the heart of the country, and drive drink from the land." Carry, for her part, announced that Moses had been a prohibitionist and a "smasher."

Dressed all in black, and with a miniature gold hatchet pinned to her bodice, the grey-haired temperance trouper stormed into several of Glasgow's best known pubs and gave the nonplussed proprietors a piece of her mind.

Attired in a black cloak and heavily veiled, the renowned "pub smasher" set forth from her hotel shortly after mid-day, and proceeded to Lauder's in Sauchiehall Street. A crowd of about a thousand was, by the time she reached it, pressing and swarming round her. As she hurriedly entered through the swing doors the mob followed and packed the bar. "This is one of the hell-homes of Scotland," she cried. "How do you get your work done at all, you business-men?" Then to the barmen – "Get out of the business; you are no credit to your mothers as long as you remain."

Her visit was a brief one. She was quickly removed out of doors. Outside she harangued the crowd, and then made off down Renfield Street to her hotel, the immense crowd, thirsting for free drinks, following in her wake.[7]

After lunch, Carry, chivalrously escorted by Edwin Scrymgeour and another male prohibitionist, descended on the Rogano, a bodega bar in Exchange Place. There she poured scorn on the heads of the astonished customers – well-heeled businessmen for the most part – until ejected by several burly attendants.

In the 1900s sensation-mongering journalists flocked to Glasgow, drawn by the reputed excesses of the Saturnalia, as a later generation of newsmen would be attracted to the city by the gang warfare of the Depression years. In 1908 a Canadian reporter wrote a piece for the Hamilton (Ontario) Spectator under the heading "Guilty Glasgow," and garnished it with lurid descriptions of Saturday night in the city centre. At the entrance to each pub was a sentinel who scrutinised "the crush of men and women driving into the place." Anyone showing signs of advanced drunkenness was turned away, or if he had got past the doorman, was promptly thrown out again. Those who had been ejected stood on the pavement, their bodies swaying, looking longingly "at the paradise of alcohol" from which they had been excluded. Some swore, but most accepted their fate "with dourness and melancholy."

It would appear that the Canadian journalist confined his researches to the unsalubrious neighbourhood of Glasgow Cross—further west, in the imposing thoroughfares of the business and commercial core, he would have found pubs as reputable as any in the kingdom. The opulent bars in Jamaica Street, Union Street, Renfield Street and Sauchiehall Street usually excluded women as well as drunken men, while the marginally higher prices kept the "submerged tenth" of the population at a respectable distance.

On Saturday night, drunks of both sexes converged on Glasgow Cross from all points of the compass; a remarkable spectacle, sociologically, as a contributor to the monthly journal of the Scottish licensed trade observed.

> Saturday night at the Cross of Glasgow is an experience that should not be missed by those who take an interest in matters of social exploration. One may travel round the globe, visit New York, the slums of San Francisco, then come to Glasgow, and he will find focussed at the Cross types of men and women as far down in the scale of being as he has seen in his travels.[8]

Argyle Street, the Trongate, the High Street and Gallowgate were notoriously drunken and rowdy on a Saturday night, and in consequence, prudent citizens steered well clear of these thoroughfares.

It is well known that between the World Wars, Glasgow was plagued with vicious gangster factions. Before the First World War, however, gangs such as the Hi Hi, the San Toy and the Village Boys flourished in various parts of the city. Each gang numbered a hundred or more members, mostly young men aged from sixteen to twenty years. A favourite ploy of the hooligan element – derisively known to law-abiding Glaswegians as "keelies" – was to accost people as they emerged from public houses and demand money from them with threats of violence. The Glasgow "keelies" were also known to enter pubs, presumably at quiet times, and demand free drink. The favourite weapons of the Edwardian gangster were the knuckle duster and the poker – the latter being carried up the sleeve until required. A particularly troublesome gang called the Redskins had several women members, one of whom was Aggie Reid, who lived in a women's model lodging house in Trongate. Aggie was frequently arrested for assault or breach of the peace, and on these occasions never less than four policemen were required to convey her to the black Maria.

The model lodging houses of Glasgow, most of which were created by the City Improvement Trust in the late nineteenth century, sheltered a motley collection of men and women, an appreciable number of whom were more or less addicted to drink. These hostels were run on strict disciplinarian lines; the accommodation was Spartan and varied in price from 3d to 4½d per night. As a counter attraction to the pubs, the indefatigable authorities laid on Saturday night lectures and music recitals, "for the amusement and improvement of the residents." Rowdy drunks who showed no aptitude for amusement or improvement were dealt with by the police, who, by arrangement with the Chief Constable, visited the "models" on Saturday nights.

Wretched industrial and social conditions encouraged many to drink themselves into a state of semi-oblivion; but regardless of the underlying causes of the scenes of drunkenness in Glasgow and in other towns and cities throughout Scotland, the immediate culprit was cheap whisky, known colloquially as "kill-the-carter." Few were so poor that they could not occasionally afford to be driven berserk by raw fiery spirits. Although whisky of better quality was readily available it was, of course, more expensive – apart from which a far from negligible number of Scots drinkers actually preferred raw whisky on account of its volatile nature. Well-matured whisky simply did not have the stupifying or inflammatory properties they were looking for. There was no legislation compelling whisky producers to mature the alcohol for a minimum period before selling it. This arrived only in 1915, when the Immature Spirits (Restriction) Act was passed to prevent the consumption of spirits until they had been matured in casks in a bonded warehouse for a minimum period of two years (by the end of the year this period of compulsory bonding had been extended to three years).

Raw spirits no doubt helped to fan the flames at Hampden Park on Saturday, 17th April, 1909, when the Celtic-Rangers Cup Final Replay culminated in a memorable riot. A raging mob stormed the pitch, uprooted the goalposts, and tore the nets to shreds. Bricks, stones and bottles rained down from the terracing. One rioter felled a policeman with a bottle, then considerately waved a white handkerchief to summon the ambulance men. The wooden fencing surrounding the terracing was set alight, as were the pay boxes, and when firemen arrived on the scene they were dragged from their appliances and assaulted. As a result of these disgraceful scenes at Hampden, the Scottish Football Association decided that there would not be a further cup replay and withheld the Scottish Cup and medals.

The spectacular Glasgow Saturnalia, grist to the temperance campaigner's mill, and food for thought for clergymen, politicians and journalists, was curtailed at last by the Great War. The return of peace saw its recurrence, but on a more modest scale. The post-war slump threw many thousands on the dole, and in the 1920s and 1930s the cinema rather than the pub was the escape route from harsh realities.

The Saturnalia's permanent memorial is the famous song "I Belong to Glasgow," which Will Fyffe, in the role of a tipsy and garrulous Glaswegian, popularised between the wars.

I belong to Glasgow, dear old Glasgow town,
But there's something the matter with Glasgow,
For its going roun' and roun'.
I'm only a common old working lad, as
anyone can see,
But when I get a couple of drinks on
a Saturday, Glasgow belongs to me.

[1] Edward Topham: Letters from Edinburgh in 1774 and 1775; letter XII, December 30, 1774.
[2] The Times, July 13, 1908.
[3] James Hamilton Muir (composite pseudonym for James Bone, Archibald Hamilton Charteris and Muirhead Bone): Glasgow in 1901, part III, chapter VIII.
[4] The Victualling Trades' Review, volume XIX (1904), page 59.
[5] James Hamilton Muir: Glasgow in 1901, part III, chapter II.
[6] ''Temperance reform: some facts and figures,'' Westminster Review, May 1908.
[7] The Scottish Licensed Trade, January 1, 1909.
[8] The Victualling Trades' Review, April 12, 1892.

Part Three

1 Design

In their heyday, and indeed for long afterwards, the late Victorian pubs of Great Britain and Ireland were frequently referred to as gin palaces; the term, although inaccurate, was not altogether inappropriate, for in some respects at least, the original gin palaces – the ornate gin shops of the 1830s and 1840s – were the forerunners of the opulent pubs of the late Victorian period. The gin shop of the mid nineteenth-century had a long bar counter and a back-fitment which incorporated spirit vats or barrels. This convenient arrangement remained popular in the 1870s and 1880s, by which time, in Scotland at any rate, whisky and not gin was being dispensed from the casks. In the early 1900s, many years after the introduction of island serving counters with central platforms for the stock, many Scottish pubs were still being fitted up in basic gin palace (or whisky palace) fashion, with long bar counters, and back-fitments incorporating barrels.

The characteristic urban English pub of the late Victorian period, several storeys in height, with a variety of socially graded bars, had no precise equivalent in Scotland. North of the Border, the urban licensed house was seldom pub and dwelling in one, for the Scottish licensing authorities did not encourage publicans to live on the premises. The Scottish urban pub was commonly situated in a flatted tenement, the ground floor of which it shared with a variety of shops. The subdivision of licensed premises on the basis of real or imaginary social distinctions was not practised in Scotland to anything like the same extent as in in England, although some pubs certainly followed the English model quite closely: the Clan Vaults (1891) in Glasgow's Jamaica Street had "ordinary" and "best" bars; it also boasted a ladies' room, a most unusual provision in a Glasgow pub of the early 1890s. Some other Scottish pubs were comprised of two drinking spaces – a main bar of generous proportions and a much smaller bar, cosier and a great deal quieter than the principal bar. The smaller of the two bars was known variously as the "private" bar, the "back" bar or the "saloon" bar; it did not always have a separate entrance. Much more usual, however, was the establishment consisting of a single public bar, sometimes with an adjoining booth where liquor could be purchased for consumption off the premises (this corresponded to the English "jug and bottle," and was generally known as the family department). In the most inferior category of Scottish pubs the single bar was not unlike the English public bar; decoration was reduced to a minimum and seating, where it existed, consisted of hard wooden benches. In pubs of a superior character, on the other hand, the single bar resembled the saloon bar of the English pub, with much applied decoration, plush seats and marble-topped tables.

Late Victorian Glaswegians, many of them of Highland or Irish stock, did full justice to the traditional Celtic potation, and the pubs of Glasgow were noted for impressive arrays of whisky barrels. From the 1880s onwards, these business-like rows of barrels were incorporated in handsome back-fitments. The casks, polished and brass-hooped, sat in aedicular niches, sharing the limelight with fancy shelving on which show bottles, glasses, china jars and knick-knacks were arranged. In licensed restaurants, theatre bars and buffet bars whisky was frequently dispensed from brilliant cut glass urns as supplied by James Cox ("the original inventor of the glass whisky urn") of the Compton House Pottery, Soho. In Glasgow and the West of Scotland the main purpose of the back-fitment was revealed by the name given to it – gantress or gauntress* (in Old Scots, a wooden stand for barrels).

Whether or not it incorporated spirit casks, the back-fitment was the most significant feature in hundreds of Scotland's late Victorian pubs – no longer simply a convenient stand for barrels and bottles but a tour de force of joinery towering up to the ceiling, aglitter with plain or decorated mirrors. In the 1880s and 1890s the craftsmen of woodcarving responsible for these elaborate and impressive fitments had usually relied on permutations of columns, pilasters, arches, niches and pediments for their effects, but in the 1900s the cabinetwork became much more sophisticated, thanks to prevailing Art Nouveau influences.

A number of lesser-known late Victorian architects made something of a speciality of pub design. In Glasgow Charles Robinson, Frank Burnet and George Bell, between them, built dozens of handsome pubs, almost all of which have since vanished. In Edinburgh Peter Lyle Henderson, John Forrester and Robert MacFarlane Cameron were responsible for many pubs of great character and charm, but sadly, little now survives of their work.

Substantial pubs and licensed restaurants proliferated in the prosperous and ebullient Glasgow of the 1890s and 1900s, commissioned by prominent publicans such as John Scouller, Gray Edmiston, Archibald Lauder, David Sloan and Philip MacSorley. The Arcade Cafe (62 Argyle Arcade) consisted of richly furnished dining rooms, coffee rooms and bars, in addition to a "cigar and tobacco divan" to which businessmen could retire in order to indulge in luxuriant pipe-dreams. The Alexandra Cafe in Buchanan Street had a particularly ostentatious back-fitment, a mass of carved mahogany and mirrors. William Reid's public house in Eglinton Street was decorated with hand-painted wallpaper depicting episodes of the Prince of Wales' visit to India. After lagging behind somewhat in the provision of liquor palaces, Scotland's largest city had at last done credit to Bacchus with spacious and glittering shrines. As the Victualling Trades' Review, referring specifically to the Glasgow bars, put it:

Has it ever occurred to our readers what a vast difference there is in the style and equipment of the modern bar as compared with the old hostelry of the past? Just take, for example, such places as the "Castle" Vaults in Renfield Street, Taylor's Bar, corner of Sauchiehall Street and West Nile Street, or the "Waterloo" Bar, down at the foot of Wellington Street and Argyle Street, and compare the luxuriant fittings, decorations, perfect ventilation, and the magnificent stained-glass work with the dingy and tumble-down "Cat and Bagpipes" of our forefathers.[1]

The Castle Vaults, at 39 Renfield Street, was the property of John MacLachlan, junior partner of the firm of brewers, wine merchants and distillers; it boasted an ornate oval-shaped bar counter and a large quantity of stained glass, and was situated in Pearl Assurance Buildings, a still extant late Victorian office block. Although much of Glasgow's Victorian and Edwardian architecture has so far survived the vicissitudes of the twentieth century the flamboyant pubs have all but disappeared; originally there were several in almost every street, their presence indicated by stained or etched glass windows, hanging lamps, and elaborate wrought-iron signs (one of the most popular of which took the form of a bunch of gilded grapes).

In recent years an important feature of the licensed houses in this city is the improvement that has taken place in their internal appearance. Artistic taste and chaste design were unknown some years ago, and the convenience and comfort of customers were simply secondary considerations. All this, however, has changed, and the licence holder who does not take cognisance of the elements of art and design will certainly lag behind in the race for success. Glasgow can boast of having the best-equipped and most completely appointed houses in the United Kingdom. The reason for this is not far to seek. A race of architects and designers have sprung up, each one vying with the other as to the thoroughness of their work. . .[2]

It was the golden age of shop design in general and pub design in particular. Architects, decorative painters, signwriters, carpenters, glass stainers and embossers, were all working within a flourishing decorative tradition. The catalogues of the art manufacturers, fruits of profitable historical gleanings, listed an abundance of fittings and accessories. No two pubs had to be exactly alike, since every licensee could command as much "artistic taste and chaste design" as he was prepared to pay for. This brings us to the subject of cost. In the absence of multiple bars, residential accommodation for a landlord or tenant, and overnight accommodation for travellers, the typical Scottish pub of the late nineteenth century was relatively small; consequently it generally cost less to build or renovate a pub in Scotland than in England. From 1871 onwards, estimates of the cost of new buildings and of alterations to existing buildings were entered in the volumes devoted to the Glasgow Dean of Guild Court Proceedings. From these entries it is apparent that, at the turn of the century, the average Glasgow pub, consisting of a large public bar, cost £1,000-£2,000, depending, no doubt, on the materials used and the quality of the craftsmanship. Occasionally the pub was incorporated in a new tenement, office block, or warehouse, in which case the financial outlay was much greater: £28,000 for Castle Chambers (1899-1902), consisting of licensed premises and offices; £32,500 for Gordon Chambers (1904-07), consisting of licensed premises, shops, offices and warehouses. These were major building enterprises by wealthy publicans and were thus exceptional. It was not, however, unusual for a publican to erect a tenement of flats, replete with shops and licensed premises, at a cost of several thousand pounds.

One by one the familiar old hostelries were transformed; structural beams and columns were substituted for partition walls, with the result that the dark, dingy and diminutive rooms in which generations of topers had sat "bousing at the nappy* . . . gettin' fou an' unco happy," were swept clean away. With mixed feelings the habitues viewed the expanse of carved and polished wood that was now the bar, the mirrored walls, richly moulded ceiling, and pendant gasaliers. Traditionalists among them undoubtedly grumbled at the demise of the plain old howff, but none could deny that the reconstituted pub had much to commend it.

Tiles – colourful, durable and easy to clean – were frequently incorporated in the exterior and interior decoration of pubs. It was typical of the Victorians, who loved ornament (sometimes to distraction), but who also appreciated value for money, to make use of decorated tiles on every possible occasion. Hotels, railway stations, theatres, town halls and hospitals all received their share, and so of course did shop premises. The latter were often embellished with tiled murals, the themes of which were witty and appropriate; frolicsome mermaids in the sea-food emporium, tea-drinking mandarins in the grocery store, and in the butcher's shop sheep and cattle, grazing in idyllic surroundings and blissfully unaware of what fate had in store for them. When the great majority of late Victorian and Edwardian shops were ousted from the nation's high streets these attractive murals and their world of whimsy and fantasy disappeared. As a means of imparting lustre to the people's palaces, tiles were ideal; large industrial potters such as Maw, Minton or Doulton offered them transfer-printed, embossed or hand-painted and many comparatively small local firms, such as that of James Duncan of Glasgow (106 West Campbell Street), also specialised in tile work. The smaller firms were generally tile decorators as opposed to tile manufacturers, and they relied on potters such as Minton for their tiles. The walls of public houses were occasionally tiled from floor to ceiling. The bar counter itself was sometimes faced with ornamental tiles. The exterior of the pub could be clad in architectural faience or terracotta (the most flamboyant surviving example in this respect is surely the Crown Liquor Saloon in Belfast's Great Victoria Street). Towards the end of the century, Doulton Lambeth Faience mural panels were features of some of the finest pub interiors.

The late Victorian decorator was also offered a wide choice of embossed materials for use on walls and ceilings. Some of the most effective of these were developed by Scotsman William Scott Morton and produced at Murieston Road, Edinburgh. The first of the Tynecastle Company's substitutes for expensive hand-worked decoration, introduced in the early 1870s, was a "stamped leather" wall covering made of canvas. A later development, Tynecastle vellum, permitted the imitation of ornament in high relief, such as rich plaster ceilings and friezes. Tynecastle canvas and vellum were in solid relief, and so too was Frederick Walton's Lincrusta, which came on the market in 1877. The original product with its rigid backing was superceded in the late 1880s by a light waterproof paper. Anaglypta, which first appeared in 1888, was made by embossing wet paper pulp and was hollow-backed; for use on ceilings it was manufactured in easy to handle lightweight sections. The various substitutes for fibreous plasterwork were inexpensive, durable, and could be obtained in a wide range of designs based on Renaissance and Georgian originals. They were extensively used in pubs, in combination with decorated glass and elaborate cabinetwork.

The handsome bar counters and display stands that were such prominent features of the late Victorian pubs were sometimes ordered from firms specialising in bar cabinetwork and advertising to that effect in the licensed trade press. Parnall and Sons Limited, of Narrow Wine Street, Bristol, occasionally advertised in the Victualling Trades' Review and had branch premises at 328 St. George's Road, Glasgow. More often, however, these fittings were supplied by local firms – joiners such as William Lightbody (42 Sydney Street, Glasgow); cabinetmakers such as William R. Clapperton and Company (59-60 Princes Street, Edinburgh), John Taylor and Son (110 Princes Street, Edinburgh), or William Patterson and Company (10 Queensferry Street, Edinburgh); builders with joinery departments such as Hutcheson and Grant (128 Pitt Street, Glasgow), Bryson and Mackintosh (5-7 Thorntree Street, Edinburgh), or William Beattie and Sons (29 Fountainbridge, Edinburgh). These and many similar firms carried out work to architects' specifications, and in some cases produced designs of their own.

The Glasgow Post Office Directory for 1903-04 lists eleven bar fitters, most of whom were suppliers of machinery, utensils and accessories rather than cabinet bar fitters specialising in joinery. For example, Messrs. Allan and Bogle (14 Clyde Street) were suppliers of beer and spirit raising engines; Robert B. Thomson and Company (54 West Howard Street) were suppliers of show bottles and urns; Beveridge Limited (11 Jamaica Street) supplied urns, mullers and pumps, while Peter McDonald and Company (4 Carlton Place) were purveyors of a wide range of spirit merchants' requisites. But some bar fitters offered a more comprehensive service. At the turn of the century John McGlashan and Company's Albany Works in Catherine Lane, Glasgow, could supply the publican with anything from a barrel spile to a fully equipped bar. McGlashan's products included beer engines and pumps; glass urns and barrels for spirits; bar tables; cabinetwork; brass spittoons; call-bells; gasogenes; boilers and geysers; gas fittings. A much requested item was the "Albany hydro-pneumatic beer self-raising engine," invented and patented by John McGlashan. As bar fitters McGlashan's were "quick-change artistes," esteemed for "first-class workmanship and solid material." They claimed to have provided "nearly all the newer and large bars in and around Glasgow" and also the bars at many exhibitions, including the Edinburgh Exhibition of 1886 and the Glasgow Exhibition of 1901.

The spirit barrels, which were supported by a back-fitment or a central platform, depending on whether the pub had a long bar or an island one, were usually ornamental as well as functional – polished or painted and gilded, with hoops of brass or nickel-silver. The manufacture of stock casks for use and display was the speciality of high-class cooperages such as the Glasgow firms of Alexander Gibb (West Regent Lane) and W.P. Lowrie and Company (works, Hydepark

Street). Lowrie and Company were also wine and spirit brokers with bonded warehouses in Washington Street.

Oval and circular island serving counters with central platforms for the whisky barrels were introduced in the mid 1880s and soon became highly popular. Far more people were able to gain simultaneous access to the bar where they could be served with the minimum of delay, while the licensee and his assistants were also admirably placed to keep them under surveillance. Archibald Lauder and John Scouller were among the first Glasgow publicans to equip their premises with island counters, and many others soon followed suit. Owing to the policies pursued by the licensing magistrates of Glasgow there were more people to each pub in Glasgow than in English cities of roughly comparable size, and the new "quick service" counters were a particularly welcome innovation. On Saturdays and at other exceptionally busy times these majestic fitments were islands in more than name, being surrounded by a noisy and occasionally turbulent sea of customers. U-shaped and semi-circular bars also became popular at this time. The long bar did not wholly go out of favour, however, for some pubs were too narrow to accommodate the new-fangled serving counters.

> While admitting the utility of the horseshoe or circular bars, now so popular, there are many of the trade whose places are perfect models in their way where this innovation has not been adopted. "The Wellington," for example, opposite the Waterloo rooms, Glasgow, might be singled out as one of the most unique and comfortable resorts of its kind in Scotland. On entering, the visitor cannot fail to observe strong evidence of good taste in the beautiful stained glass panels on every side. A range of sitting-rooms lies to the right; or, should the front bar be crowded, passing straight in you can have a quiet "hauf" and a snack in the back saloon, where there is a bar fitted up in a way that even the grim teetotaler might admire.[3]

Art tiles, embossed wall and ceiling coverings and fine joinery made important contributions to the inviting interior of the liquor palace, but glass, and mirror-glass in particular, gave it its characteristic glitter and sparkle.

> The embellishment and decoration of our hotels, restaurants, bars, and public-houses has been almost entirely revolutionised during the last decade. Instead of dark, low-roofed, and often insanitary premises, we find elegant, airy, light apartments, whose decorations, being "things of beauty," may be presumed to be, to the customers and owners alike, "joys for ever."
> The principal factor in these much-to-be-desired improvements is *glass* – glass in all its varied forms of design, colour, and shape. Easily cleaned and *kept* clean, there is no better form of decoration for a busy hostelry, "where men do mostly congregate."[4]

"Glass in all its varied forms" was supplied to the pubs of the 1890s and early 1900s by craftsmen who specialised in techniques such as embossing (etching with white and hydrofluoric acids), brilliant, or deep, cutting, bevelling, silvering, staining and sandblasting. The pub's stained, embossed or brilliant cut glass windows were an important part of its allure, and they also served a functional purpose, admitting the light without exposing the customers to the scrutiny of passers-by or the sneers of the unco guid. Architects occasionally supplied designs for these windows, but the craftsmen were capable of producing thoroughly self-assured work on their own.

Towards the end of the nineteenth century there was a marked increase in the demand for decorated glass of every description and by the turn of the century the products of the glass stainers and embossers could be seen almost everywhere, in town halls, public libraries, churches, shops, pubs, restaurants and cafes.

The Glasgow Post Office Directory for 1880-81 lists only four firms specialising in glass staining, embossing and gilding, while the Directory for 1899-1900 lists no fewer than fifty-eight; ranging from modest ateliers such as that of James P. Hunter (162 Eglinton Street) to influential firms such as J. & W. Guthrie and Andrew Wells, Ltd. (237 West George Street). Among the Edinburgh firms specialising in glass staining and embossing in 1901 were: Ballantine and Gardiner (42 George Street), Cunningham and Company (18 Leith Street and 60 Howe Street) and Ciceri and Company (57 Frederick Street). Messrs. Ciceri (the head of the firm, Joshua Ciceri, was of Italian origin) were also fine art and curio dealers.

Stained glass windows were features of very many Scottish pubs; the Four Seasons were a favourite theme and were usually personified by stately damsels, demurely posed, and surrounded by rich borders of appropriately seasonal fruit and flowers. Other popular subjects were sportsmen, inventors, statesmen, historical personages, explorers, and soldiers. Rabbie Burns was depicted in stained glass, and so too were those notable rascals Rob Roy and Deacon Brodie. Many publicans were keen on athletics and the windows of their premises were accordingly decorated with scenes of boating, cycling, football and other pursuits. Obscure glass was also highly popular; the etched designs—which were generally provided with sparkling deep-cut accents – ranged from simple but effective arrangements of scrolls and festoons or hops and grapes, to elaborate compositions of historical or topographical interest.

Inside the pub, carefully arranged mirrors created the semblance of spaciousness and multiplied the images of customers, staff, fittings, bottles, glasses and ornaments. Entire walls were occasionally panelled with large mirrors from the dado upwards, conveying the impression that a looking-glass pub co-existed with the familiar everyday one. Like the stained or embossed glass window panels, the wall mirrors were functional as well as decorative – with their help the publican and his assistants were able to keep a discreet eye on all parts of the house. The acme of mirror decoration was represented by the polychromatic mirror panel, a lush development of the late 1880s and 1890s. The composition was painted on the back of a sheet of glass, which was then silvered over. Some London pubs retain extremely handsome back-painted mirrors, but in Scotland the finest specimens were consigned to the rubbish heap long ago.

Advertisement mirrors, known in late Victorian Scotland as mirror showcards, were distributed to pubs by brewers, distillers and spirit wholesalers. At the turn of the century lavishly decorated mirrors were widely used for advertising purposes and they could be seen, not only in licensed premises, but in the shops of confectioners, grocers, tobacconists, and other retailers.

Mirrors advertising defunct breweries or extinct whisky merchants still adorn the walls of quite a number of Scottish pubs, but countless decorated mirrors, including most of the larger and more elaborate examples, were sacrificed some time ago to the then prevailing fashion for extremely plain pub interiors. Having rid themselves of authentic Victorian advertisement mirrors, some licence holders are now displaying replicas, so the wheel of fashion has turned full circle. Brewers' or spirit dealers' advertisement mirrors, like all things pertaining to the licensed trade, were of interest to the Victualling Trades' Review and its readers.

Just before going to press we made a call at the show-rooms of Mr. H. B. Macphail, mirror show-card manufacturer of London Street, Glasgow. A visit to Mr. MacPhail's silvering works, always an interesting function, was on this occasion rendered doubly so from the fact that a handsome mirror, destined for a firm of brewers' agents in Egypt, has just been completed and was on view.

The mirror is one that does credit to Mr. MacPhail's artistic taste and to the skill of his designers. The name of the firm of brewers, Messrs. William Younger and Co., of Edinburgh, surmounts a rich emblazoned trade mark, and underneath, in appropriate lettering, that of the agents, Messrs. J. E. Mortimer and Co., Egypt, is engraved. A chaste silver border encircles the whole, and in the four corners (sic) the busts of Scott, Byron and Tannahill lend it that national character which it so well merits.[5]

In the early 1890s MacPhail's showrooms and workshops were situated at 112-127 London Street (now London Road), near Glasgow Cross. From frequent references to the firm in the Victualling Trades' Review we know that the young proprietor (he was "scarcely thirty" in 1892) took an interest in his employees and personally supervised their work. Once a year, on the 19th of May (Queen Victoria's birthday), he led them into the country for a picnic, which was followed by manly sports. MacPhail's became a limited liability company in 1896 and moved to more extensive premises at 79 Finnieston Street; alas, their pub mirrors are now seldom seen in situ. One can more readily come upon examples of the work of another Glasgow firm – Forrest and Son. "The most extensive business of the kind in the United Kingdom" was the proud claim of Forrest and Son in the 1890s, when they supplied large quantities of decorated mirrors to retailers, wholesalers and manufacturers, as well as to brewers, distillers and whisky merchants for distribution to bars, licensed restaurants and hotels up and down the country. Typical of the firm's output was a series of mirrors produced for an English restaurant and featured in the National Guardian for November 26, 1896. These advertised McConnell's Old Irish Whiskey ("the embossing and gilding is unique and beautiful, the shamrock naturally predominating"); Melrose Old Highland Whisky, incorporating "a lovely view of the historical Melrose Abbey by moonlight;" Tennent's Pilsener Lager Beer ("seventy-five feet of glass . . . the fruit and flowers, which enter largely into the design, are richly coloured and embossed"), and Robertson, Sanderson and Company's Celebrated Mountain

Dew ("recommended in a bold and spirited oil painting of two Highland sportsmen enjoying a mild and doubtless well-earned refreshment after the labours of the chase.")

In the 1890s Forrest and Son occupied a four-storey range of offices, showrooms and workshops at 355 Argyle Street, between York Street and James Watt Street. The establishment was featured in "Glasgow and its Environs, a Literary, Commercial and Social Review" (Stratten and Stratten, 1891), in which the various stages in the manufacture of an advertisement mirror were described. The plate glass was first cut to the exact size required; the sheet of glass was then placed on top of the design, which had been rendered in reverse on paper. The lettering and ornamentation were carefully traced onto the glass with a protective substance. Next came submersion in a bath of hydrofluoric acid which etched those areas of the glass that had been left exposed. The design was finished off with colours and gold leaf, after which the sheet of glass was transferred to the silvering department where it was cleaned, prepared, and laid on the silvering table. This consisted of a steam chamber with a slate-covered top; the steam chamber heated the slate, causing the silver solution to adhere when it was poured over the glass. After the silvering had been done the mirror was dried and backed with several coats of protective. The finished advertisement mirror was then removed to another workshop to be fitted with a heavy and ornate oak frame.

In 1907 Forrest and Son transferred their operations to 11-25 Bishop Street, Anderston Cross; to this substantial building (it had formerly been a warehouse) they added a casemaking and shopfitting works. The Bishop Street premises were demolished in 1968. The firm also had offices in Edinburgh (4 North Bridge) and London (24 Gray's Inn Road).

Among the other Glasgow firms which specialised in the design and manufacture of mirror showcards were Knox brothers (16 York Street), William Meikle and Sons (19-21 Wellington Street), and Alexander McLaughlan and Company (works, 87 Pitt Street; offices and warehouse, 9 Bothwell Circus). McLaughlan also ran a successful wine and spirit business and owned the Clydesdale Bar in West Nile Street. William Meikle and Sons described themselves as "licensees for the patent sand-blasting system of embossing." In this process fine sand was blown, under pressure, against the glass plate, zinc stencils being used to cover those parts of the plate which were to be left clear. Varying densities were obtained by the use of different grades of sand.

In the 1890s, when the trade of the glass stainer and embosser was a flourishing one, there was plenty of scope for ambitious young craftsmen. Having served his apprenticeship in Glasgow "with satisfaction to his master and credit to himself," Harry S. Donald embarked on a tour of "the best art circles, Paris, Amiens, Boulogne, Lyons, Antwerp, &c.," with a view to "making himself conversant with whatever was likely to prove useful to him, and assist him in his future career." (The Victualling Trades' Review, March 12, 1896). He then returned to Glasgow, and while still in his early twenties, "he pluckily began business for himself – having the confidence inspired by self-acquired knowledge – and opened premises at 57 South Portland Street." The business prospered, necessitating a move to larger premises at 19 Rutherglen Road. Donald's work, the Review noted, was "to be found all over England, Ireland, and Scotland, as well as in all our colonies."

In place of engraved mirrors, some wholesale spirit merchants supplied their customers with novelties such as outsize bottles for advertising purposes. Alexander McConnell and Company of Glasgow (showrooms and offices, 27 Oswald Street; works, 11-18 Brown Street) specialised in "large one, two and four gallon crystal show bottles and barrels fitted with superior silvered taps." These containers were set up on the bar counter or display stand, after the fashion of cut glass whisky urns in pubs of the highest class. They were decorated with a hand-painted representation of the wholesale merchant's label or trade mark, "executed only by experienced artists." Whisky merchants also supplied pubs with framed colour prints, "combinations of art and advertising," such as the Glasgow firm of Watson and Middleton's "Bonnie Lass of Ballochmyle."

> The figure is that of a handsome damsel chastely attired, and bears a striking contrast to those voluptuous and scantily-clad females so fashionable in colour prints nowadays. We understand that the firm are possessors of the original painting, which was recently purchased at one of the London art galleries for a large sum. Needless to say, it is registered, and forms a fitting representation of the famous Ballochmyle blend of Scotch whisky whose message it bears.[6]

It was by no means a rare occurrence for sentimental Victorian or Edwardian paintings to be utilised in this manner by shrewd businessmen – "Bubbles" (of Pears' Soap fame) and "His Master's Voice" are two well-known examples. William Teacher and Sons, perhaps despairing of finding anything suitable in the art exhibitions of the day, advertised for "a highly artistic show tablet" for their "Australian Bonded" and "Highland Cream" whiskies. A prize of fifty guineas was offered to the artist, "male or female, professional or amateur," who could come up with the most effective design.

Decorative paintings embellished some of the more substantial late Victorian pubs, but unlike decorated glass or tiles, they lost their bloom fairly quickly in the gaslit and smoky interiors. When Victorian design subsequently became unfashionable, dingy wall or ceiling paintings were considered to be particularly distasteful, and they rapidly disappeared. Nothing now survives of the output of decorative painters such as Andrew Gardner of Glasgow, whose premises were situated in Clyde Street, Calton. According to the Scottish Wine, Spirit and Beer Trades' Review (August 23, 1887), he "studied the finest specimens of his art in Paris, Brussels and the Netherlands, and gained invaluable suggestions from some of the productions of the most famous decorators, and was specially delighted with the magnificently painted floral decorations of the cafes and cabarets." Among the more popular subjects for decorative paintings were landscapes or seascapes, stylised flora and fauna, sporting activities, and stirring military scenes such as the Battle of Omdurman or the Relief of Ladysmith.

Towards the end of the period under review, the Scottish licensing authorities increasingly concerned themselves with the layout of pubs. When considering whether or not to grant or renew licensing certificates their decisions frequently turned on the applicants' willingness or reluctance to carry out structural improvements. After the passing of the Licensing (Scotland) Act of 1903, alterations to licensed premises of the sort designed to provide increased facilities for drinking or conceal from view any part of the premises required the approval of the licensing courts, the members of which could insist on seeing plans of the proposed alterations. With regard to applications for the renewal of certificates, the members of the licensing court could also require plans of the premises to be made available for their perusal, and on renewing certificates they could order such alterations as they saw fit. If a court order for structural alterations was made and complied with, it was understood that no further orders of a similar nature would be made for at least five years (in the event of the certificate being renewed from year to year during that period). Failure to comply with such an order rendered the certificate holder liable to prosecution. Long before the passing of the 1903 Act, Glasgow publicans had to apply to the licensing magistrates for permission to make alterations, and it had been customary for the magistrates to send two of their number to inspect the premises before granting or refusing permission.

North of the border, the principal bugbear of the late Victorian licensing authorities was the pub with a small bar and numerous "boxes" – self-contained private sitting rooms which made supervision difficult if not impossible. In Glasgow and elsewhere, the magistrates strongly condemned such pubs and exerted pressure on the licence holders to make the necessary alterations. In the early 1900s the Glasgow magistrates also conducted a campaign against family (jug and bottle) departments. To be sure, regarding alterations and extensions to licensed premises, the attitude of the Scottish licensing authorities varied considerably from place to place. In some towns, in the case of an extension to premises, an application had to be made for a new licence, even when the proposed extension was a relatively insignificant one.

It is notable that the late Victorian Scottish pub was a more democratic institution than the English pub of the same period. At the turn of the century a great many English pubs were subdivided by means of partitions, the island counters being ringed with multiple bars. In the private and saloon bars of the class-conscious pubs of London, Birmingham or Manchester the well-heeled customers were separated from the public bar commoners by partitions, while privacy screens shielded them from the eyes of inquisitive barmaids. Privacy screens (dubbed "snob screens" by the irreverent working class toper) generally consisted of embossed or brilliant cut glass panels set in a framework of carved wood; they were erected on top of the counter, small openings being provided below eye level for the passage of liquors and the receipt of monies. In the England of modern, more egalitarian times, the character of many a surviving late Victorian pub has been greatly eroded through the removal of the partitions and "snob screens".

Some English pubs had five, ten, or even fifteen box-like bars; for the customers, snugly ensconced behind partitions and screens of polished mahogany and engraved glass, the arrangement was highly satisfactory, but it was not entirely to the advantage of the publican, who was liable to be taken to task if drunkenness, betting or other malpractices occurred on his premises.

"Agriculture and Horticulture" – Doulton tiled mural from the St. Mungo Vintners' (Glasgow Herald) (right).

Elevation of tenement incorporating pub (the Old Ship Bank Tavern), Saltmarket, Glasgow (R. W. Horn, 1904) (right).

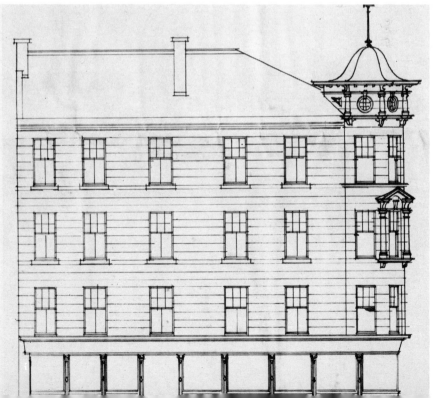

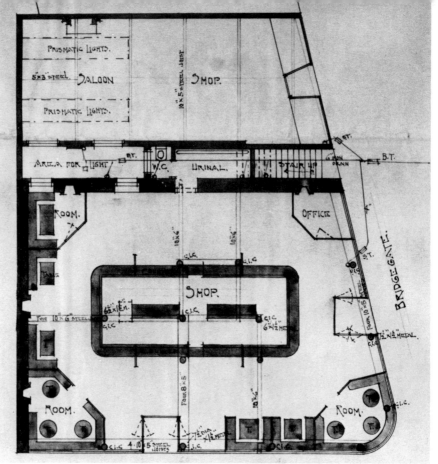

Plan of Old Ship Bank Tavern (R. W. Horn, 1904) (right).

Exterior of Old Ship Bank Tavern (opposite page).

Ground floor and Upper floor plans of tenement incorporating pub (the Bull Inn), New Street, Paisley (W. D. McLennan, 1900) (below right and left).

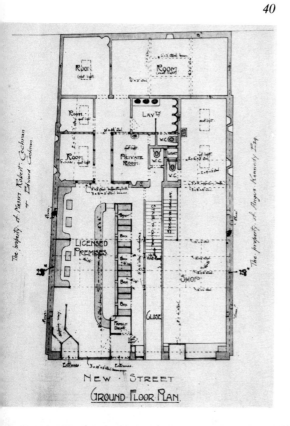

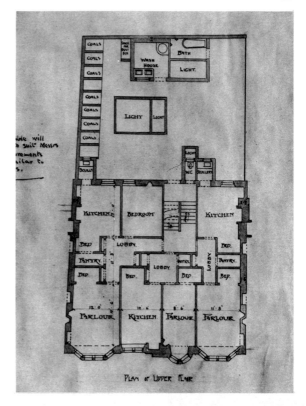

Front elevation of the Bull Inn (W. D. McLennan) (left).

Exterior of the Bull Inn, New Street, Paisley (opposite page).

Detail of the exterior of the Bull Inn (below).

Interior of the Bull Inn.

The fireplace at the Bull Inn (left).

46

*The Rowantree Inn,
Mill Road, Uddingston,
remodelled by
Alexander Cullen in
1902–03 (right).*

*The Burgh Bar,
Glasgow Road, Paisley
(Brand and Lithgow,
1905) (below).*

*The Old Crow Tavern,
Kirkintilloch Road,
Bishopbriggs
(Alexander McDonald,
1902–03) (above).*
51

*The Nineteenth Hole,
High Street, Renfrew
(Whyte and Galloway,
1910–11) (left and
below).*

53

*The Central Bar, Main
Street, Renton
(c. 1893) (left and
below).*

54

55, 56 *The interior of the Railway Tavern (Saddle Bar), West George Street, Kilmarnock (C. E. Robinson, 1902–03) (top). The Union Inn, Camelon, Falkirk (above). Public bar of the Union Inn, remodelled by George Page in 1901 57 (right).*

Advertisement mirrors
in the public bar of the
Union Inn; the Younger
and Co mirror (above
left) is appropriately
decorated with hops and
barley.

59, 60

58

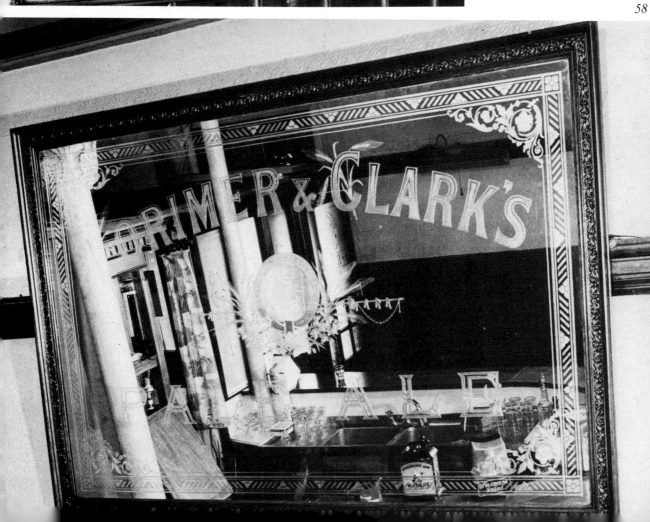

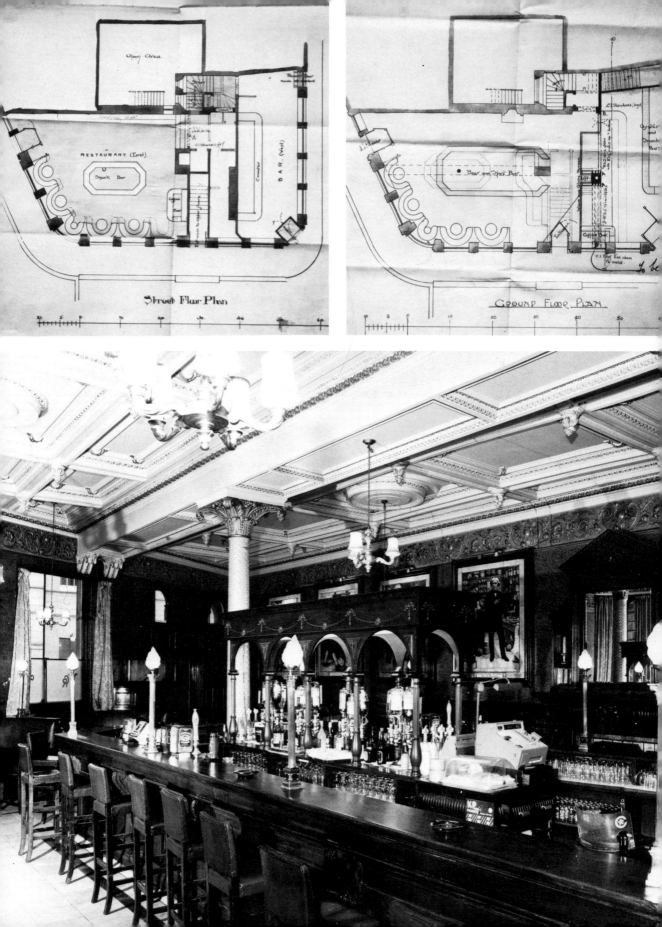

Street Floor Plan

Ground Floor Plan

*The Café Royal, West
Register Street,
Edinburgh (opposite
page top left). Plan
showing alterations (J.
M. Henry, 1898).*

*The Café Royal, West
Register Street,
Edinburgh. Plan
showing subsequent
alterations (J. M.
Henry, 1900) (opposite
page top right).*

*Café Royal, West
Register Street,
Edinburgh; the Circle
Bar (opposite page
bottom right and
above).*

61, 62, 63, 64, 65

Café Royal, West
Register Street,
Edinburgh; the Oyster
Bar (above).

"Rugby Football and
Cricket" – stained glass
window in the Café
Royal's Oyster Bar (far
left).

"Daguerre and Niépce"
– Doulton tiled mural in
the Café Royal's Oyster
Bar (left).

67
68

*The Guildford Arms,
West Register Street,
Edinburgh (1895–96):
Cameron's original
proposals.*

*Rutherford's Bar,
Drummond Street,
Edinburgh (J. M.
Henry, 1899) (bottom).*

*Plan showing R. M.
Cameron's original
proposals.*

69

70

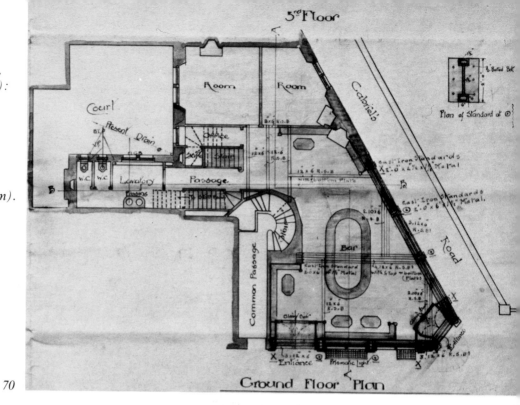

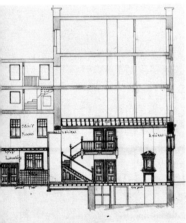

Section B.B.

Elevation showing R. M. Cameron's original proposals (top left).

The Guildford Arms, West Register Street, Edinburgh; plan, section and elevation showing Cameron's reconsidered proposals, which were duly carried out (right, above and top left).

71, 72,
73, 74

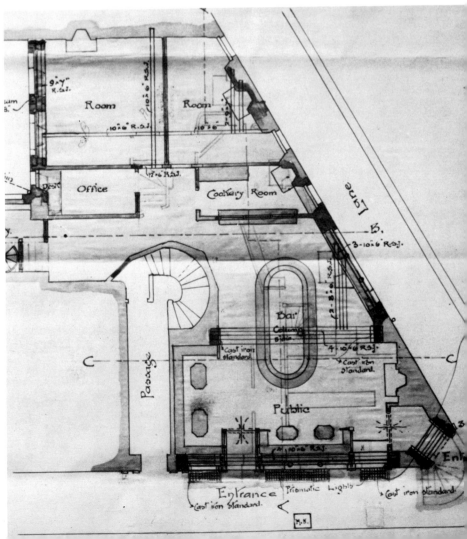

The Scottish licensing authorities advocated open planning for the sake of easier supervision by the licence holders and the constabulary; they placed considerably more emphasis on overall supervision than their opposite numbers in England. In Glasgow, that stronghold of the temperance party, the magistrates were notoriously high-handed in their dealings with the licence holders; characteristically, they deplored the multiple bar system, forcefully insisting that public houses should be as open as possible to supervision both from the inside and the outside. The result was a pub with relatively few screens or partitions, lacking in facilities for exclusive drinking, but not necessarily devoid of character on that account. Magisterial restrictions on screens and partitions brought the counter and display fitment into greater prominence; anyone who pushed open the pub's glass-paned swing doors had an unimpeded view of these features. At its most impressive and stylish, the one-bar Scottish pub was a spacious and lofty saloon, with fittings and ornamentation on a proportionate scale. To compensate for the rather daunting lack of cosy intimacy there were attractive and bold features such as mural paintings, faience tiled pictures, elaborate ceilings and ornate mirrors.

From the point of view of the customer who liked to relax with his glass and pipe, the new-style pubs of the 1880s were unsatisfactory in one respect: the provision of seating was woefully inadequate. The earliest of the palace pubs were geared to perpendicular drinking, the feverish tempo of which is conveyed by T. L. Peacock's definition of drunkenness:

> Not drunk is he who from the floor
> Can rise alone and still drink more;
> But drunk is he who prostrate lies,
> Without the power to drink or rise.

The old-fashioned licensed houses had frequently been badly lit and poorly ventilated, but at least their tiny sitting rooms or snuggeries had offered ease and privacy.

> No doubt the old secret sitting room arrangement – still in use in some houses – was not to be admired. It was neither to the advantage of the publican nor the public. But why should all sitting rooms be abolished? That certainly has scarcely been achieved yet, but it is what we are tending to. In some of our principal public houses it is almost impossible to get a comfortable seat. You must stand at the bar within the view of every intrusive person, and occasionally forced to hear the most insane babble – the drivelling of insanity – and open to the annoyance of every beggar and match seller who slinks alongside, beyond the reach of the shopman's watchful eye. It is just possible to carry this bar system too far. Why not have a few more large public rooms, well supplied with newspapers, where people can meet to discuss the news of the day, like gentlemen of the good old times.[7]

Some of the more bloody-minded magistrates were positively averse to the prospect of comfortable pubs, since they believed that by compelling people to drink standing up they were advancing the cause of temperance (they greatly underestimated the drinking man's enthusiasm and stamina). Most magistrates, to give them their due, had nothing against seating as such, as long as the customers were not seated in back rooms where the licence holder could not keep them under surveillance.

In place of private sitting rooms with walls of brick and plaster and doors which could be shut tight to exclude draughts and prying eyes, architects increasingly substituted snugs which were separated from the body of the pub only by a light wooden screen which was usually about seven feet high and thus did not go right up to the ceiling. Unfortunately the stained or engraved glass panels that were the most popular form of glazing for these screens rendered the inmates of the snugs almost invisible, and so many publicans – prompted by the hyper-critical licensing magistrates – substituted clear glass.

It was, of course, up to the architect to find a happy medium between the requirements of the publican and his patrons on the one hand and those of the licensing authorities on the other hand. In the process of doing so he was able to create pubs as inviting as Ye Olde Three Tuns, Hanover Street, Edinburgh. It consisted of a front bar, with a saloon and an adjoining lounge at the rear of the premises. The "wide well-kept bar" was "flanked by a longitudinal counter," while the "spacious saloon" had walls that were "literally covered with memorials of Edinburgh, both in picture and literature." The saloon, incidentally, featured "a good supply of the latest reading matter." (The Victualling Trades' Review; December 1907, page 170).

Apart from the usual sitting rooms, many pubs had one or more rooms of a "special" nature – a smoking room, a reading room, or a large room suitable for smoking concerts, presentations and club or committee meetings. Although billiards had a great many devotees in the 1890s and 1900s comparatively few Scottish pubs were equipped with billiard rooms; this was probably because the Scottish licensing authorities frowned on pub games and amusements (in Glasgow, for example, there were strict rules against pub games, other than dominoes or draughts.) Public billiard saloons, many of them licensed, were certainly plentiful enough; in some cases they were run by publicans as a side-line. In 1905 the magistrates of Glasgow ruled that no drinking should be allowed to take place in public billiard saloons after ten o'clock at night (the closing hour of the public houses).

Some pubs had linoleum-covered floors, others floors covered in mosaic tiles. Sawdust was generally sprinkled on pub floors, a sensible practice, since beer was frequently spilled on the floor, and pipe-smoking or tobacco-chewing customers did not always take the trouble to use the spittoons.

In the eighteenth century licensed house any conveniently situated room had done duty as the liquor store, but in the nineteenth century, as pubs became more substantial in order to attract trade, more attention was paid to the design of the stock room, for badly kept beer was likely to damage the reputation of the house, no matter how attractive the decor or how friendly and efficient the bar staff. While people could be enticed into a pub by the combined skills of the architect, the bar cabinetmaker, and the glass stainer, it took the expertise of the cellarman – an individual whose main task was to bring the ale, porter and stout to the peak of condition – to turn them into regular customers. The architect was able to assist, however, by providing a well-designed beer cellar in which uniformity of temperature could be obtained. Slow-maturing "stock" beers and fast-maturing "running" beers had to be stored at different temperatures, and so if only one cellar was available it had to be partitioned and a portion reserved for each type. In the late Victorian period the floor of the cellar was covered with asphalt or concrete and the walls were limewashed or faced with white glazed tiles. The large urban pubs had proportionately roomy cellars accommodating bottling and blending plant in addition to quantities of hogsheads (54-gallon capacity) and barrels (36-gallon capacity) containing whisky, rum, brandy, gin, stout, porter and ale. Wines and liqueurs, owing to their value, were usually kept under lock and key in a separate part of the cellar. The casks of beer were stacked on wooden trestles (gauntrees or gantries – Anglice, stillions), for if they had been allowed to rest on the floor the temperature of the latter, especially if cold, would have been imparted to the contents, while any dampness present would have rotted the wooden staves of the casks and rusted the hoops.

The rich decor of many a late Victorian pub was enhanced by a cheerful accumulation of bric-a-brac – potted plants, ornaments, pictures, and stuffed specimens of birds, beasts and reptiles. Seaport pubs were noted for fine collections of curios, acquired over the years from thirsty but impecunious matelots. The most remarkable public house "museums" were to be found in London. The Edinburgh Castle, Mornington Crescent (Camden Town), housed a most comprehensive collection which ranged from medals, suits of armour and uniforms, through paintings and tapestries, to skeletons and two-headed freaks, and included 80,000 butterflies and moths, a Benin bronze, three great auk's eggs, gold buckles from Nelson's shoes, the trumpet which sounded the charge at Balaclava, and the spear that dispatched General Gordon. In 1908 the entire collection was auctioned off, lot 1, appropriately enough, being "The Day of Judgement," in carved frame.

Few publicans could aspire to the ownership of great auk's eggs, but most were able to display a few steel-engravings or chromolithographs. In the public bar of Stuart Bell's (formerly Paxton's) licensed restaurant in Glasgow's Argyle Street the walls were covered with crimson canvas and hung with valuable paintings, including works by Samuel Bough and Sir Lawrence Alma-Tadema. Pub collections were not infrequently limited to specific subjects, such as sport, militaria, or music hall. The proprietor of one well-known Edinburgh pub – the Old Abbey Tavern at the foot of the Canongate – was more enterprising than many of his peers: he exhibited a richly embroidered waistcoat and insisted, against all the evidence to the contrary, that it was the handiwork of Mary, Queen of Scots, and had once belonged to no less a personage than Lord Darnley. Scottish publicans were particularly keen on Burnsiana, even spurious Burnsiana; Alexander Ancell Wright of the Blythswood Bar, 97 Hope Street, Glasgow, proudly displayed an ornate snuff box, alleged to have been made from the left hind hoof of Tam o' Shanter's "gray mare Meg." The Hole i' the Wa' Inn, High Street, Dumfries, boasted "probably one of the largest private collections of Burns relics in the country." (The Victualling Trades' Review, June 1908). The Glasgow publican who wanted to obtain a few conversation pieces in the shape of flintlock pistols, claymores, targes or quaiches, could take his pick from the shelves of Hunter's (later Chisholm's) curio warehouse, 305-309 Argyle Street (corner of Robertson Street).

At the turn of the century public house entertainment frequently took the form of the disc music box, a German invention. The console model was often very tall and stately, and for use in pubs it was fitted with a penny-in-the-slot mechanism. At first the metal discs had to be changed by hand, but by the late 1890s fully automatic machines were available. These could play twelve popular melodies and were operated by means of a dial which was marked with numbers, corresponding with the numbers allotted to the musical offerings. All the customer had to do was move the lever on the dial to the number of the disc he wished to hear and insert his penny in the slot. The disc music box was thus the forerunner of the modern juke box; admittedly, it emitted tones of a comparatively pleasant and dulcet nature, but like the much more strident and offensive juke box of today, it was cordially detested by peace-loving citizens.

Having exhausted the repertoire of the "musical automaton," enthusiasts of pub entertainments could turn their attention to the mutoscope. The devotee dropped a penny into the slot, placed his eyes to the binocular viewer, and slowly turned the handle – to watch the great Eugene Sandow going through his regular body-building exercises ("by stopping the machine at any time, any particular pose or muscle development may be thoroughly studied.") Then there was the popular express train sequence, so realistic that it was feared that the operator of the mutoscope would feel obliged "to step back to avoid the smoke and breeze from the rushing engine."

In the early 1900s a gramophone on the premises was a star attraction; it was enough to make even the most bibulous of patrons momentarily forget the dram at his elbow when the voice of Harry Lauder emerged from the depths of the trumpet. The Scottish Polyphon Company marketed coin-operated gramophones and picture machines, in addition to music boxes. A more bizarre amusement than the music box, the mutoscope or the gramophone was the battery-operated electric shock machine – "an American novelty" which proved very popular with the clientele of at least one Glasgow pub. The person who desired a shock could "so manipulate the instrument as to make the current light or heavy." Fortunately for both the licence holder and the customers, the current could also be readily stopped.

Until the early 1890s the interiors of most Scottish pubs were illuminated by open-flame gas burners. The incandescent gas mantle was a considerable improvement, and since the simple attachment could be adjusted to fit most types of gas apparatus, it was soon being used extensively. In the mid 1890s incandescent gaslight was advertised as being "superior to electric light and one-eighth the cost."

Notwithstanding the fact that electric light was initially very expensive, it was being installed in many bars in the late 1890s. Publicans were keen on "the light of the future" for several reasons: it was a novelty which attracted custom, it was the healthiest form of illumination for crowded premises, and it was perfectly clean, so that the decorations in an electrically-lit pub were certain to stay fresh for a long time.

Heating, in the late Victorian pub, was usually by means of one or more open fires, although cast-iron stoves or steam pipes were not uncommon. The chimneypiece, of marble or carved wood, sometimes had a deep shelf for the accommodation of ornaments such as heavy bronze or cast-iron figurines; in the grander pubs it was surmounted by an ornately carved and mirrored overmantel.

The exterior of the substantial late Victorian public house was particularly impressive at night. The large windows with their rich embossed decoration were infused with the colours of the tinted globes which shaded the gas jets or incandescent mantles, and viewed from the dimly-lit street, the sight was tantalising indeed.

The era of the palatial pub was all too brief, at least in Scotland where the early Victorian gin shops had never been as opulent as their counterparts south of the border. Essentially it lasted from the mid 1880s until the eve of the First World War. Ornate late Victorian and Edwardian pubs were still plentiful in the 1930s, but they were by then unfashionable, and their doom was sealed. In the 1960s they were fast becoming something of a rarity, and by the mid 1970s they had almost totally disappeared. A small number have survived in whole or in part, dispersed over a wide area, and it is now time for us to turn our attention to a representative selection of these.

*Duly colloquialised to "gantry."
*Strong ale.

[1] The Victualling Trades' Review, February 12, 1890.
[2] The Victualling Trades' Review, January 1894, page 22.
[3] The Victualling Trades' Review, February 12, 1899. The Wellington Bar was situated at 78 Wellington Street.
[4] The Victualling Trades' Review, April 13, 1896.
[5] The Victualling Trades' Review, October 13, 1890.
[6] The Victualling Trades' Review, April 13, 1896.
[7] The Scottish Wine, Spirit and Beer Trades' Review, July 19, 1887.

Part Three

2 Examples

A plan of a suburban pub of the 1870s is shown in Plate 1 (Partick Dean of Guild Court Records, Strathclyde Regional Archives). It was prepared, in May 1879, for licence holder James Stevenson by architect John Smellie, the premises being located on the south side of Dumbarton Road (now Old Dumbarton Road). There were two entrances, one of which also led to a "jug and bottle" compartment. The single, public, bar was flanked by two small sitting rooms, and there were three more rooms at the rear of the premises (a central passageway, through bar counter and stock fitment, allowed the customers to gain access to these).

A similar arrangement is shown in Plate 2 (Glasgow Dean of Guild Court Records, Strathclyde Regional Archives). The plan, an unsigned one, is that of a pub which was situated at 55-57 Candleriggs in the heart of Glasgow, as it appeared in the mid 1880s. Here also there were two entrances, leading to public and jug bars. Both bars were quite small, but customers could pass through to the back of the pub where there were sitting rooms of various sizes. In 1887 the premises were acquired by William Brechin and Sons, wine and spirit merchants, and after alterations, emerged as the Stag Vaults, with a large island serving counter and a central fitment for the stock casks.

In the late 1880s large open-planned pubs with mirrored walls and island counters were coming into fashion, but extreme simplicity still characterised many new pubs, especially those belonging to the licensed trade's small fry. William Bowman's premises in Weaver Street, Partick, were remodelled in 1886 by John MacCormack and Company of Glasgow (ground plan and elevation, Partick Dean of Guild Court Records, Strathclyde Regional Archives; Plates 3 and 4). This pub, which was situated on the ground floor of a four-storey tenement, had an exceedingly plain frontage. The interior consisted of a low-ceilinged public bar with an L-shaped counter and a back-fitment for the stock of spirits and bottled beer. Across from the bar counter there was a small sitting room and an adjoining beer store.

When the indomitable Carry Nation visited Edwardian Glasgow she was doubtlessly incensed by the sight of pubs of all classes, shapes and sizes, and the temptation to stave in whisky barrels, reduce mirrors to smithereens and make matchwood of mahogany fitments must have been well nigh irresistible. Carry need not have worried – a later generation of architects and bar-fitters would ultimately prove more destructive than several battalions of hatchet-wielding amazons. Their vandalism, however, would not stem from a fanatical hatred of pubs, but from an excess of Functionalist zeal. The elaborate frontages of many old-established Glasgow licensed houses now conceal drab modern interiors, and it is sometimes difficult to believe that the same pubs were once repositories of high quality craftsmanship, having been richly decorated inside as well as outside.

The typical Glasgow pub of the late 1890s boasted a large island counter, in the centre of which was the stock platform supporting spirit casks. Ornately decorated mirrors hung on the walls, and illumination was provided by gasaliers. Open fires heated the interior, and there were comfortably upholstered seats, screened off from the bar circulating area.

The model for many of the large Glasgow pubs of this type was the Horseshoe Bar, 17-19 Drury Street (Plates 5-10). The premises had been licensed for some forty years before being taken over in 1884 by John Scouller (1849-1923), one of the most notable of the city's late Victorian and Edwardian licence holders. Under a previous owner, John Young, the early Victorian hostelry, one of the last places in Britain where a sedan chair could be hired for festive or ceremonial occasions, had been considerably altered. The premises were again remodelled between 1885 and 1887.

The pub was given two entrances, one leading to the left of the oval-shaped island bar and the other leading to the right. To facilitate quick service the spirit casks on the central stock platform were placed on their sides, with taps at each end. On either side of the bar there was a partitioned-off sitting area with tables, leather-upholstered seats and a fireplace. At the rear of the pub were another two fireplaces, above which the wall was fitted with mirrors. Tall gasaliers rose from the bar counter and branched into triple lamps. No plan of the Horseshoe has survived, and it is a matter of conjecture who was responsible for these alterations. The Scottish Wine, Spirit and Beer Trades' Review (February 13, 1888) gave much of the credit to Scouller himself, remarking that caterers from as far afield as Dundee, Aberdeen and Inverness, having inspected the Horseshoe Bar and thoroughly approved of it, were "forever calling for measurements and plans for buildings of their own," all of which the worthy proprietor supplied with good grace. If Scouller was not in fact his own architect, then it is certainly quite likely that he suggested the "horseshoe" theme to the architect or builder, for he was, by all accounts, a keen equestrian. The Snaffle Bit, 21 Howard Street, and the Spur, 84 Polmadie Street, were another two Scouller-owned pubs with "horsy" themes.

In 1901 the partitions between the sitting rooms and the bar were removed. The counter was enlarged at the rear; it also lost its gasaliers, but gained a shelf carried on miniature columns.

By the early 1900s the pub had become something of a Glasgow institution, as popular with prosperous merchants as with impecunious clerks. Current newspapers and magazines were always on hand for the use of the patrons, and telegraphic bulletins containing information on share price fluctuations were posted up for the benefit of city businessmen. The proprietor was a kenspeckle figure, impeccably dressed, with a bushy military moustache, and latterly, gold pince-nez. He was born in College Street, his ancestors having been members of the Hammermens' Incorporation as far back as 1536. Before acquiring the premises in Drury Street, Scouller had been the Glasgow agent for the Falkirk Brewery (James Aitken and Company). An enthusiastic civilian soldier, he served with the Lanarkshire Yeomanry Cavalry for 47 years, retiring from Volunteering shortly before the outbreak of the Great War with the rank of captain. When war came "he willingly offered his services," was put in charge of the Yeomanry Depot at Yorkhill, "and held that position till he was well past the age limit." (The Bailie, October 12, 1921). He was an avid collector, his tastes, according to The Bailie, "embracing everything from Andreas Ferraras (sic) to Tappit Hens." In his Pollokshields residence, The Moss, 30 Dalziel Road, he had an impressive collection of glass, pewter, medals, flintlocks, targes, and swords – among the latter, no fewer than twenty-five being attributed to Andrea dei Ferrari of Belluno.

Two other well-known Glasgow publicans were also associated with the Horseshoe Bar in its heyday. David Sloan was manager there before becoming proprietor of the Arcade Cafe, while John Y. Whyte, another former manager, succeeded Captain Scouller as proprietor of the Horseshoe in 1923. Between the wars, Whyte owned several of the finest pubs in Glasgow, including the Union Cafe (116 Union Street) and the Cecil (70 Renfield Street), both of which have since vanished. As proprietor of the Horseshoe he literally left his mark on it, superimposing his initials on the mirrors and incising them into the woodwork. Since Whyte's day, the pub has remained substantially intact (it is now the property of Tennent Caledonian Breweries, a Scottish subsidiary of Bass Charrington). The casks on the stock platform have been empty since the 1930s; the speciality of the house in former days was the "Lachie" blend of ten-year-old Highland malt whiskies. Horseshoe emblems abound; they decorate the mirrors, the capitals of the pillars, the chimney pieces, and the surrounds of the two clocks. A farrier (a familiar sight in the Glasgow of the 1880s) works at his anvil beneath one of these clocks. The huge mirrors once reflected flaring gas jets, white-aproned bartenders, and an exclusively masculine clientele.

Two Union Jack pendants in stained glass are preserved in the Horseshoe as mementoes of the Union Cafe (1901), which latterly belonged to John Y. Whyte but was originally the property of a restaurateur by the name of William Hunter. The Union Cafe, long since destroyed, was formerly situated at 116 Union Street.

Dominated by a monumental serving counter, the handsome and well-preserved interior of the Horseshoe Bar fittingly commemorates Glasgow's democratic late Victorian liquor palaces, of which there were once dozens in the vicinity of Drury Street.

The Blane Valley (now the Change House, 76 Glassford Street and 9 Garthland Street) was designed by Frank Burnet (1848-1923), an architect who was responsible for many of the larger Glasgow bars of the 1880s and 1890s. The pub is located on the ground floor of an early nineteenth century warehouse, and prior to being remodelled by Burnet in 1887 (at an estimated cost of £500!) it was typical of the older and more conservative type of Glasgow hostelry (plan and elevations of the existing premises, made by Frank Burnet, Glasgow Dean of Guild Court

Records, Strathclyde Regional Archives; Plate 11). There were entrances in Glassford Street and Garthland Street. The principal, Glassford Street, entrance gave access to a small bar-room, from which passageways led to a number of sitting rooms, several of which were windowless. By the 1880s pubs such as this one, similar in many respects to the old-time taverns, were proving unacceptable to the licensing magistrates of Glasgow and other Scottish towns and cities. Most of the drinking was done in the privacy of the sitting rooms, and by coming and going via the side entrance, people could by-pass the bar altogether. The publican and his assistants could not therefore exercise overall supervision, which was what the licensing authorities had come to expect.

Burnet's designs for the Blane Valley, one surmises, would have met with the wholehearted approval of the authorities (ground plan and elevation to Garthland Street, Glasgow Dean of Guild Court Records, Strathclyde Regional Archives; Plates 12 and 13). Three comfortable and well-lit sitting rooms were provided in the front of the premises. The new pub's principal feature, however, was a large island counter with an ornately carved central fitment for the stock casks. The rear wall of the pub was panelled with large mirrors, alternating with pilasters, and the doors and windows of the sitting rooms were filled with stained glass. Like the Horseshoe in Drury Street, the Blane Valley was essentially a pub for perpendicular drinkers, many of whom worked in nearby shops, warehouses and offices. In the 1890s the leisurely "meridian" was, by and large, a thing of the past; most people now stood at the bar counter where they were able to help themselves to free biscuit and cheese snacks, a welcome accompaniment to the Blane Valley's Old Heather Blend of whiskies.

The interior of the Blane Valley has been considerably altered, but the original arcaded frontage is relatively intact (Plate 14), and the cipher of the late Victorian proprietors, Buchanan, Scott and Company, can still be seen above the doors. Peter Buchanan and James Scott also owned the Strathendrick, Dundas Street, and the Old Hayhouse, Bridgeton; they were primarily spirit merchants and their pubs were termed "spirit stores." Their partnership continued until 1890 when Scott retired; Buchanan continued to run the business until his death in 1909. The owner of a stud of racehorses, Buchanan "took a healthy and active interest in the sport of kings, and his successes on the Turf were both popular and numerous." (The Scottish Licensed Trade, August 1909).

The Glasgow of the late nineteenth century was predominantly a city of tenements, huge cliffs of red or yellow ashlar which, in a heavily polluted industrial atmosphere, were all too soon coated with disfiguring soot and grime. In the 1880s and 1890s Frank Burnet built several hundred of these imposing blocks of flats, as a business speculation on his own account as well as on behalf of clients. In Dalmarnock, Parkhead, Alexandra Parade and other working class districts Burnet's tenements consisted of flats of one or two apartments, usually with one water closet between several households. He also built tenements of a superior character in districts such as Queen's Park, Battlefield and Woodside, with an average of three apartments per flat, water closets and baths. The Glasgow Corporation Improvements and General Powers Act of 1897, by which seven congested and insanitary areas in the city were scheduled for demolition and reconstruction, also increased Burnet's workload. The red sandstone tenements at the top of the High Street, Scottish Baronial in character, are a good example of his "model flats for the working classes" – they were built, at the turn of the century, on the cleared site of some of the most atrocious slums in the United Kingdom. Undeniably more attractive than the rather dour tenements in the High Street is the red sandstone tenement at the junction of St. George's Road and Woodlands Road, near Charing Cross, designed by Burnet in 1900. With a roofline enlivened by cupolas and sinuous fin de siecle ironwork it serves as an appropriate foil to the spectacular range of buildings known as Charing Cross Mansions, the work of another and more successful Glasgow architect named Burnet – John James Burnet who designed the King Edward VII Galleries at the British Museum and was duly rewarded with a knighthood.

Frank Burnet appears to have maintained close links with members of the Glasgow licensed trade; between 1887 and 1910 he certainly received an appreciable number of commissions for pubs. In 1898, by which time he was in partnership with William Boston (1866-1937) and James Carruthers, he designed Castle Chambers for brothers George and John MacLachlan. The MacLachlans – brewers, distillers and whisky blenders as well as wholesale and retail wine and spirit merchants – required an appropriately imposing headquarters, and this Burnet provided – eight storeys in height, built of red sandstone ashlar and polished Peterhead granite, it was completed in 1902 and still stands at the junction of West Regent Street and Renfield Street. The ground floor originally consisted of the opulent Palace Restaurant.

In 1903 the head of the firm of Burnet, Boston and Carruthers received another important commission from a prominent Glasgow publican and whisky merchant – David Ross, one-time proprietor of the Waterloo Bar at the corner of Wellington Street and Argyle Street. This was for Gordon Chambers, an eight storey (including basement) red ashlar Edwardian baroque pile, with facades to Mitchell Street, Mitchell Lane and Gordon Lane. The cost of this building was estimated at £32,500. In the course of construction the initials of David Ross, together with the date 1905, were inscribed on the principal, Mitchell Street, facade. The basement of Gordon Chambers consisted of a billiard saloon (grandiloquently called the Imperial Billiard Conservatory) and wholesale stores; the ground floor was let as motor car showrooms, with licensed premises at the corner of Mitchell Lane, and the upper storeys were let as offices and warehouses. The corner pub, the Gordon Bar (Plate 15), was opened in 1906; it replaced an earlier pub of the same name which had stood on the site prior to redevelopment and which had also belonged to Ross. The prosperous-looking exterior – a dignified combination of polished granite, carved wood, ornamental ironwork and decorated glass – indicates that the Gordon was a lavish pub in its day, but the interior, alas, has been modernised and is now plain and unadorned.

Born on the Inner Hebridean island of Islay, David Ross emigrated to Australia while still a young man. There, between cattle dealing and gold mining, he "succeeded in acquiring a very fair amount of money, but not quite enough to satisfy his ambition." (The Bailie, January 3, 1906). He therefore went to New Zealand, "in which Colony – sticking to the former lines – his career was even more successful than in Australia – so successful that, after a few years, he bethought himself of home." Returning to Scotland in 1868, he settled in Glasgow, where he set up a large wholesale and retail fleshing business. After eight years "he determined to apply his capital and energies in a new direction," and in 1875 he started a wholesale and retail wine and spirit business. Ross, who "always recognised great possibilities in building enterprises," and was "possessor of many valuable blocks and tenements throughout the city," was a personal friend of Frank Burnet and was associated with the architect in numerous property transactions.

"One of the most handsome bars in Glasgow" was how the Victualling Trades' Review (May 1, 1893) described the Old Toll Bar, 1 Paisley Road West, shortly after it had been completed (in actual fact the Burgh of Kinning Park, in which the pub was situated, was not incorporated in the City of Glasgow until 1905). The plan submitted to Kinning Park Dean of Guild Court in August 1892 has not survived, but the pub itself is relatively unspoilt (Plates 16-20); it has, however, been re-fronted in an unprepossessing modern style. Two entrances in Paisley Road West lead to a single bar-room. A third entrance, round the corner in Admiral Street, gives access to a disused jug and bottle compartment as well as to the bar. The main features of the interior are a long bar counter and a back-fitment incorporating whisky barrels. Small spirit casks were originally accommodated in the recesses beneath the large barrels. The arrangement of a straight bar counter and an ornate back-fitment, replete with barrels, mirrored centre-piece, pediment and clock, was still a very popular one in the Scotland of the early 1890s. The mirrors in the recessed middle section of the fitment were often richly decorated; sometimes they carried an embossed, coloured and gilded advertisement for the products of a brewer or distiller.

According to The Scottish Licensed Trade (September 1903) part of the cornicing of the Old Toll Bar ". . . at one time did duty in the old City of Glasgow Bank, . . ." an institution which had some 133 branches throughout Scotland in 1878, the year in which it collapsed, with economically disastrous results. Possibly the decorative feature alluded to by the licensed trade's monthly journal was removed from the Bank's Head Office at 24 Virginia Street, Glasgow, or it might have been salvaged from the branch office at 158 Paisley Road.

Above the dark polished wood panelling the walls are covered with a Lincrusta-type paper. The glazed portions of the pub's inner doors are embellished with painted decoration based on Empire motifs such as ribbons, swags, scrolls and cornucopias full of fruit and flowers. The four large advertisement mirrors, enriched with colours and gilding, were made by Forrest and Son of Glasgow. Apart from being highly decorative, late Victorian pub mirrors are frequently informative; one of the mirrors in the Old Toll Bar bears the inscription "pressure filtered Black and Gold, the aristocrat of whiskies," a reminder of the fact that before it became compulsory to mature spirits in bond for a minimum period before retailing them, whisky was sometimes treated by means of air pressure or chemical additives to render it more palatable and less toxic.

David McCall who commissioned the alterations of 1892-93 was a well-known Glasgow publican and restaurateur – in partnership with George Fair he ran the popular Victoria Restaurant, which used to be situated in Union Street – and in the heyday of the Old Toll Bar the customers could have sampled some choice liquors. The whiskies included Smith's Glenlivet, Coleraine Irish whiskey ("as supplied to the House of Commons since 1843") and the Old Toll Bar Special – all drawn from the wood. There was Gamle Carlsberg lager and Robert Younger's famed 90s ale, in addition to ales and stouts from Bass, Barclay and Perkins, Worthington, and William Younger. And as indicated by an inscription on one of the mirrors, "very old vintage port, brandy, champagnes and clarets" were provided for the more fastidious patrons.

The Old Toll Bar perpetuates the memory of the Parkhouse Toll, which, in bygone days, operated the turnpike roads from Glasgow to Greenock, via Govan, and from Glasgow to Paisley, via the village of Halfwayhouse (a cast-iron post – a relic of the toll barrier – still stands at the side of Govan Road, not far from the pub). Some of the toll-houses were formerly licensed, thus enabling people who were about to set out on a journey to have "one for the road" beforehand, but the Forbes Mackenzie Act helped to put a stop to the practice, since under its provisions no licensing certificate could be granted to the occupant of a toll-house if there was a conventional public house within two or three miles on the same road.

Monday, 6th February, 1899 saw the formal opening of one of Glasgow's most splendid late Victorian pubs – MacSorley's. Situated at the corner of Jamaica Street and Ann Street (now Midland Street), it occupied the ground floor and basement of a fine new red ashlar commercial building, commissioned by Philip MacSorley and designed by George Bell (basement and ground floor plans and elevation to Ann Street, Glasgow Dean of Guild Court Records, Strathclyde Regional Archives; Plates 21 and 22).

On the ground floor there was a large island bar counter and a much smaller snack and oyster counter. Behind the main counter the heavily carved mahogany stock fitment reached almost to the ceiling. The overall effect was sumptuous; the walls were partly panelled, partly stencilled and frescoed; there was an enriched cornice, and the ceiling, painted blue, was patterned in gold. The floor was covered with mosaic tiles. Round the periphery of the bar-room shallow partitions divided the seating into sections and afforded a measure of privacy to sedentary drinkers. The principal light fittings were electric, but gaslight was also provided, for use in the event of an electrical fault. The basement consisted of a kitchen, beer and wine cellars, and a vast tiled lavatory (to which one could descend from either the interior or the exterior of the pub, since it was designed for the convenience of the general public as well as for that of the bar patrons).

Work on the upper floors of the building continued after the completion of the ground floor bars, and by 1903 there was an attractive dining-room, in addition to a well-upholstered smoking-room and a suite of ladies' rooms. An American bar – "in charge of an expert barman from New York" – was also added to the amenities, and suave sophisticates were able to indulge their tastes for exotic transatlantic concoctions such as the "cocktail," the "mint julep," and the "corpse reviver."

Unfortunately the elaborately decorated interiors of MacSorley's were destroyed some time ago; the elegant exterior woodwork and the brilliant cut and embossed glass of the windows are virtually all that survives of what was once a magnificent pub (Plate 23). These fragments are nostalgic reminders of the nights of oysters and champagne – or "corpse revivers." In 1908 Philip MacSorley disposed of the Jamaica Street establishment, which had been his headquarters, but retained his other licensed premises in Holland Street, off Sauchiehall Street, and in Pollokshaws Road, on the south side of the city. The new owner, Malcolm McIntyre, ran the business until shortly after the First World War, when it was taken over by a Mr. Neil Gillies.

George Bell F.R.I.B.A. (1854-1915) was the head of the long-established firm of Clarke and Bell, of which his father, George Bell senior, had been co-founder (at the turn of the century the other members of the firm were Robert Alexander Bryden and James Hoey Craigie). His works included Paisley's County Buildings (1890) and the reconstructed north, Ingram Street, end of Glasgow's City and County Buildings (1895). He also built tenements, some of which were stately blocks of commodious flats in middle class districts of Glasgow, such as Woodside, Strathbungo, and Pollokshields. An enthusiastic civilian soldier for many years, Bell served in the 3rd Lanark Rifle Volunteers and the 1st Lanark Volunteer Artillery. In 1895 he designed the headquarters of the 1st Lanark Rifle Volunteers; the building, at 261 West Princes Street, Glasgow, now accommodates the Scottish Ballet. He was President of the Glasgow Institute of Architects from 1908 to 1910.

In 1904 two identical and adjoining tenements were erected to Bell's designs in Dumbarton Road, Partick (elevation to Dumbarton Road, Partick Dean of Guild Court Records, Strathclyde Regional Archives; Plate 24). These tenements are still extant; they have three flats on each of their three upper floors, and each flat contains two rooms, together with a connecting passageway (lobby) and a bathroom. The ground floor consists of shops, closes (the usual means of ingress to Scottish tenement flats) and licensed premises.

The pub, still known by its original name, the Hayburn Vaults, has a well-preserved sub Art Nouveau frontage (Plate 25). The interior, however, has been completely modernised in execrable taste. The former arrangement was that of a large island serving counter, rather like a hollow L in shape, with an L-shaped central stock fitment. A small portion of the bar counter was screened off to form a cubical for jug and bottle sales. On one side of the bar-room there were bench-type seats, and more seats were provided in two tiny snugs. Two sitting rooms of much larger dimensions were located at the rear of the premises.

The Exchequer, formerly the Roost Bar, 59 Dumbarton Road, Partick (Plate 26), was commissioned by the well-known Glasgow publican Philip MacSorley in 1899 and completed the following year. Designed by James Hoey Craigie of Clarke and Bell, it is Art Nouveau in character, occupies a corner site, and was formerly part of the ground floor of a mid-Victorian tenement – the upper storeys of the building have been demolished. Its two entrances lead to a low-ceilinged public bar with bench seating, a longitudinal serving counter and a carved and mirror-backed display fitment. In recent years, alas, the exuberantly carved wooden frontage has on several occasions been crudely redecorated and the elegant signwriting which for many years graced the fascia has been destroyed.

Still in quite good condition is the Corona Bar, Shawlands Cross, Glasgow.

Built by Clarke and Bell in 1912-13, and probably designed by J. H. Craigie, it is situated at the junction of Pollokshaws Road and Langside Avenue; south of the border a similar corner site would almost certainly have accommodated a brewery-owned establishment of several storeys, but the typically Scottish Corona Bar has only one storey and consists of a large public bar, together with sitting rooms and a jug and bottle compartment (plan of ground floor, Glasgow Dean of Guild Court Records, Strathclyde Regional Archives; Plate 27). The pub was commissioned by spirit merchant James O'Malley and the cost of construction was estimated at £1,724. It has a prominent Art Nouveau exterior, the main feature of which is a turret crowned by a lead cupola (Plate 28). Above the Corona's two doorways there are sculptural representations of a right hand, palm outward, on which is superimposed a Passion-Cross. These are allusions to the curiously named village of Crossmyloof which once occupied a site which stretched roughly from Minard Road to Shawlands Cross and which was largely swept away, in the course of major redevelopment, at the end of the nineteenth century. "Cross my loof" is old Scots for "cross my palm," and there have been several ingenious attempts to explain how the village of Crossmyloof came by its unusual name. In one version Mary, Queen of Scots passed through the district shortly before the Battle of Langside, displayed her rosary in the palm of her hand, and declared that by the cross in her loof she would prevail over her enemies. In another no less fanciful version the defeated Queen, on being informed by some of her followers that in consequence of the position occupied by the victorious rebels she would be unable to reach the comparative safety of Dumbarton, placed her crucifix in the palm of her hand and passionately exclaimed – "By the cross in my loof I will be there tonight in spite of yon traitors!" In actual fact the district had been known as Crossmyloof for centuries before the troubled times of Queen Mary; it is believed to take its name from a wooden cross erected on the site by the Celtic Saint Moluag.

The interior of the Corona Bar (Plates 29 and 30) is of considerable interest, despite the erosion of quite a lot of the original decorative detail. The windows – which retain their stained and etched glass – are exceptionally large, and there is also a lantern light, carried on a series of cast-iron columns and elliptical arches. The capitals of the columns are ornamented with reversed volutes and stylised pomagranates. Upholstered seats and bolted-down tables are arranged in full view of the U-shaped bar counter, and of the pub's three original sitting rooms two are still in use.

In the early years of the twentieth century, Glasgow's splendid system of electric trams, city improvement schemes, public spirit and sound finances won it the high-sounding title of "the model municipality". Nor was that all, for the "Glasgow School" of painters and designers had achieved recognition at home and abroad, and the completion, in 1909, of Charles Rennie Mackintosh's Art School was an architectural event of international significance. Towering Art Nouveau buildings testified to the commercial acumen and expansive mood of Edwardian Glasgow, and the shops, tea-rooms, restaurants and pubs also reflected the city's avante-garde image. The great majority of the Edwardian shops, tea-rooms and restaurants have long since vanished, and as for the pubs, although a number of them retain their Art Nouveau frontages, the interiors are generally now redolent of late twentieth-century banality.

In 1903 Messrs. Howard and Wyndham's King's Theatre was under construction in Bath Street, and this prompted Duncan Tweedley, whose licensed premises were situated almost directly opposite, at the north-east corner of Bath and Elmbank Streets, to commission expensive alterations with a view to securing the patronage of discerning theatre-goers. Designed by architect William Reid and completed the following year, the King's Arms (now known as the Griffin) has a flamboyant Art Nouveau exterior with etched and embossed glass windows set in elegant woodwork (Plate 31). The interior must formerly have been extremely handsome; alterations in the crass and insensitive 1960s did nothing to improve its appearance. Some of the original features can still be seen, including the U-shaped bar counter (marred, however, by a modern bar canopy), the moulded oval-shaped ceiling, and the decorative wood dado. Until the mid 1950s Glasgow and neighbouring towns such as Clydebank and Paisley retained a substantial number of Art Nouveau pubs, the work of architects who had evidently been influenced to a greater or lesser degree by C. R. Mackintosh and other protagonists of the Glasgow Style; these pubs would themselves have merited a book-length study had they survived in good condition until the present day.

Between 1900 and 1912 William Reid designed a series of pubs in the Burgh of Partick (the Burgh was incorporated in the City of Glasgow in the latter year). Wilson's Bar, 4 Byres Road (Plate 32), was opened in April 1904. The original owner, Mrs. Jane Mitchell, had previously held the licence of the long-established Californian Tavern, demolished when Byres Road was widened. At her behest Reid had built a four-storey tenement of red ashlar masonry, with a shop and licensed premises on the ground floor, and flats on the upper floors. Of the Art Nouveau pub only the frontage has remained relatively intact; all that survives of the original interior is the wood-panelled dado. There was formerly a U-shaped bar counter (placed at right angles to the entrance) with a central fitment for barrels, bottles and other articles. Part of the counter was screened off to provide a jug and bottle compartment. On one side of the bar-room there were bench seats and bolted-down tables. A small sitting room occupied one corner, and at the rear of the premises there was a large saloon suitable for smoking concerts and other functions.

Before being remodelled by architects Ninian MacWhannel and John Rogerson in 1904 (at an estimated cost of £1,000), the licensed premises at 9 Queen Street, Glasgow, belonging to the St. Mungo Vintners' Company, consisted of no fewer than eleven sitting rooms, together with a reading room and a small front bar (plan of the existing premises, made by MacWhannel and Rogerson: Glasgow Dean of Guild Court Records, Strathclyde Regional Archives; Plate 33). Commercial travellers had been accustomed to meeting their customers in the small cubicals at the back, eight in number, connected by a long corridor like the compartments of a railway coach. In the Glasgow of the 1870s "compartmentalised" pubs had been very numerous, but by the early 1900s they were fast disappearing. The licensing magistrates strongly disapproved of them since the activities of the people in the booths could not be supervised from behind the bar.

The new St. Mungo Vintners' pub had a frontage of red Peterhead granite, with leaded glass windows and a mosaic fascia in green, gold and white; this replaced a plain and unprepossessing exterior with a central doorway and two small windows. Inside, the transformation was even more complete (plan, Glasgow Dean of Guild Court Records, Strathclyde Regional Archives; Plate 34). The box-like sitting rooms had been abolished; all the seating was now at the front of the premises, most of it in full view of the bar. The booths at the rear and the reading room had been replaced by a kitchen, urinal and dining saloon. The long bar counter, embellished with carved enrichments, ceramic inlay and sinuous brasswork, was of a pronounced Art Nouveau character, while the display stand was in a contrasting Renaissance style with segmented pediments and twisted and fluted colonnettes. The walls were painted white, but the ceiling, divided into compartments and delicately moulded, was coloured. Two Doulton Lambeth Faience tiled mural panels, fixed to the wall opposite the bar, represented "Commerce and Industry" and "Agriculture and Horticulture." They were painted by John H. McLennan who worked at the Doulton Company's Lambeth Studios for many years, in the course of which he designed and painted tiled murals for the King of Siam and the Czar of Russia, as well as for the Birkbeck Bank and the Children's Hospital, Great Ormond Street. At the Paris Exhibition of 1900 three "vitreous fresco" panels painted by him from the designs of A. E. Pierce depicted the adventures of Sir Galahad, as described by Malory in his "Morte d'Arthur."

The St. Mungo Vintners' closed down in 1974 and the fittings were dismantled for removal to the United States, but some aspects of the interior were photographed beforehand by the Glasgow Herald (Plates 35 and 36). In spite of its name the pub was an ordinary Glasgow bar, in which beer and spirits were the principal drinks offered for sale. The interiors of wine bars, such as the bodega bars belonging to the Glasgow firm of Rogano Limited, were characterised by rows of wooden barrels, from which the various ports and sherries were drawn as required.

Ninian MacWhannel (1860-1939) and John Rogerson (c.1862-1930) specialised in the design of hospitals and schools. The Royal Samaritan Hospital for Women (1896) and Alexandra Parade Public School (1904), both in Glasgow, are notable examples of their work. At the turn of the century they were also responsible for some of the most attractive pubs in the Greater Glasgow area. The Barrachnie Inn (formerly called Gilbert Stewart's Vaults), on the eastern outskirts of the city, was probably MacWhannel and Rogerson's finest achievement in pub design. Predictably, the original bar fittings have been destroyed; as is evident from a photograph which appeared in the Victualling Trades' Review for August 1906, they closely resembled those of the pub in Queen Street.

The Old Ship Bank Tavern, at the corner of Saltmarket and Bridgegate, forms part of a Victorian tenement which was remodelled in 1904 by Robert William Horn A.R.I.B.A. for Bernard McAnulty who owned the property and had licensed premises on the ground floor. Horn, who later became one of Glasgow's Directors of Housing (1928-1932), altered the exterior of the tenement, which had been severely rectangular, and made some additions, including a corner tower with cupola (elevation to Saltmarket, Glasgow Dean of Guild Court Records,

Strathclyde Regional Archives; Plate 37.) The flatted upper storeys were modernised and the flats, which had formerly only had water closets, were equipped with bathrooms. On the ground floor of the building, McAnulty's pub was also remodelled and enlarged. It had previously consisted of a small bar, entered from Saltmarket, with an extremely plain frontage, an island serving counter and two sitting rooms. The premises were converted into a spacious public bar with entrances in both Saltmarket and Bridgegate, a much larger island counter, and a better provision of seats and tables (ground floor plan, Glasgow Dean of Guild Court Records, Strathclyde Regional Archives; Plate 38). There was no family (i.e. – jug and bottle) department, for around 1900 the licensing magistrates of Glasgow, having previously been in favour of family departments, changed their minds and called for the removal of these appendages whenever pubs changed hands or underwent alterations (they later relaxed this strict rule). The Glasgow magistrates also insisted that the space around the bar counter should be as open as possible to facilitate supervision, but pub architects were able to provide a modicum of privacy by sub-dividing the counter by means of shallow partitions, as may be seen from the plan of the Old Ship Bank Tavern. All that survives today of Horn's pub of 1904 is the attractive frontage (Plate 39); the interior is quite modern. The tenement in which the pub is situated was built on the site of the Ship Bank, one of several banks which were established in eighteenth century Glasgow by wealthy and influential citizens – hitherto the existing banks had been Edinburgh-based. The Ship Bank, founded in 1750, was the earliest of the Glasgow banks, and it enjoyed an independent existence for many years. Eventually, however, it was swallowed up by the Bank of Scotland. The notes issued by the Ship Bank bore the device of a full-rigged merchant vessel, and to this day the same insignia appears on Bank of Scotland notes. The Old Ship Bank building had consisted of three storeys and an attic, and it had been part of the duties of the youngest apprentice to mount guard over the premises during the night, for which purpose he was supplied with a pistol to repel intruders and a bugle to sound the alarm. For this irksome and potentially dangerous service his canny employers rewarded him with an annual gratuity of £1. 10. 6d.

The pub's etched glass windows are decorated with a representation of the Ship Bank corner as it would have appeared in the eighteenth century, when wealthy merchants had their dwellings and counting houses in the Saltmarket – men of the stamp of Scott's immortal Bailie Nicol Jarvie.

Paisley's Victorian and Edwardian pubs, like those of neighbouring Glasgow, have suffered cruelly at the hands of a later generation of architects and bar fitters. At the turn of the century the town boasted many noteworthy pubs, not the least interesting of which was James McLay's Museum Bar, 5-6 Old Smithhills, where stuffed zoological specimens returned the barfly's glassy stare. Today, unfortunately, the prominent frontages of Paisley's older pubs usually conceal sadly altered interiors.

The Bull Inn, 7 New Street, is a notable exception. In 1900 a wine and spirit merchant by the name of Charles Stevenson commissioned W. D. McLennan, a local architect, to prepare plans for a tenement, incorporating, at ground floor level, a large pub. This was a familiar procedure in late Victorian Scotland where licence holders who were also property developers (if on a relatively modest scale) not infrequently combined the two roles, erecting tenements or warehouses replete with pubs.

The New Street property originally consisted of a pub, a shop, and three flatted storeys (plan of ground floor and front elevation; Local History Department, Renfrew District Libraries; Plates 40 and 41). The shop is no longer in existence, having been transformed into a lounge bar adjunct of the pub. The flats, two-apartment and three-apartment, were designed to accommodate artisans and their families. Bed recesses were provided in the kitchens and parlours – these, like the shared water closets (situated on the half-landings) being characteristics of a working class tenement. Most Scottish tenements had backcourts with facilities for washing and drying clothes; since the space normally reserved for these facilities was taken up in this instance by the sitting rooms of the pub, the backcourt, with its communal wash-house and bathroom (!), was elevated to first floor level (plan, Local History Department, Renfrew District Libraries; Plate 42).

Built of red sandstone ashlar, the tenement has an asymmetrical facade, Art Nouveau in style, with oriel windows and a conical-roofed turret (Plate 43). The slightly recessed frontage of the Bull Inn retains its carved woodwork and leaded glass and bears the date 1901 (Plate 44). In place of the more usual lettered fascia there is an enamelled sign, suspended from a sinuous iron bracket. It is interesting to note that the completed pub differs in some respects from the pub as shown in the ground floor plan and front elevation, submitted to the Paisley magistrates in 1900 (see Plates 40 and 41). For example, two entrances are indicated on the plan – one leading directly to the public bar, the other serving the family department as well as the bar.

The well-preserved interior is rich in Art Nouveau detail (Plates 45 and 46). It consists of a wood-panelled bar-room (to which women were unable to gain admittance until recent legislation made such discrimination illegal), with wood-panelled snugs at the rear of the premises. The pillared back-fitment acts as a support for elongated whisky barrels, now disused. Opposite the long bar counter, wooden screens with leaded glass panels are employed to form draught-free alcoves, furnished with chairs and tables. The dark stain of the panelling and cabinetwork is relieved by cream-coloured paintwork and a collection of photographs of Old Paisley.

W. D. McLennan's surviving architectural works in Paisley include villas, tenements and churches. Orchard Street United Free Church, now a factory annex, dates from 1905; it is Art Nouveau in character, as is St. Matthew's Church of Scotland, Violet Street (1910).

The Burgh Bar, 64 Glasgow Road, Paisley, still has its attractive Edwardian exterior (Plate 47). Inside, however, the roomy public bar shows unmistakeable signs of latter day "improvements". The original bar counter and stock platform have been removed, but there is still quite a lot of authentic detail, including some finely engraved glass panels bearing the Paisley Burgh arms. The Burgh Bar was designed by the Glasgow firm of Brand and Lithgow in 1905, having been commissioned by a spirit merchant called Isaac Buchanan.

The Rowantree Inn (Plate 48), at 60 Old Mill Road, Uddingston, near

Glasgow, preserves the external appearance of a suburban pub of the mid nineteenth-century. In the latter part of the century many similar hostelries disappeared as outlying districts became more populous and single-storey buildings were torn down, to be replaced by tenements of three or more flatted storeys. The interior of the pub was remodelled in 1902-03 by a Hamilton architect, Alexander Cullen, and is Art Nouveau in style. There is a longitudinal bar counter and a carved display stand, to which are attached two etched advertisement mirrors with back-painted centrepieces, commemorating the Fisherrow Brewery (William Whitelaw and Sons), Musselburgh, and the Waverley Brewery (James Jamieson), Edinburgh, both of which are now defunct. Originally the customers' side of the bar was divided into two equal-sized drinking spaces by a centrally-placed jug and bottle compartment, but this unusual feature was recently removed. The Scottish Licensed Trade (March 1910) remarked on the Rowantree Inn's advantageous situation, "amid a perfect hive of tenement houses of the working class, who know where to go for a good dram and a refreshing glass of 90s ale."

The Old Crow Tavern, Kirkintilloch Road, Bishopbriggs, was remodelled in 1902-03 by Alexander McDonald of the Glasgow firm of McDonald and Currie – "a young man rapidly making a name for himself" in pub renovation work, according to the Victualling Trades' Review (February 1903), which added that the promising young architect was "meantime altering a number of public houses in the City of Glasgow." McDonald gave the simple vernacular wayside inn a more sophisticated, sub Art Nouveau, character (Plate 49), organising the ground floor drinking space along the lines of an urban public bar, open-planned, with an island serving counter.

The Nineteenth Hole, 103 High Street, Renfrew, is situated on the ground floor of a three-storey red sandstone tenement (Plate 50). Glasgow architects James Whyte and Gordon Galloway built both tenement and pub in 1910-11 for a Mrs. McCormack. The pub formerly comprised a public bar with two adjoining sitting rooms and a small jug and bottle compartment with a separate entrance; the sitting rooms have since been converted into a games room and the bar fittings, inevitably, have lost their dark stain, but the interior is otherwise in excellent condition.

The decorative treatment can perhaps best be described as Edwardian Classical. Behind the U-shaped bar counter there are two structural columns with moulded capitals. The central display stand, the pub's most prominent feature (Plate 51), is like a miniature shrine of Bacchus; two rows of colonnettes, the capitals of which are ornamented with a bunch of grapes motif, support a heavy entablature. Attached to this fitment are antique electric light sconces with globes suggestive of flaming torches. The window glass is etched with a simple but pleasing arrangement of wreaths and ribbons. On two sides of the pub there are built-in seats of the bench type and tables with bolted-down cast-iron supports.

The Central Bar, situated in Main Street, Renton (Dunbartonshire), dates from c.1893. It forms part of a two-storey red ashlar tenement property which was erected by Peter Macintyre, who, we are told, combined the responsibilities of a publican with those of "a family grocer, wine importer, and purveyor to public gatherings such as the local ploughing match" (The National Guardian, January 24, 1894).

The pub originally consisted of a public bar with two entrances and a jug and bottle cubical – the latter had its own entrance and was "further kept in privacy from the public bar by a wooden partition and a dark red curtain suspended from a brass rod." Adjoining the bar there were "four sitting rooms, with oak-stained doors surmounted by little glass windows, small paned, and varied in colour." Only two of these sitting rooms have survived intact to the present day, but in other respects the interior is well-preserved and is an attractive example of a small-town pub of the period (Plates 52 and 53). In 1893 Renton had some 6,000 inhabitants.

The panelled bar counter is semi-circular in shape with a brass rail round the top. Set into the back-fitment there is a row of whisky barrels, interspersed with Ionic colonnettes which carry an entablature. The walls are largely lined with tongued and grooved boarding, and the ceiling and cornices are of an elaborate character. Above the chimney piece in the public bar a painted and gilded mirror, designed by Forrest and Son of Glasgow, commemorates the Old Oak Tree Blend of Scotch Whisky (Plate 54).

Kilmarnock's late Victorian and Edwardian pubs, like those of many another medium-sized Scottish town, have mainly succumbed to progress, but until recently the Railway Tavern (now known as Fifty Waistcoats), 22 West George Street, retained much of its original Edwardian character (Plate 55). In 1902, when it was acquired by Malcolm McCulloch, a long-established Glasgow publican, the property consisted of licensed premises with cellarage underneath and rooms overhead. The existing pub was of an old-fashioned character, with a small bar-room and several sitting rooms.

McCulloch promptly commissioned Charles H. Robinson, also of Glasgow, to reconstruct the property. The building's plain ashlar exterior was extended and considerably altered, while the interior was entirely gutted out. On the ground floor of the premises there was formed a spacious and well-lit public bar. This was furnished with a large island counter and a central display stand. At the rear of the premises there was a snug for sedentary drinkers and a small office for the proprietor. Underneath there was a beer cellar, a wine store, a blending cellar and a bottling room. On the upper floor there were a number of private sitting rooms and a large saloon which was admirably suitable for smoking concerts, Burns Nights, and other Edwardian beanos, but which could be sub-divided for more intimate gatherings. The new Railway Tavern (so-called because of its proximity to the station of the Glasgow and South Western Railway) was completed in May 1903.

Charles H. Robinson was responsible for some of the most opulent pubs in late Victorian Glasgow, including the Arcade Cafe, 62 Argyle Street (1900). The National Guardian (January 3, 1894) described him as "one of the most successful designers of the new bar". Time has not dealt kindly with his work. The Railway Tavern was essentially intact until 1980 when the handsome oval-shaped bar counter was reduced in length by eight feet on either side. The attractive frontage is composed of three broad window bays, with pilaster-flanked entrances at either end. Inside, there are four cast-iron columns with Corinthian capitals; in its original form the serving counter was built around three of these structural members.

In its heyday the Union Inn, Camelon, Falkirk, was one of the best known hostelries in Scotland. Three storeys in height, the Inn is built of dressed stone, with a rusticated ground floor and strongly emphasized quoins at the angles of the two upper floors (Plate 56). Situated at Lock 16 on the now derelict Forth and Clyde Canal, it originally contained overnight accommodation for travellers, living quarters for the proprietor and his family, and, of course, licensed facilities.

In the pre-railway days the Forth and Clyde Navigation, completed in 1790, was of inestimable service to the western and central regions of Scotland; raw materials and commodities such as salt, sugar and flour went by the Canal to Glasgow, Falkirk, and other industrial towns, while manufactured goods were conveyed eastwards to Grangemouth for shipment. Passenger traffic was also brisk – if that is the right word, for the horse-drawn boats originally took five and a half hours to travel the twenty-five miles between Lock 16 and Port Dundas (Glasgow). In the early 1800s "swift" passenger boats were introduced, each of which was drawn by two thoroughbred horses, changed every two miles, and these did the journey between Glasgow and Falkirk in three and a half hours. By 1814 as many as 2,000 passengers frequently travelled between Port Dundas and Lock 16 in a single week; the leisurely voyage along the Canal was also popular with honeymoon couples of modest means.

In 1822 the Edinburgh and Glasgow Union Canal was completed; this waterway, which ran from Port Hopetoun, Edinburgh, to a junction with the Forth and Clyde Navigation at Lock 16, greatly increased the volume of passenger traffic, and by 1836 the number being carried was close on 200,000 per annum. A service of night boats between Glasgow and Edinburgh had been inaugurated in 1831; known as "hoolits," (Anglice, "owls,") they were fitted with sleeping bunks. In 1841 it cost six shillings (cabin fare) or four shillings (steerage) to travel by "swift passage" boat from Port Dundas to Edinburgh. The journey from Port Dundas to Falkirk could be made for three shillings (cabin fare) or two shillings (steerage).

1840-41 probably marked the peak of the passenger traffic, with five boats leaving Glasgow for Edinburgh every weekday, supplemented by three night boats, but the opening, in 1842, of the Edinburgh and Glasgow Railway dealt a severe blow to the Forth and Clyde Navigation; substantial reductions in fares did not stop travellers from deserting en masse to the Railway. A considerable number of horse-drawn pleasure craft continued to make use of the Canal, however. In 1866 the first screw steamer was introduced, and by the mid 1880s, pleasure steamers were making daily trips to and from Port Dundas.

At the turn of the century, therefore, the long-established Union Inn was reaping benefits from a new breed of canal users, the day trippers and holidaymakers, and in 1901 the licensee, Catherine Struthers, commissioned George Page, a Falkirk architect, to make alterations to the bar, which at that time comprised two separate drinking spaces, both of which were located on the ground floor, at the front of the premises. These consisted of a bar-room with a small counter, and a sitting room, respectively situated to the right and left of a corridor which led from the entrance to the rear of the premises, where there were private apartments and stairs communicating with the upper floors.

Page completely remodelled the bar interior, substituting cast-iron columns for the partition walls, and utilising all of the available space for an open-planned public bar with an island serving counter in the shape of an elongated 0.

Once inside the tiled entrance porch there are doors straight ahead, leading to the "family" department, while to the right and left there are doors leading to the bar. Until recently this arrangement was also common to the Rowantree Inn, Uddingston, but the latter has since lost its jug and bottle cubical. The interior of the pub is in quite a good state of preservation (Plate 57). Above a wood-panelled dado the walls are covered with a Lincrusta-type paper and there is a frieze and ceiling decoration in the same material. The carved and mirror-backed display stand is built into one side of the bar counter, evidently because the counter was too shallow to accommodate a central stock fitment. Of the four structural cast-iron columns, two – those which flank the display unit – have ornate capitals. Originally tiny snugs, each of which was provided with a table and bench seat, were fitted into three of the four corners of the room, but only one of these snugs, now disused, is in existence today. The brilliant cut glass window and door panels are of an interesting sub Art Nouveau character, and the mirror-advertisements include some attractive examples of brewers' mirrors, products of several long extinct Glasgow and Edinburgh firms of glass stainers and embossers (Plates 58-60). The William Younger's mirror, by Forrest and Son of Glasgow, is appropriately ornamented with conventionalized representations of hops and barley. At the back of the bar-room doors give access to the domestic apartments, which were unaffected by the alterations of 1901-02. In late Victorian and Edwardian Scotland a very general rule prevailed that licensees of public houses were not allowed to reside in the premises, but this stricture, for obvious reasons, did not apply to hoteliers or innkeepers.

In the Edinburgh of the early nineteenth century the public houses were by no means conspicuous. It was necessary to descend to some, because they occupied cellars or basements, while others were located in backcourts or narrow wynds. The Victorians gradually changed all that, and by the turn of the century the Scottish capital was particularly well endowed with handsome and convenient pubs and licensed restaurants. The Cafe Royal and the Guildford Arms were named after earlier and less opulent establishments. The original Guildford Tavern had been celebrated for tripe suppers served with an accompaniment of prime Edinburgh ale, while the Cafe Royal Tavern had been popular with hunting and racing enthusiasts.

Edinburgh's first Cafe Royal was opened in 1826. It was situated on the first floor of a two-storey building on the north side of West Register Street and originally consisted of wine, coffee and dinner rooms. At a slightly later date the premises were enlarged and sleeping accommodation was made available, but it was not until 1859 that the Cafe Royal was first described, in the Edinburgh Post Office Directory, as an hotel. In 1863 a new Cafe Royal Hotel, consisting of a basement, three storeys, and a double attic, was opened at 17 West Register Street. This building, an essay in the style of the Second French Empire, with curved angles to the richly modelled facade and a steep Mansard roof, was designed by Robert Paterson (1825-1889), Edinburgh's Assessor of Rates. In 1865 the Cafe Royal was advertising dinner "off the joint" and a bed for the night, each at 1s 6d.

It was in the 1890s and early 1900s that the Cafe Royal underwent a series of alterations which left it with some of the most sumptuous bar and restaurant interiors in the United Kingdom. The process began in 1893, when a new owner,

George McLaren, commissioned Alexander W. MacNaughton to make alterations to the ground floor apartments, which at that time consisted of a luncheon room, a smoking room, and a bar (the latter was located at the west end of the premises, where the Oyster Bar is today). MacNaughton enlarged the luncheon room by incorporating the smoking room, and since this measure entailed the removal of a bearing partition, the ceiling and structural wall overhead were supported by means of steel girders and the elegant cast-iron pillar with fern leaf capital which is still a feature of the present Circle Bar.

Two years later the Cafe Royal was sold to Alexander MacPherson for the sum of £14,000. MacPherson, who had previously held a position under Charles Clark, the proprietor of the Royal British Hotel in Princes Street, immediately embarked on extensive improvements. The apartments on the ground floor were redecorated; reading, smoking and dining facilities were provided on the first floor, and on the floor above several bedrooms were converted into four private luncheon and dining rooms, which MacPherson named the "Argyle," the "Buccleuch," the "Hopetoun," and the "Rosebery" Rooms, in honour of the four principal Earls of Scotland. The architect, as before, was Alexander MacNaughton. The alterations were evidently completed by May 1895, for on the 10th of that month the National Guardian described them in some detail. The Scotsman of July 13th carried an advertisement for the refurbished Hotel.

In the latter half of the 1890s, thanks to the efforts of McLaren and his successor MacPherson, the Cafe Royal enjoyed considerable popularity as a wining and dining establishment; the hotel side of the business, on the other hand, was no longer very remunerative.

In 1898 the Cafe Royal was acquired by Charles Clark, whose Royal British Hotel had recently been rebuilt to put it on a more competitive footing with its rivals. Clark planned to sever the Cafe Royal's hotel connection entirely and concentrate on the lucrative restaurant and bar trade (people who had previously stayed at the Cafe Royal were to be recommended to the Royal British Hotel in future). He therefore commissioned James MacIntyre Henry, who had been his architect at the Royal British Hotel, to make alterations to the premises (street floor plan, Edinburgh Dean of Guild Court Records, Edinburgh City Archives; Plate 61). The ground floor restaurant was converted into a quick-service buffet; solid and liquid refreshments were served at an octagonal island counter, and there was also a smaller counter at which coffee was dispensed. Comfortable seating was provided in five semi-circular bays. Henry also made alterations to the public bar and gave it a more imposing entrance with a pediment and flanking pillars, located at the north-west corner of the building; the old, south-west entrance to the bar was made into a window. The Cafe Royal's original main entrance (on the north side of the building, inscribed with the date 1862) was altered so that it only communicated with the stairs leading to the upper floors, which Clark intended to let for warehouses and business offices (in 1908, however, the upper floors became the Register Commercial Temperance Hotel, and continued as such until 1946). These alterations, completed in February 1899, were described in the National Guardian of February 19th.

In March 1899 the coffee bar in the buffet was replaced by a somewhat larger sandwich bar, then, in the autumn of 1900, the ground floor of the premises was again subjected to thorough-going alterations. Once more, the architect was J. M. Henry (ground floor plan, Edinburgh Dean of Guild Court Records, Edinburgh City Archives; Plate 62). The buffet bar was transformed into a vast public bar with two entrances, and, in place of the two existing counters, a beer and spirit counter of impressive dimensions. The seating, as formerly, was arranged in semi-circular bays. The old public bar in turn became a buffet bar, "refitted on the latest London models," according to The Scotsman (March 25, 1901), with a handsome bar counter at which food, particularly shellfish, could be obtained, along with "wines, spirits and beers of the finest quality only." There was also another counter, smaller and much plainer, at which coffee was served. The old main stair in the middle of the building was removed at this time, and a new staircase connecting with the upper storeys was provided at the south-west end of the premises, where the entrance to the public bar had been located prior to the alterations of 1898. An account of these changes appeared in the National Guardian of March 22, 1901, and the premises were re-opened on Monday, March 25th.

The Cafe Royal's opulent ground floor bars, classics of fin de siecle interior decoration, are fortunately still in superb condition. An impressive feature of both bars are the Doulton Lambeth Faience tiled murals; these were painted by John Eyre and Esther Lewis, highly accomplished designers who produced a wide range of work for the Doulton Company in the 1880s and 1890s.

From its marble floor to its panelled and moulded ceiling the Circle Bar, as the public bar is called, is redolent of middle class prosperity and confidence at the end of Queen Victoria's long reign (Plates 63-65). Of the seven large tiled murals by John Eyre six are on display here. They appropriately portray men who in their time were in the vanguard of the forces of material progress – William Caxton, Benjamin Franklin, Robert Peel, Michael Faraday, George Stephenson, and James Watt. Readers of Samuel Smiles would have relished these colourful representations of the genius as inventor, engineer or scientist, far-seeing, persevering, and ultimately triumphant. "There is no limit to the speed if the works can be made to stand," is the inscription beneath the portrait of Stephenson. According to the National Guardian (March 22, 1901) the panels were originally exhibited at the 1891 Royal Naval Exhibition, Chelsea. The Circle Bar's majestic octagonal island serving counter, like the fireplace and the screen separating the two bars, was installed in 1900, but the central stock fitment is a pastiche of Victorian bar cabinetwork, dating only from 1979. The fireplace boasts a formidable architectural overmantel, replete with columns, niches, balconies and a deeply moulded pediment, in addition to a tall mirror, not unlike the one through which a bemused Alice gained access to looking-glass world. The ornately-carved walnut screen, fitted with bevelled mirrors on the Circle Bar side and both bevelled and engraved mirrors on the Oyster Bar side, was made to Henry's specification by John Taylor and Son of Princes Street, the mirrors being supplied by Ciceri and Company, Frederick Street. Wood panelling, a rich scrolled frieze and an elaborate ceiling with gilt embellishments add to the visual delights of the Circle Bar.

In Luckie Middlemass's cellar dedicated Georgian followers of fashion had eaten oysters by the light (and smell) of tallow candles and washed them down with draughts of London porter. Affluent Edwardian patrons of the Cafe Royal's Oyster Bar could eat their succulent bivalves at a marble-topped counter while admiring eight large stained glass windows depicting elegantly accoutred protagonists of bowling, tennis, archery, shooting, hunting, fishing, rugby football and cricket (Plates 66 and 67). Archery is represented by a member of the Royal Company of Archers in his distinctive green uniform. The tennis player, the footballer and the cricketer are gentlemen amateurs; at the turn of the century many people still equated professional sport with vulgar "panem et circenses". These beautiful windows were produced by Ballantine and Gardiner of 42 George Street (the same firm also manufactured windows for the House of Lords); if they compare favourably with late Victorian ecclesiastical stained glass windows this is perhaps because of the robust nature of the theme – empire-builders valued sport for its character-forming qualities and in his well-known poem Vitai Lampada, Sir Henry Newbolt drew an analogy between cricket and active service.

There are three Doulton tiled murals in the Oyster Bar, one of which was painted by John Eyre (Plate 68). The seventh in the splendid series devoted to great innovators, it commemorates the association of Joseph Nicephore Niepce and Louis Daguerre, which began in 1829. The subsequent fame of Daguerre obscured the important contribution of Niepce, who died in 1833, but the Doulton panel sets the record straight with the inscription "joint discoverers of photography." The other two murals represent a Liverpool paddle steamer and the Cunard liner Umbria. They were painted by Esther Lewis who specialised in seascapes. The Umbria panel recalls the Golden Age of Clydeside, when it was the largest shipbuilding centre in the world. Built by Fairfield of Govan, Umbria made record-breaking Atlantic crossings in 1884 and 1887. Her sister ship Etruria also won the coveted Blue Riband. Like the luxury Atlantic steamships of the rival White Star Line, Umbria and Etruria were "floating hotels," lavishly furnished and decorated. The apotheosis of the "floating hotel" was of course the ill-fated White Star liner Titanic. For many years Cunard relied on Fairfield for their crack liners, the "greyhounds of the Atlantic."

The geometric ceiling of the Oyster Bar, Scottish Renaissance in character, has enrichments in the form of gilded pendants and painted heraldic devices (emblems of the United Kingdom). The revolving door at the entrance to the Oyster Bar was installed in the 1920s when Charles Venus Clark, son of the late Victorian proprietor, commissioned J. M. Henry to make further alterations to the Cafe Royal (thankfully, the most important of these alterations were confined to the first floor of the building).

It seems scarcely credible that the Cafe Royal was under threat of demolition as recently as 1969. F. W. Woolworth hoped to acquire the site for an extension of their premises at the east end of Princes Street. The danger was averted only after a long drawn out battle in which the preservationists for once were victorious.

In the 1890s Rutherford and Company were old-established and highly reputable licensed victuallers with branches in Leith, Edinburgh and Glasgow. The firm's premises at 3 Drummond Street, Edinburgh, were remodelled by J. M. Henry in 1899; regrettably, they have since been modernised, and all that survives today of Henry's pub is the wooden frontage, surmounted by a segmented pediment and balustrades (Plate 69). A plan preserved in the City of Edinburgh Archives shows that the interior was originally furnished with a U-shaped bar counter and an island stock fitment.

A native of Dunkeld, Perthshire, James MacIntyre Henry carried out a considerable amount of work in that county, including Dunkeld House, erected for the Duke of Atholl in 1902. He was architect of the Midlothian County Buildings in Parliament Square, Edinburgh (1900), and from 1912 to 1917 he held office as the city's Lord Dean of Guild. Before going into practice on his own account he was for some time a draughtsman in the office of David Bryce, one of Scotland's most eminent Victorian architects. Henry died in 1929; in an obituary notice (R.I.B.A. Journal, November 23, 1929) T. F. MacLennan, his partner over a period of twenty-five years, referred to his "sound knowledge of materials and methods of construction," adding, however, that he was "slow to adopt new materials or new methods."

The Guildford Arms, 1 West Register Street, was designed by Robert MacFarlane Cameron and completed in 1896. It superceded the Guildford Arms Hotel, a long-established hostelry which, in the mid 1890s, numbered among its attractions Miss Lizzie Veitch, a barmaid who had carried off first prize in a beauty competition organised by a London newspaper.

In 1895 the Guildford Arms Hotel was acquired by James Dodds, proprietor of the Beehive Inn in the Grassmarket, and since the existing premises were unsuitable for his requirements – he wanted a large, up-to-date public bar with additional facilities for smoking concerts and the like – he consulted Cameron, who prepared designs for a pub comprised of a spacious bar (dominated by a fashionable island counter) and two generously-proportioned sitting rooms (ground floor plan and elevation to West Register Street, Edinburgh Dean of Guild Court Records, Edinburgh City Archives; Plates 70 and 71). Apparently Cameron and his client were not altogether satisfied with these designs; at any rate the architect reconsidered his proposals (amended plan, section, and elevation to West Register Street, Edinburgh Dean of Guild Court Records, Edinburgh City Archives; Plates 72-74). This time he incorporated the first floor of the building. "The work of demolition and subsequent reconstruction was one of great difficulty," remarked the National Guardian of June 26, 1896, "but it was carried out without the slightest accident." The new Guildford Arms consisted of a lofty ground-floor bar and a mezzanine. The frontage was suitably imposing, its tall, wide, round-headed windows alternating with fluted pilasters, and the main entrance was flanked by granite columns and surmounted by an elaborately-carved freestone pediment (Plate 75). There were two sitting rooms on the ground floor and two more on the mezzanine. By means of a folding screen the rooms on the upper level could be transformed into a small hall, capable of seating about a hundred people. By 1908, however, the mezzanine was being utilised as a dining saloon.

The main feature of the ground-floor bar, its ornate island counter, was removed during alterations in 1940; the present counter, which is set against the back wall, dates only from 1970 when alterations were made to the premises by a London architect. The magnificent ceiling, lavishly decorated in the Jacobean manner, is now the principal reminder of the Guildford's late Victorian opulence.

R. M. Cameron sat on the town council of Edinburgh for a number of years, and between 1901 and 1904 he served as a bailie or magistrate of the city. The publicans of Edinburgh considered councillor Cameron to be "a firm friend of the Trade" – meaning, no doubt, that unlike many of his fellow councillors, he was not entirely obsessed by the Drink Question. For this reason, perhaps, his talents as an architect were occasionally puffed by the licensed trade journals, and he was often invited to carry out pub renovation work. During the 1890s and 1900s (with the exception of an adventurous interlude as a Volunteer member of the British forces in South Africa) he designed a good number of pubs, including the Three Tuns, Hanover Street (1899) and the new Golf Tavern, Wrights' Houses, Bruntsfield (1899).

The Northern Bar at 1-3 Howard Place was designed by Cameron in 1903 as a replacement for an old-fashioned pub which occupied part of the sunk storey of a tenement – as some Edinburgh pubs do to this day. The new pub extended over the area, which became the beer and wine cellar. As the architect had incorporated part of the ground floor of the tenement, removing several walls in the process, the upper floors of the building had to be supported by steel beams and cast-iron columns. Decorative pilasters divided the pub's attractive exterior into seven bays, two of which consisted of entrance porches (Plate 76). The interior, now considerably altered, was originally highly ornate, with an island bar counter and central display fitment of carved walnut, a panelled dado, an enriched ceiling and frieze, and much leaded glass. The bar counter was of unusual design, tapering at one end to a boat-like prow. There were two enclosed snugs, located at the back of the premises.

The charming Edwardian public bar and private bar of the Haymarket Inn were designed by Cameron in 1906 for Messrs. Ryrie and Company, whisky merchants. The oldest portion of the Inn (Plate 77) was built in 1862 next door to the terminus of the Edinburgh and Glasgow Railway, which later became the North British line and extended its operations into the heart of the capital. Until recently both bars were in immaculate condition, and the public bar (Plate 78) was particularly inviting with its long counter with bolection-moulded panelling, carved and mirrored display stand, beamed ceiling and stained glass windows, but the woodwork in this bar has since been deprived of its dark stain.

In 1897 Antonin Siffre, an Edinburgh caterer of French extraction who purveyed for Parliament House, the Faculty of Advocates, and the Polo Club, applied for a full public house licence for his establishment at 32A Castle Street, the Cafe de Paris, which was only licensed for the sale of wine and beer. His credentials included certificates of recommendation from a French marquise, from the Hotel Victoria, London, and from the chef to Her Majesty the Queen – notwithstanding all of which the licensing magistrates, who were not easily swayed in their judgements, refused his application.

Six years later, in 1903, M. Siffre became proprietor of the Grosvenor Buffet, or West End Wine Vaults, as the premises were alternatively styled, at 28 Shandwick Place. This was an excellent location for a pub, close to the Caledonian Railway Company's Princes Street Station.

As fitted up by William Beattie and Sons, a Fountainbridge firm of builders, carpenters and contractors, the Grosvenor consisted of buffet bar, dining room and servery, the last two apartments being situated at the rear of the premises. Scottish Brewers, who now hold the licence, recently remodelled the frontage in a style more suggestive of Pickwickian London than Edwardian Edinburgh, and the interior has also been partly reorganised, but the buffet bar has been retained; it has a long counter, behind which there looms a display fitment of great panache, a splendid representative of the vanishing species of ornamental bar backs (Plate 79). Here the shelving which every pub requires has been incorporated in an exceedingly elaborate structure, Jacobean in character, heavily carved and mirror-backed to reflect glasses, show bottles and miniature spirit barrels. Originally some ferns in china pots, sundry pictures and knick-knacks, and one of James Cox's glass whisky urns would have added the finishing touches to this attractive bar.

Round the corner from the Grosvenor – at 1 Queensferry Street – there is an Edwardian pub of considerable distinction, originally owned by a spirit merchant called Hugh Mather and still known as Mather's Bar. It is located on the ground floor of an imposing five-storey red ashlar building, designed in 1900 by Sydney Mitchell for the National Commercial Bank of Scotland and the Caledonian United Services Club. Mather's Bar (1901-1902) is neo-Georgian in style, as befits a pub which is situated in close proximity to Robert Adam's Charlotte Square. Above a granite plinth there are five small-paned windows, an elegant arrangement now marred by ugly modern glass; these windows, together with the entrance to the bar, are surmounted by two large fanlights. The interior is reasonably well-preserved, and the graceful Edinburgh of the Augustan Age is reflected in the treatment of the ceiling, frieze and cabinetwork (Plate 80). Behind the long bar counter the towering display stand is architectural in character with bevelled mirrors set in niches, aedicular arches and a broken pediment.

In the 1890s and 1900s Sydney Mitchell and his partner George Wilson were engaged on a comprehensive range of widely distributed architectural projects, including country houses, churches, hospitals, assurance offices and banks. A. G. S. Mitchell (1856-1930), the senior partner, was a Fellow of the Society of Antiquaries of Scotland and had been trained in the office of Sir Rowand Anderson. He restored the Mercat Cross in Edinburgh's High Street in 1885 and designed "Old Edinburgh" for the Edinburgh Exhibition of 1886. Among his more important architectural works in the Scottish capital were the Commercial Bank of Scotland, North Bridge Street (1898), Edinburgh University Student's Union, Teviot Row (1887-89), University Hall, Ramsay Garden (1893-96), the Diamond Jubilee Pavilion at Edinburgh Royal infirmary (1900), and the picturesque group of "model working class houses" in the Dean Village, known as Well Court (1884).

At the turn of the century, Edinburgh-born architect, engineer and surveyor Peter Lyle Henderson (1848-1912) was known throughout Scotland as "the brewers' architect". Henderson, who commenced practice in 1881, was an expert in the construction of breweries, and in the brewing boom years of the late nineteenth century he certainly did not lack commissions. He pioneered Duddingston as a brewery site and designed many of the breweries which were established there, including the North British Brewery (Blyth and Cameron, 1897) and the Pentland

124

Brewery (T. Y. Paterson, 1901). Among his breweries elsewhere were Ballingall's Park Brewery in Dundee (1881), Aitken's Brewery in Falkirk (1900), and the Slatefield Brewery (1881), the Anchor Brewery (1889), and the Home Brewery (1895), all in Glasgow. As well as being functional, Henderson's breweries were pleasing to the eye – St. Leonard's Brewery (1889-90), for example, situated in St. Leonard's Street, Edinburgh, and built of rubble masonry, with red ashlar dressings, was Scottish Baronial in style.

P. L. Henderson also carried out a great many commissions for new pubs, and his workload, in this respect, was said to be the largest of any in Edinburgh. Like some other architects who enjoyed a rapport with prominent members of the licensed trade, Henderson was an enthusiastic Freemason – in 1900 he converted a late Georgian house at 75-77 Queen Street, Edinburgh, into a Masonic temple. The National Guardian (October 25, 1895) praised him for his achievements in "over-hauling and modernising" pubs, adding that "for the past eighteen years or so" he had carried on a "regular crusade in improving the public houses of Edinburgh."

One of Henderson's earliest pubs was the Old Abbey Tavern, 1-3 Canongate, which was ornamented with hand-painted tiles depicting scenes in the history of Holyrood Palace; he had a marked penchant for decorated tiles and made use of them on many subsequent occasions. Later known as the Lord Darnley's Waistcoat in honour of the garment of that name which was displayed within, carefully preserved in a glass case, for the delight of American tourists and day trippers from Glasgow, this particular hostelry was badly damaged by fire in 1950 and demolished in more recent times when the area was redeveloped. The waistcoat, which actually dates from the mid eighteenth century, is now exhibited in a modern pub of pseudo-traditional character, the Lord Darnley in the West Port district of Edinburgh.

In 1894 P. L. Henderson designed a substantial new pub for one Donald Stewart; situated in a typical Old Town "land," at the corner of the Lawnmarket and Bank Street, it is now known as Deacon Brodie's Tavern, in remembrance of William Brodie, Deacon of the Incorporation of Wrights (or carpenters), who lived nearby, in a house located at the foot of the close which still bears his name. The Deacon was executed for burglary on October 1st, 1788; shortly before his arrest, he had improved on the method of dispatching criminals by substituting a trap door for the ancient practice of the double ladder.

The public bar on the ground floor was equipped with a long counter, curved at the ends, and an elaborately carved display fitment; to the left of the entrance there was a tiny compartment for jug and bottle transactions. Two small snugs were provided at the rear of the premises, and there were also sitting rooms upstairs (plan, Edinburgh Dean of Guild Court Records, Edinburgh City Archives; Plate 81). Subsequent alterations at a considerably later date have robbed the pub of much of its late Victorian character, but some of the original features have been retained, including the ornate ceiling and bar cabinetwork. The contrast between the brightly-painted exterior of Deacon Brodie's Tavern and the time-stained rubble masonry of the building's upper storeys (Plate 82) was not one which Henderson intended, for at the time of building he observed that "the use of glaring colour in cement or paint at this prominent corner will not be permitted."

In 1895 a small-time property investor by the name of Colin McAndrew commissioned P. L. Henderson to build a four-storey tenement at 283-287 Causewayside. On the ground floor, provision was made for licensed premises and a small shop. The pub, at 283 Causewayside (now 45 Ratcliffe Terrace), which Henderson designed for a spirit merchant called Donald Cameron, was acquired in 1902 by John Leslie; it survives in impeccable condition, and is still known as Leslie's Bar (Plates 83 and 84). The premises originally consisted of public and saloon bars, with two small rooms at the rear, and a separate compartment for jug and bottle sales, but at a much later date the neighbouring shop was annexed and converted into a sitting room adjunct of the public bar. The long, rectangular bar counter, centrally-placed to separate the two drinking spaces, boasts a form of "snob screen" which prevents customers in the public bar from seeing what is going on in the saloon bar – and vice versa. The people in the saloon bar obtain their refreshments by applying at several small hatches, not unlike the ticket windows in an old-fashioned railway booking office. The decorative detail is of an admirably restrained neo-classical character which effectively highlights the solid craftsmanship of the bar cabinetwork and bolection-moulded panelling.

The Central Bar at 7-9 Leith Walk was built as a replacement for an earlier pub of the same name. Situated at the junction of Leith Walk and Duke Street, this had been acquired by the North British Railway Company in 1898; it was duly demolished when the North British built Leith Central Station at the foot of the Walk. The railway company arranged to provide the Central Bar's proprietor, John Doig, with a new and larger place of business, which was to occupy an advantageous position, immediately adjoining the station. Designed, like its predecessor, by P. L. Henderson, this pub, consisting of a lofty and spacious public bar and two sitting rooms (located at the back of the premises), was completed in 1899.

Unlike Leith Central Station, the second Central Bar is still in use. The frontage is relatively plain, with two large window bays, flanked by entrance doorways. The windows are ordinary plate glass, but positioned a little way behind them there are screens of carved wood, embellished with mirrors and stained glass. These are low enough to let passers-by catch a tantalising glimpse of the inviting interior with its lustrous polychrome tiles and sparkling mirrors. Inside, the wall surfaces are entirely covered with tiles, except where pub fitments intervene, or where bevelled mirrors have been introduced (Plate 85). Most of the tiles, manufactured by the Stoke-on-Trent firm of Minton, Hollins and Company, are patterned and embossed, fawn, green and blue being the predominant colours, but there is also a series of tiled murals depicting various sporting pursuits, including yacht racing and golf (the latter sport is represented by a portly Prince of Wales, later King Edward VII). Beneath the ceiling – which is of the low-relief Lincrusta type – there is a tiled frieze in an elaborate scroll pattern. The walls of the earlier Central Bar had also been decorated with mirrors and hand-painted tiles.

On one side of the pub the built-in seating, well padded with horsehair and upholstered in black leather, is divided into four U-shaped sections, offering an agreeable measure of autonomy to convivial groups; on the opposite side the seating is of the bench type, also upholstered in leather. The U-shaped bar counter

126

is of generous dimensions, as befits a pub which, originally at any rate, enjoyed a brisk passing trade. The entablature of the bar display unit, which is set up against the back wall, is obligingly supported by a quartet of griffins. In Edinburgh and Leith the late Victorian pub's ornately carved stock fitment frequently incorporated one or more glazed cupboards, handy for displaying cigars and other small items of stock. The fitment in the Central Bar is of this description; unfortunately it, like the rest of the bar cabinetwork, has been deprived of its original finish – dark stained and highly polished woodwork added considerably to the charm of the late Victorian pub, contributing to the overall richness of the decoration.

The Mitre, 133 High Street, was designed by P. L. Henderson in 1901. Before reconstruction the premises, which were very narrow, consisted of a small low-ceilinged bar and a long saloon—situated at the rear of the premises – where the seats were arranged to form convivial nooks. Henderson left the saloon pretty much as it was as far as the seating arrangement was concerned. The bar he enlarged considerably, taking in an adjoining shop and the flat overhead (in 1901, after these alterations, there remained three storeys and an attic above the Mitre, but the upper stages of the building have since been demolished). The remodelled pub stretched from Carrubber's Close to Bishop's Close. The handsome stone frontage (Plate 86) is intact, except for the fenestration, which has been somewhat spoiled by modern glass of a bogus "olde worlde" character. The interior, in spite of incongruous modern additions, is still of considerable interest. There is good-quality panelling and cabinetwork, some engraved glass, and a splendid Jacobean-style ceiling with enriched cornices.

It was in Carrubber's Close, immediately to the west of the Mitre, that the elder Alan Ramsay tried to establish a playhouse. In the puritanical Edinburgh of 1736 this was a highly optimistic venture, premature, and doomed to failure; the following year Ramsay's theatre was closed down by order of the city magistrates.

The Edwardian Abbotsford Bar, 3-5 Rose Street, has an exceptionally well-preserved interior and is arguably the most attractive surviving example of the work of that prolific designer of pubs, P. L. Henderson. This delightful hostelry is Abbotsford II, having been built as a replacement for the earlier Abbotsford Arms, designed by William Hogg in 1887. Commissioned by licensed victualler John Rigg, the Abbotsford Arms had a two-storey frontage in the Flemish Renaissance style (ground floor plan and elevation to Rose Street, Edinburgh Dean of Guild Court Records, Edinburgh City Archives; Plates 87 and 88). It primarily consisted of a public bar, a jug bar, and a dining saloon; the bars were on the ground floor and the dining room, which could accommodate up to a hundred people, was on the floor above. By means of folding shutters the dining room could be made into two smaller apartments. The old Abbotsford was situated at 2-4 Rose Street, almost directly opposite its successor. When Jenner's Princes Street warehouses went up in flames on the night of Saturday, November 26, 1892, firemen fought the spectacular blaze from the roof of the Abbotsford Arms, one of the few buildings in the immediate vicinity to escape serious damage. In 1897 a later proprietor, J. S. McTavish, removed the jug bar and diverted the staircase to the main entrance (marked "public entrance" on the plan), so that his customers could gain access to the dining room without having to pass through the public bar.

The old Abbotsford Arms was demolished in 1902, when additions were being made to Jenner's department store, but the company employed Henderson to build an extension onto another one of their properties, situated on the opposite side of the street, incorporating a new set of licensed premises (front elevation to Rose Street, Edinburgh Dean of Guild Court Records, Edinburgh City Archives; Plate 89). The extension was built of red sandstone ashlar, in Scottish Baronial style, to correspond with the style of the existing warehouse.

The new Abbotsford, named, like its predecessor, after Sir Walter Scott's baronial mansion in Roxburghshire, also consisted of a bar and restaurant. The bar, on the street floor of the building, was furnished with two counters — a large counter, on the island model, at which drinks were dispensed, and a much smaller snack counter. At the rear of the premises there was a lounge and a smoking room.

The Abbotsford Bar has changed little since the early years of the twentieth century, when it was a favourite resort of music hall artistes. Jacobean in character, it has dark, rich Spanish mahogany fittings and panelling, wall mirrors, and a lavishly ornamented ceiling (Plate 90). The dominant feature is the island bar counter, which is exquisitely modelled, with carved enrichments and an ornately detailed superstructure. The National Guardian of October 16, 1903 contained an interesting description of the new premises, from which we learn that the Abbotsford's original colour scheme was pleasantly restful and subdued; the upper parts of the walls were painted green and the ceiling was decorated in tints of cream, with gilt embellishments.

The Kenilworth, 152-154 Rose Street, bears the name of one of the Waverley novels, and so Rose Street pays tribute to the "Wizard of the North" with two pubs of outstanding quality. Designed by Thomas Purves Marwick F.R.I.B.A. (1854-1927) and completed in 1900, it replaced an earlier pub which had been designed in 1893 by P. L. Henderson. Both pubs were commissioned by a wine and spirit merchant called Peter Fisher.

Rose Street had been planned in the late eighteenth century for the better class of artisans, but by the middle of the nineteenth century it had become an oasis in the relatively dry New Town and was virtually lined with pubs. The hostelry which preceded the present Kenilworth consisted of a public bar and a jug bar; it occupied the ground floor of one of Rose Street's original Georgian houses, a three-storey dwelling with an attic floor and bow dormers. Patrons of the public bar could either stand at the long counter or withdraw to one of the small sitting rooms which were provided at the rear of the premises (plan of the earlier premises, made by Thomas Marwick in 1899, Edinburgh Dean of Guild Court Records, Edinburgh City Archives; Plate 91).

With a view to enlarging and extending his premises, Fisher acquired the flat on the second storey, together with an adjoining property. In the course of the alterations the sitting rooms at the rear of the existing pub were cleared away and the floors of the flat overhead were removed. The result was a lofty public bar, the walls of which, to a considerable height, were richly clad in embossed and decorated tiles of superb quality. The windows of the second-floor flat, now situated under the pub's elaborate Jacobean-style ceiling, were turned to decorative account by means of stained glass.

The imposing frontage
of the Guildford Arms
(above).

The Northern Bar,
Howard Place,
Edinburgh (R. M.
Cameron, 1903) (left).

The public bar of the
Haymarket Inn
(above).

The Haymarket Inn,
Edinburgh, remodelled
in 1906 by R. M.
Cameron (right).

*Mather's Bar,
Queensferry Street,
Edinburgh (Mitchell
and Wilson, 1901–02)
(left).*

*The Grosvenor Buffet,
Shandwick Place,
Edinburgh (William
Beattie and Sons, 1903)
(below).*

79

Deacon Brodie's Tavern, Lawnmarket, Edinburgh (P. L. Henderson, 1894) (right).

Plan of Deacon Brodie's Tavern (P. L. Henderson, 1894) (below).

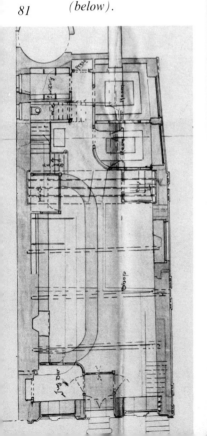

Leslie's Bar; the saloon bar (above).

Leslie's Bar, Ratcliffe Terrace, Edinburgh (P. L. Henderson, 1895); the public bar (right).

85

The Central Bar, Leith Walk, Edinburgh (P. L. Henderson, 1898–99) (above).

The Mitre, High Street, Edinburgh (P. L. Henderson, 1901) (right).

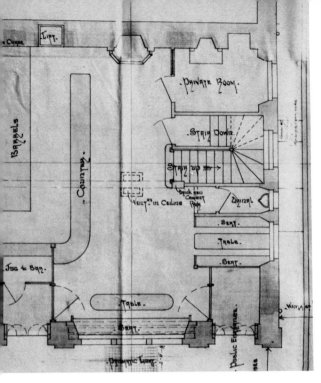

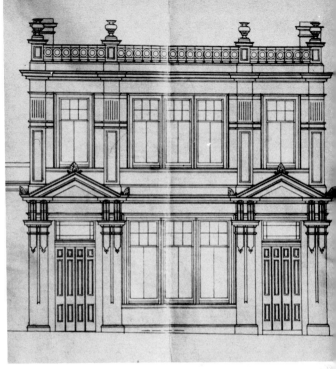

*The original Abbotsford
Arms, 2–4 Rose Street,
Edinburgh. Ground floor
plan and front elevation
(Robert Hogg, 1887)
(top left and right).*

*The Abbotsford Bar and
Restaurant, 3–5 Rose
Street, Edinburgh.
Front elevation (P. L.
Henderson, 1902)
(left).*

The public bar of the Abbotsford (1902) (left).

Exterior of the Kenilworth, Rose Street, Edinburgh (Thomas Marwick, 1899–1900) (below).

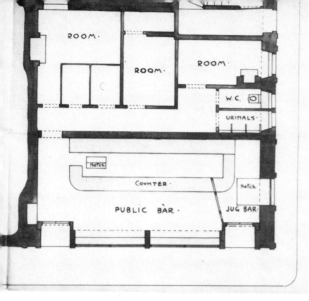

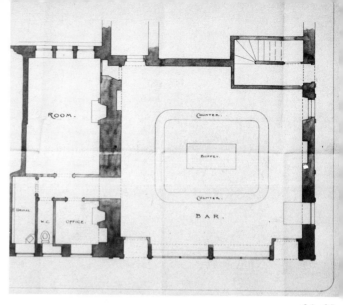

91, 95

The Kenilworth, Rose Street, Edinburgh. Plan of the original pub, designed by P. L. Henderson in 1893 (Thomas Marwick, 1899) (top left).

Ground floor plan of the Kenilworth (Thomas Marwick, 1900) (above right).

The island bar counter (left).

The richly ornate stock fitments (below).

93

*The Barony Bar,
Broughton Street,
Edinburgh (John
Forrester, 1898–99)
(left, bottom and
opposite page top).*

Greyfriars' Bobby's Bar, Candlemaker Row, Edinburgh (Dunn and Findlay, 1893) (below).

The Windsor Buffet, Elm Row, Edinburgh (c. 1899) (left).

The back fitment in Bennet's Bar, Leven Street, Edinburgh (Lyle and Constable, 1891 and 1906) (below).

Richly modelled mirrors in Bennet's Bar with tiles by Simpson and Sons of London.

The Piershill Tavern,
Piershill Place,
Edinburgh (c. 1893)
(top).

Noble's Bar,
Constitution Street,
Leith (William
Thomson, 1897–98)
(left).

The Speedwell Bar,
Perth Road, Dundee
(John Bruce and Son,
1903) (opposite page
bottom).

106

Public bar of the Bay
Horse, Henderson
Street, Leith (William
Thomson, 1899) (left).

The Star and Garter,
Crown Street, Aberdeen
(George Coutts, 1901);
detail (below).

108

107

The Prince of Wales, St. Nicholas Lane, Aberdeen (c. 1909) (right).

The Grill Bar, Union Street, Aberdeen (Jenkins and Marr, 1925) (bottom).

The unspoilt frontage of the Kenilworth (Plate 92) consists of four window bays, with entrances at either end. The painted fascia is carried on consoles with enriched capitals, and there is a hanging sign in the shape of a knight's plumed helmet. It is, however, the Kenilworth's opulent interior which makes it one of the most evocative late Victorian pubs in the Scottish capital (Plates 93 and 94). Behind the pillared island bar counter there is a display stand of pronounced panache, exuberantly carved, mirrored, and adorned with palm fronds. Although the present arrangement of the bar counter and central fitment agrees with Marwick's intentions as revealed in a plan dated March 1900 (Edinburgh Dean of Guild Court Records, Edinburgh City Archives; Plate 95) the counter was subsequently altered, when the drinking space was re-organised in terms of public and lounge areas, and it only reverted to the island pattern in 1966.

Thomas Marwick's practice was a large and varied one and his works included churches, country houses, offices, warehouses and industrial buildings. As architect to the National Commercial Bank of Scotland he designed many branch offices, including the still extant Trongate, Glasgow, branch, a distinguished four-storey building, Scottish Renaissance in style (1903). Marwick was President of the Edinburgh Architectural Association from 1918 to 1921 and President of the Incorporation of Architects in Scotland from 1922 to 1924. In an obituary notice which appeared in the I.A.S. Quarterly (1927 – number 27) he was described as "a prodigious and untiring worker," with "little use for slackers or assistants who did not show a real enthusiasm for the profession." It was also observed that "with strong leanings to Renaissance he could handle classic and gothic with considerable facility." The possessor of "a fine architectural library," and "most widely read," he "took a keen interest in antiquities, and was well known as an authority on Old Edinburgh."

John Forrester was an architect who, like P. L. Henderson and R. M. Cameron, did an appreciable amount of pub renovation work in the Edinburgh of the late nineteenth century. Forrester, who was held in high esteem by the city's publicans and was a frequent guest at licensed trade functions, was the architect of some of the best known late Victorian and Edwardian pubs in the Edinburgh area, including the Robbie Burns (sic), at the foot of Leith Walk, the Crown Inn, Piershill, the Globe Tavern, in the Kirkgate, Leith, and the Black Bull Tavern, 45 Leith Street, Edinburgh. The latter, a basement pub of great character, was sacrificed to redevelopment a number of years ago, but the bar counter and display fitment survive, having been transferred to the Antiquary, a pub and restaurant in St. Stephen's Street. In the early 1900s the Black Bull Tavern had a novel sign; this took the form of a bull's head with eyes which, being lit by electricity, glowed fearsomely in the dark.

The Barony Bar, 83-85 Broughton Street, Edinburgh, was designed by Forrester in 1898 and completed the following year. Commissioned by the trustees of one George Sinclair, a deceased wine and spirit merchant, it consisted of a public bar and a jug and bottle compartment. The well-preserved frontage of the pub is of teak and is topped with a heavy and ornate entablature (Plate 96). Of the two original entrances, one has fallen into disuse. The interior was partly re-organised some time ago, but a good deal of the late Victorian decor has been retained (Plates

97 and 98). There were formerly two snugs at the back of the premises, but these have been incorporated in the main drinking space. The bar fittings are of oak; behind the long counter there is a carved, pedimented and mirrored display fitment which, with its ornamental balustrades and ball finials, is reminiscent of the exterior woodwork. The dado consists of polychrome tiles, including tiled pictures of Scottish scenery. The walls are hung with attractive mirrors advertising Old Scotch Whisky and India Pale Ale.

The locality of the Barony Bar was once the ancient baronial burgh of Broughton, a place notorious as a haunt of witches. Barony Street, directly opposite the pub, is built on the site of a row of thatched cottages, one of which was popularly known as the "witch's howff". The cellars of the Broughton Bar, 46 Broughton Street, were formerly the dungeons of the burgh tolbooth (demolished 1829) in which practitioners of the black arts were incarcerated while awaiting execution.

Greyfriars' Bobby's Bar, 34 Candlemaker Row, is one of the best known pubs in Edinburgh, if only because it is situated just a few yards away from the famous drinking fountain surmounted by a bronze effigy of the faithful little Skye terrier which lay on or near its master's grave in Greyfriars' Churchyard almost continuously until its death in 1872. The memorial fountain was provided by the philanthropic Baroness Burdett-Coutts.

The pub, which was designed in 1893 by the firm of Dunn and Findlay, architects, occupies the ground floor of a row of early Georgian rubble-built houses which adjoin the Candlemakers' Hall (1722) and has a frontage which is relatively unspoilt (Plate 99). Unfortunately the interior has been completely modernised – ironically, in olde worlde style. The premises originally consisted of a public bar and a jug bar, each with its own entrance, and four self-contained snugs. The public bar, low-ceilinged and narrow, was fitted with a long counter and a low, arcaded back-fitment.

James Dunn was architect of the opulent Grand Restaurant (1890), 3-5 South St. Andrew's Street, which, according to the Victualling Trades' Review (April 11, 1891) consisted of a buffet bar, a dining room, and a smoking room, all of which were decorated and furnished on a no-expense-spared basis, with a lavish use of coloured marbles, ornately carved woods, and rich Morocco leathers.

The Windsor Buffet, 45 Elm Row (Plate 100) dates basically from 1899. The only existing plan of that date – a licensing court plan preserved in the Edinburgh archives – is unsigned; it shows, however, that the interior of the pub has changed little over the years, although, as later plans indicate, minor alterations were in fact made to the premises in 1903, 1906 and 1923. The Windsor, which has only one entrance, originally consisted of a buffet bar, a jug bar, and three sitting rooms, one of which was located at the far end of the premises. In 1903 the jug bar was removed and in 1906, when a back bar was installed, the enclosed snug at the rear of the pub also ceased to exist.

The installation of the back bar provided additional facilities for drinking, but the Windsor remained essentially a luncheon bar, offering a good range of quick snacks as well as alcoholic refreshments. Evidently the Windsor Buffet was formerly much more lavishly decorated that it is at present; the bar fittings are of excellent quality and there is an elaborate series of enriched cornices and brackets, but the colour scheme is now unco-ordinated and the woodwork has been deprived of its dark stain. The pub is more intimate than the immediate bar circulating area would suggest, since there are also several alcoves, furnished with seats and tables and well suited to relaxed drinking.

With its highly ornamental woodwork, coloured and gilded advertisement mirrors, hand-painted tiles and stained glass windows, Bennet's Bar, 8 Leven Street, exemplifies the finest traditions of Victorian and Edwardian pub design (Plates 101-103). It became the property of James Bruce Bennet in the mid 1920s and has remained in the hands of the Bennet family ever since – the original owner, however, was a publican called George Marshall.

The pub, which is situated next door to the King's Theatre, has a narrow frontage with a central doorway flanked by window bays. The interior consists of a sumptuously decorated public bar and a tiny jug and bottle compartment. The bar is Italian Renaissance in character, with a long counter and a handsome display fitment, ornamented with niches, pilasters and scallop shell pediments. Opposite the counter there are bench seats, well padded and upholstered, with tables placed at intervals in front of them. Above the seating the wall dissolves into a fantasia of arches, bevelled mirrors, slender Aeolic columns and Raphaelesque tiled pictures.

Bennet's, nee Marshall's, Bar was designed in 1891 by George Lyle, of the firm of Lyle and Constable, and altered by the same architect in 1906. The 1891 layout largely corresponded with that of the present pub, the jug and bottle compartment and the bar counter being placed to the left of the entrance. Situated at the front of the pub, to the right of the doorway, there was a small snug, and at the rear of the premises a much larger sitting room was provided. In 1906 a back bar (known as the saloon bar) was installed, in anticipation, no doubt, of a considerable increase in trade, due to the proximity of the newly completed King's Theatre. The richly modelled arcading opposite the serving counter, which is not indicated on any of the surviving plans, may also have been a 1906 addition, in sympathy with the style of the earlier bar-fittings. The charming decorative tilework was executed by the well-known firm of William B. Simpson and Sons of 97 and 99 St. Martin's Lane, London. Simpson's were strictly tile decorators, using biscuit (i.e.– fired but unglazed tiles) made by Maw and Company, the Shropshire tile manufacturers, for whom they were the London agents. They were responsible for the tiled interiors of some of the finest late Victorian pubs in the metropolis, including the still extant Princess Louise, Holborn (1891). The frontage of the pub, altered in 1906, features leaded glass door-panels advertising Jeffrey's lager beer, introduced in 1903.

The Piershill Tavern, 7 Piershill Place, has an unspoilt public bar dating largely from c.1893. In its heyday this bar was the haunt of cavalry officers from Piershill Barracks, which used to be situated directly opposite the pub. The Barracks were acquired by Edinburgh Corporation in 1934, but long before that date they had ceased to be used for cavalry purposes. In the late 1930s the Corporation cleared the site and built a municipal housing estate, using large quantities of the old stone from the Barracks—which they had cannily salvaged – to face the three and four-storey tenement blocks.

The Tavern formerly belonged to a spirit merchant called George Mills, and when he made alterations to the premises, Mills incorporated another pub, the property of a competitor whose licence had been revoked. "He acquired the adjoining property which had, during his tenure of the next door, lost its licence. He also equipped the stables in the best style, and there has generally been a scrimmage amongst officers of successive regiments for loose-boxes, harness-rooms, coach-houses, and other accommodation." (The National Guardian, March 18, 1898). The pub was sold in 1898 to Andrew Porter, who subsequently made alterations to the premises, preserving, however, a good deal of the original character of the establishment. His descendants still hold the licence.

The interior of the bar (Plate 104) is very pleasant, with dark stained woodwork, leaded glass screens, mirror-advertisements and marble-topped tables with ornate cast-iron supports incorporating the Scottish thistle. The sitting rooms which adjoin the bar were later additions, made at different periods; the large saloon at the rear of the premises dates from about 1910. A small jug bar, the leaded glass screen of which has a horseshoe-shaped opening, is reserved for the off-sales trade.

Noble's Bar, 44A Constitution Street, Leith, was commissioned by Archibald Noble in 1897 and opened in May 1898. The architect was William Thomson of Leith. The pub's lofty and ornate frontage, almost Art Nouveau in style, has been crudely painted but is intact in other respects (Plate 105). There are two entrances, flanking an elliptical-arched window. The late Victorian stained glass has survived, and amid the sinuous fin de siecle abstractions there are representations of medieval merchant vessels, an allusion to the history and traditions of the Port of Leith. The interior, now slightly altered, formerly comprised an open-planned public bar and a jug and bottle compartment. A small sitting room, with a skylight overhead, was provided at the rear of the premises. Regrettably, the original bar counter no longer exists; it consisted of two long parallel sections which curved inwards at the ends furthest from the doors. In 1972 it was replaced by a smaller, U-shaped counter of traditional design. The public bar, with its dark polished teak panelling, wall mirrors, frieze depicting medieval shipping, and Jacobean-style ceiling, is otherwise well-preserved.

Leith was once particularly well-endowed with handsome late Victorian and Edwardian pubs, many of which were of a pronounced Art Nouveau character, but wartime bombing, post-war redevelopment, and the assaults of modern bar-fitting specialists have greatly reduced their numbers. W. N. Thomson was responsible for some of the port's finest pubs. The Victoria Bar, 265 Leith Walk, an exceptionally interesting example of his work, was illustrated in the Victualling Trades' Review of June 15, 1897. Decorated and equipped, according to the Review, "in a consummate and sumptuous manner," with stained glass windows, ornamental tiles, a long mahogany counter, the front of which was embellished with latticework in gilt metal, and a towering bar display unit, carved with architectural motifs and adorned with mirrors, it has since been completely modernised.

The Bay Horse, 63 Henderson Street, Leith, was designed by Thomson in 1899 and originally consisted of a public bar, a jug bar and two sitting rooms. There are two entrances, the one giving access to both bars, the other communicating solely with the public bar; the latter (Plate 106) has lost a good deal of its original character, which must have been quite rich, judging by what has survived. The charming little jug bar, on the other hand, is completely unspoilt. The counter which serves both bars has been re-fronted in a contemporary style and fails to live up to the late Victorian display stand, which is mirror-backed, with fluted Corinthian colonnettes supporting a carved entablature.

W. N. Thomson's architectural works included the United Presbyterian Church, Junction Street, Leith (1895). He also built an extension to Leith Hospital (1899) and converted an existing church in Graham Street, Edinburgh, into a synagogue (1898).

Most of Dundee's Victorian and Edwardian pubs have been modernised, but a few retain their elaborate frontages and stained or etched glass windows. One of the most noteworthy of the city's Edwardian pubs was the Old Bank Bar, 25-27 Murraygate. Opened in 1903 by George E. Telfer, it consisted of a public bar with an immense octagonal island counter, and an adjoining private bar which was a favourite haunt of music hall entertainers. The walls of the public bar were adorned with mirrors, pictures, and antlered deerheads (the proprietor had a somewhat exaggerated feeling for the decorative qualities of deerheads en masse and added to the collection at every opportunity). The Old Bank Bar was demolished in 1968.

The Speedwell Bar at 165-167 Perth Road, Dundee (Plate 107), is an unspoilt Edwardian pub of considerable merit. Situated on the ground floor of a Scottish Baronial style four-storey tenement, it was designed in 1903 by architects John Bruce and Son, for James G. Speed of William Speed and Son, wine and spirit merchants. The premises comprise a public bar, sub-divided by means of a glazed wooden screen, and two sitting rooms. The bar counter and display stand are L-shaped, the Lincrusta-type ceiling and frieze are enriched with Jacobean-style decoration in low relief, and the cornices are ornamented with dentil courses. The bar cabinetwork and dado panelling were produced by W. & R. Brownlee, builders and manufacturing joiners. The National Guardian of January 29, 1904 devoted several paragraphs to the newly-opened Speedwell Bar.

The Victorian and Edwardian pubs of Aberdeen have largely disappeared. Among the most impressive of them was the public bar of the Exchange Restaurant (c.1897), known as "the lang bar". The premises stretched from Stirling Street to Exchange Street and were equipped with an exceptionally long bar counter, behind which were arranged spirit barrels and mirror-backed shelves. Private and bodega bars, a dining room and a smoking lounge, all lavishly appointed, were also features of the Exchange. Another handsome Aberdeen hostelry was the Bon Accord (c.1901), which was situated at the corner of George Street and Hutcheon Street, on the ground floor of a four-storey granite-built property. Designed by George Brown and Alexander Watt and decorated by Edward Copland for a spirit merchant called Thomas Gibb, the Bon-Accord had stained glass windows representative of various sports, including horse racing, cycling, football, golf, boating, tennis, and croquet. The bar was large and lofty, with mahogany fittings, an ornate ceiling and frieze in high relief, and walls that were decorated with ornamental tiles to a height of about five feet and then adorned with a richly patterned Oriental-style paper.

Fine old Aberdeen pubs such as the Royal Oak (7-9 Marischal Street), the Elite

Bar (9-10 Back Wynd), the Palace Bar (1-3 Bridge Place), and the Central Bar (415 Great Northern Road), retained their island counters or long bars and preserved much of their traditional atmosphere and character until the 1960s and beyond. Typical in this respect was the Criterion Bar, 54 Guild Street, at one time a popular resort of audiences and artistes from the nearby Tivoli Variety Theatre. Prior to modernisation in the 1960s, the Criterion boasted a handsome oval island serving counter and a lofty central display stand, and the upper parts of the walls were decorated with murals depicting Aberdeen harbour landmarks.

In its Edwardian heyday the Star and Garter, 6-8 Crown Street, was one of the most splendid pubs in the "granite city". The work of George Coutts, who also designed the four-storey commercial block in which it is situated, it was completed in 1901. The imposing granite-built ediface was erected by a Mrs. J. Webster, who duly became the first licensee of the ground-floor pub. The interior of the Star and Garter, we learn from the National Guardian (December 6, 1901), was originally lavishly decorated, with wall panelling and bar fittings of carved mahogany. Elaborately-carved screens separated the public, private and buffet bars, and the seating throughout was upholstered in dark morocco leather. In the early 1970s much of the evidence of the Star and Garter's original character was destroyed in an ill-conceived renovation scheme which substituted flimsy pseudo-traditional bar furniture for the massive and solid products of late Victorian craftsmanship. An interesting feature of the pub, however, is its deeply coffered ceiling, which survives intact and incorporates Anaglypta panels (Plate 108). The Dean of Guild records of the period show that, at the turn of the century, George Coutts' practice was a successful if unspectacular one, with business premises, factories, warehouses and villas to his credit.

The Prince of Wales, 7 St. Nicholas Lane, of which both the date and the architect are conjectural, is in a reasonably good state of preservation. The bar interior (Plate 109) is long and low-ceilinged, with rooflights overhead. The serving counter – the longest in Aberdeen – is in three sections and runs the full length of the pub, and there are two display fitments, richly modelled, with mirror-backed arches and fluted colonnettes carrying entablatures. Much of the seating has been renewed, but two high-backed wooden settles, located at the rear of the pub, are still in use.

The premises, known until 1909 as the Prince of Wales Hotel, were taken over in that year by a spirit merchant named John McKay. It is possible that the interior was remodelled shortly afterwards at the behest of the new proprietor, though it must be admitted that the bar fittings do not suggest such a late date. The architect may have been George Milne, whose office was situated in nearby Union Street. Milne was certainly employed by McKay in 1913, when he did some work at the rear of the premises; the Dean of Guild records for that year contain a cryptic reference to "outbuildings," which leads one to surmise that Milne may have extended the existing bar on that occasion.

Strictly speaking, the Grill Bar, 213 Union Street, has no right to consideration in a book dealing with Victorian and Edwardian pubs. It is included here as a rare and particularly fine example of pub design in the early inter-war years, when the exacting standards set by the Victorians and Edwardians had not wholly been abandoned. In 1925 John Innes acquired the old-established Grill Restaurant and commissioned architects Jenkins and Marr of Bridge Street to remodel the premises. The pub which emerged from these alterations survives in excellent condition and is representative of the lush 1920s phase of Art Deco – in the 1930s the style was destined to develop along lines of increasing angularity and severity.

The Grill has two entrances, one at the front of the premises and the other at the rear (Langstane Place). The frontage in Union Street is clad in bronze and sparingly ornamented with neo-classical motifs. The interior (Plate 110) is long and fairly narrow, with a bar counter and back-fitment which stretch almost the full length of the premises. The ceiling is enriched with simple plaster decoration, and the walls are decorated with bevelled mirrors and elaborately figured, highly varnished veneers. There are upholstered bench seats opposite the counter, and similar seating is provided in recesses at either end of the pub, behind arches of elliptical form.

Pubs such as the Grill marked the end of a confident and versatile decorative tradition: ornamentation was greatly reduced in the pubs of the 1930s, the latter being characterised by simple geometric patterns, plain glazed tiles, unframed mirrors and chromium-edged bar counters.

Conclusion

Money was scarce in the Scotland of the inter-war years, and so relatively few pubs were built or refurbished at that time. A very substantial number of Victorian and Edwardian pubs therefore survived in a remarkably good state of preservation until the second half of the twentieth century. The years 1955 – 1975 were the locust years during which the Affluent Society did colossal damage to the nation's historic buildings and townscape and also wrecked hundreds of pubs of architectural merit and historical interest.

Not, perhaps, since the iconoclastic heyday of John Knox had so much irreplaceable craftsmanship been wilfully destroyed. Intricately-carved bar furniture, hand-painted tiles, stained glass windows, moulded plasterwork, finely engraved glass mirrors and panels, all were deliberately smashed to pieces, as pubs which only required a minimum of timely restoration were torn apart. It was folly to discard such a magnificent legacy of craftsmanship, folly compounded by the fact that the principal culprits—brewery architects and designers, and firms of bar-fitting specialists—consistently proved themselves to be incapable of creating pubs with a fraction of the atmosphere and character of the ones which they swept away.

Although the leading Scottish brewers were notorious vandals in this respect, it would be unfair to cast them in the role of sole villains of the piece; the individual licence holder was equally contemptuous of the "old-fashioned" pub, the solid and ornate fittings of which required the occasional application of elbow-grease and occupied space which could otherwise be filled with electronic amusements. It is also a fact that in several Scottish towns and cities some long-established pubs were victims of comprehensive redevelopment: in the 1960s and 1970s hundreds of Victorian tenements were demolished, and in many cases pubs—mostly modern, but with a number of exceptions—had formed part of these buildings.

The palace pubs were products of an age of brimming self-confidence, low taxation and abundant craftsmanship—a fortuitous combination which in all probability will never occur again. They were destroyed en masse at a time when Victorian and Edwardian architecture and interior decoration were greatly underrated, having been previously condemned by advocates of Functionalism—representatives of the "ornament is crime" school of thought—who poured scorn on ornate pubs and shops, ornamental street furniture, decorative architecture, and other foibles of our ignorant and irrational forebears.

In many instances the pubs which the vandals despoiled were not merely delightful expressions of Victorian or Edwardian gemütlichkeit, but works of art in their own right (this was especially true of the Art Nouveau pubs of the early 1900s). It was tragic that the vast majority of these pubs were "improved" out of existence precisely at a time when pub design standards were abysmally low.

From Thurso to North Berwick, the old-established hostelries with their complex ornamentation, visual richness and local colour were demolished or drastically altered. The pubs which replaced them mainly consisted of lounge bars (with formica surfaces, piped music or juke-boxes, pool tables, gambling machines and garish illuminated keg beer taps), disco bars (with go-go dancers and flashing coloured lights), and so-called "theme" bars (thinly disguised as Wild West saloons, Swiss ski lodges, Tudor inns, or Teutonic beer cellars; ironically, having presumably exhausted their repertoire of ludicrous "themes", brewery architects and bar-fitting specialists are now busy creating fake Victorian pubs).

The outrageous attack on pubs of traditional Scottish character coincided with an equally disgraceful assault on the traditional Scottish pint. In the 1930s there were over forty Scottish brewing companies, producing a remarkable range of naturally-conditioned draught beers; today there are fewer than a dozen, and the main products are now bland, fizzy keg beers, as devoid of local and regional characteristics as the plastic pubs in which they are usually dispensed.

Happily, cask-conditioned ales of excellent quality can still be obtained in Scotland. Since the advent of processed beers in kegs and cans they have not been widely advertised, for the giant brewing concerns which dominate the market prefer to promote the sale of the "national" products in which they have invested enormous amounts of capital, but the Campaign for Real Ale has done much to publicise them, and their popularity has soared in recent years. Indeed, several large Scottish brewing companies have now started to reinstall hand-pumps in their tied houses, a volte-face that would have been unthinkable a few years ago. It is satisfying to know that in at least some of Scotland's remaining traditional pubs one can still enjoy traditionally-brewed Scottish ales.

Today, alas, Scotland's Victorian and Edwardian pubs are sadly depleted: the survivors represent only a small fraction of what was once in existence—a few dozen out of thousands. With one or two notable exceptions they are not listed buildings, and as this book goes to press it is more than likely that several of the pubs featured in its closing chapter will be added to the casualty list. After all, it is usually the authorities who single out buildings as being worthy of preservation, and the authorities have virtually ignored pubs, although nineteenth century pubs are quite as much a part of our social history as nineteenth century houses, railway stations, banks, exchanges and town halls. If Scotland retained only a very limited number of well-preserved Victorian and Edwardian villas, churches, or tenements, then we can be tolerably certain that these buildings would be reasonably well-protected by legislation. Yet the pubs of the same period, regardless of their scarcity value and intrinsic worth, have largely been denied such protection. This is a deplorable state of affairs, since to an even greater degree than the villas, the churches and the tenements, these pubs embody the spirit of their age. Whatever they designed, from bollards to bridges, and from lamposts to locomotives, the Victorians and Edwardians gave due consideration to both function and decoration. Their pubs, however, were arguably their most effective synthesis of functional and decorative elements.

In the absence of adequate statutory safeguards, the fate of these splendid old pubs hinges on the attitude of their owners, the brewery companies and members of the "free trade". When contemplating "improvements" of one sort or another they would do well to bear in mind the investment in materials and skills which Victorian and Edwardian pubs represent—craftsmanship which our great-grandfathers took for granted could only be duplicated today at prohibitive expense. Here, as in so many comparable situations, conservation, far from being impractical or uneconomical, is sound common sense.

SUGGESTIONS FOR FURTHER READING

Andrews, Allen. The Whisky Barons (1977)

Barnard, Alfred. The Noted Breweries of Great Britain and Ireland (1889-91)
     The Whisky Distilleries of the United Kingdom (1887, reprinted 1969)

Barnard, Julian. The Decorative Tradition (1973)

Brander, Michael. The Original Scotch (1974)

Donnachie, Ian. A History of the Brewing Industry in Scotland (1979)

Girouard, Mark. Victorian Pubs (1975)

Graham, Henry Grey. The Social Life of Scotland in the Eighteenth Century
     (1899, reprinted 1969)

Longmate, Norman. The Waterdrinkers, a History of Temperance (1968)

"Shadow" (Alexander Brown). Midnight Scenes and Social Photographs (1858,
     reprinted 1976)

Spiller, Brian. Victorian Public Houses (1972)

Stuart, Marie. Old Edinburgh Taverns (1952)

NOTES ON PRIMARY SOURCES AND BACKGROUND MATERIAL

1 PARLIAMENTARY PAPERS

Those which deal either directly or indirectly with drink and the licensed trade in Victorian and Edwardian Scotland are too numerous to list in detail here. A representative selection of reports, returns, etc., including some of the most important, is given below (arranged in chronological order). For further information, readers are referred to the General Index to British Parliamentary Papers, published by H.M. Stationery Office.

1846 XV Report from the Select Committee on the system of granting certificates for public houses in Scotland.

1852-53 LXXXI Number of persons taken into custody for drunkenness and disorderly conduct in each city and town in the United Kingdom, 1841 to 1851.

1857-58 XXXIV Number of persons taken drunk to the police offices of Glasgow, Edinburgh, Dundee, Greenock and Paisley, 1857-58.

1860 XXXII, XXXIII Report from the Royal Commission on the licensing system.

1873 LIV Return of convictions for drunkenness for each county and borough in England, Wales, Scotland and Ireland, from 1st July 1871 to 1st July 1872.

1874 LIV Return for each Royal Burgh in Scotland, for each year, 1869 to 1873, of the number of licences granted by the justices of the peace under appeal from the magistrates of the burgh.

1874 LXII Return of particulars of liquor licences issued in Scotland, 1871-72.

1875 LXII Return of the number of persons arrested as (1) drunk and incapable, and (2) drunk and disorderly, in each burgh and county in Scotland, 1874-75.

1877 XLIX Amount of revenue derived from Scottish grocers' and public house licences, 1876-77.

1877 XI, 1878 XIV, 1878-79 X Reports from the Select Committee of the House of Lords on Intemperance.

1878 XXVI Report of the Royal Commission on the laws regulating the sale and consumption of exciseable liquors, sold for consumption off the premises in Scotland.

1883 LV Return showing the arrests for drunkenness during 1882 in each burgh and county in Scotland.

1884 XLVII Return of the number of inns and hotels, public houses, and other licensed premises, in each county, city, and burgh in Scotland, 1841, 1851, 1861, 1871, and 1881.

1887 LXVII Return of the number of persons arrested as (1) drunk and incapable, and (2) drunk and disorderly, in each burgh and county in Scotland during 1886.

1890 LXIII Return of liquor licences issued in the cities, burghs, and counties of Scotland, 1886-89.

1890 LXIII Return of particulars relating to licensed premises in the City of Glasgow, 1890.

1890 X, 1890-91 XI Report from the Select Committee on British and Foreign Spirits, 1890-91.

1893-94 XVII Report from the Departmental Committee on the Treatment of Inebriates.

1893-94 LXXIV Return of the number of persons arrested as (1) drunk and incapable, and (2) drunk and disorderly, in each burgh and county in Scotland during 1892.

1897 XXXIV, XXXV; 1898 XXXVI, XXXVIII;

1899 XXXV Reports of the Royal Commission on the Liquor Licensing Laws (for Scottish Evidence, see 1898 XXXVIII).

1899 XII Report of the Departmental Committee on Rules for Scottish Inebriate Reformatories.

1899 XXX Report of the Departmental Committee on Beer Materials.

1899 LXXIX Regulations for certified Scottish Inebriate Reformatories.

1908 LVIII; 1909 XLIX Reports of the Royal Commission on Whisky and other Potable Spirits.

2 SOLICITORS' RECORDS

Among the old legal documents which now repose in Scottish civic or regional archives, there are a considerable number which throw light on the financial affairs of Victorian and Edwardian publicans. The most important of these are sederunt or minute books, records of trust dispositions and settlements, with (in most cases) inventories and valuations of the deceaseds' heritable and moveable property. Occasionally the trustees of the deceased wine and spirit merchant (who were empowered to manage or otherwise dispose of his or her estate) obtained a transfer of the licence and continued to run the pub, so that sederunt books sometimes contain particulars of drawings from licensed premises and details of outlay on stock, wages, alterations, etc. Of these and other solicitors' records which have been deposited in Strathclyde Regional Archives and which were consulted in the preparation of this book, the following documents proved to be particularly useful.

Baird, Alexander; Glasgow wine and spirit merchant (died 1873). Sederunt book of trust covering period 1871-1892. Contents include inventory and valuation of house furniture, particulars of income derived from investments in property, inventory and valuation of fittings and stock of licensed premises situated at 169 Gallowgate, Glasgow, and pub accounts, with details of weekly drawings and total drawings per annum.

Craig, James Jnr; Glasgow wine and spirit merchant (died 1884). Book of trust covering period 1883-1947. Contents include inventory and valuation of fittings and stock of licensed premises situated at 131 St. Vincent Street, Glasgow. A separate ledger, covering the years 1884-1891, contains particulars of bank deposits, business debts, etc.

Dunbar, Stewart; Glasgow wine and spirit merchant. Two small account books covering period 1855-1868. Contents include particulars of financial outlay on stock.

Eunson, George; Glasgow wine and spirit merchant (died 1879). Minute book of trust covering period 1871-1892. Contents include inventory and valuation of household furniture and effects, details of investments in property and shares, and inventory and valuation of fittings and stock of licensed premises situated at 182 Trongate, Glasgow.

Loudon, J. Bryce; Glasgow wine and spirit merchant (died 1860). Sederunt book of trust covering period 1860-1884. Contents include inventory and valuation of house furniture and personal effects, particulars of income, and inventory and valuation of fittings and stock of licensed premises situated at 3 Melville Place (132 Trongate), Glasgow.

McAllister, Peter; Glasgow wine and spirit merchant (died 1837). Sederunt book of trust covering period 1837-1851. Contents include printed catalogues of wines, spirits, etc. – McAllister's stock, which was auctioned off shortly after his demise.

McKay, D. G.; Partick wine and spirit merchant (died 1881). Sederunt book of trust covering period 1880-1887. Contents include inventory and valuation of house furniture and other domestic effects, particulars of income derived from investments in property and other sources, and inventory and valuation of fittings and stock of licensed premises situated at 127 Dumbarton Road, Partick.

McLaren, William; Glasgow wine and spirit merchant (died 1872). Book of trust covering period 1871-1908. Contents include details of drawings from several sets of licensed premises and particulars of sale of goodwill of same.

Meikle, John; Glasgow wine and spirit merchant (died 1905). Sederunt book of trust covering period 1848-1867. Contents include inventory of personal estate and details of property investments.

Naismith, John Hall; Clydebank wine and spirit merchant (died 1891). Sederunt book of trust covering period 1891-1909. Contents include inventory and valuation of household furniture, and inventory and valuation of fittings and stock of licensed premises situated in Victoria Place, Clydebank.

Pender, John; Glasgow wine and spirit merchant (died 1871). Sederunt book of trust covering period 1871-1877. Contents include inventory and valuation of fittings and stock of two sets of licensed premises, respectively situated at 5 Adam's Court Lane and 12 St. Enoch Square, Glasgow.

Smith, Lilias; Greenock wine and spirit merchant (died 1899). Sederunt books (8) of trust covering period 1898-1955. Contents include inventory and valuation of fittings and stock of licensed premises (James Watt Bar) situated at 30 East Hamilton Street, Greenock, details of pub drawings and remuneration to staff, account of alterations, etc. A separate ledger, covering the years 1901-1905, contains the accounts of the James Watt Bar for that period.

3   ARCHITECTS' AND BUILDERS' DESIGNS

Large numbers of plans, elevations, etc., of late Victorian and Edwardian pubs are preserved in Strathclyde Regional Archives, Glasgow, and Edinburgh City Archives. Known collectively as lining plans, they were originally submitted to the Dean of Guild Courts, accompanied by applications for permission to erect or alter buildings (lining petitions). Strathclyde Regional Archives has Glasgow Dean of Guild Court lining plans from 1885 onwards, Govan Dean of Guild Court lining plans from c.1870-1912, and Partick Dean of Guild Court lining plans from 1877-1912. Edinburgh City Archives has Edinburgh Dean of Guild Court lining plans from 1880 onwards and Leith Dean of Guild Court lining plans from 1877-1920 (in the latter year Leith was merged in Edinburgh and Leith Dean of Guild Court was abolished); the Leith series of plans is, however, incomplete. In the case of licensed premises, the lining plan may be no more than a simple pen-and-ink drawing on a single sheet of waxed paper; on the other hand it may consist of several sheets of colour-washed plans, elevations and constructional details, vividly depicting the "before and after" appearance of the premises. In addition to lining plans, Edinburgh City Archives has Edinburgh Licensing Court plans from 1899 onwards. These plans, made by architects or builders at the publican's expense, and produced at sittings of the Licensing Court, enabled the licensing magistrates, when considering whether or not to issue a new licence or sanction the transfer or renewal of an existing one, to see at a glance if the premises in question measured up to their exacting standards. The earliest Licensing Court plans correspond to the most rudimentary Dean of Guild Court lining plans and consist of pen-and-ink drawings on single sheets of waxed paper.

4   LICENSED TRADE PERIODICALS

Hotel and Caterer. Monthly, 1912-13
The National Guardian. Weekly, 1889-1975
The Scottish Wine, Spirit and Beer Trades'
Review. Monthly, 1887-1888
The Victualling Trades' Review. Monthly, 1889-1908

These publications are an exceedingly valuable source of information on all aspects of the late Victorian and Edwardian licensed trade. The contents include illustrated descriptions of pubs and licensed restaurants, articles on breweries and distilleries, potted biographies of publicans, restaurateurs and whisky merchants, and publicity puffs on behalf of architects, bar-fitters, decorative painters, glass embossers, and other craftsmen involved in pub renovation work.

5   DOCUMENTS RELATING SPECIFICALLY TO THE LICENSED TRADE IN GLASGOW AND ITS IMMEDIATE ENVIRONS. A SELECTION FROM STRATHCLYDE REGIONAL ARCHIVES.

Glasgow. Minutes of the Licensing Court, 1897-1961.
    Reports of Proceedings of the Licensing Court, 1912-1966.
    Public house certificates: ale, 1779-1824.

Public house certificates: spirits, 1818-1824.

Public house certificates: ale and spirits, 1824-1898.

Public house certificates: register of applications, 1898 onwards.

Volumes (3) of ward-maps marking licensed premises, 1902, 1913 and undated.

Govan. Public house certificates, 1904-1912.

Minutes of Burgh Licensing Court, 1904-1912.

Partick. Public house certificates, 1904-1912.

Pollokshaws. Public house certificates, 1904-1912.

Minutes of Burgh Licensing Court, 1904-1908.

6   POST OFFICE DIRECTORIES

Victorian and Edwardian Post Office Directories usually have a section devoted to trades and professions, in which are listed the names and addresses of local wine and spirit merchants, architects, bar-fitters, etc. The central reference libraries of Glasgow, Edinburgh, Aberdeen, Dundee, and other smaller Scottish towns have full runs of Post Office Directories for their respective localities.

GLOSSARY OF TERMS RELATING TO ARCHITECTURE AND INTERIOR DECORATION

Aedicule, an opening framed by columns or colonnettes carrying a pedimented entablature

Aeolic column, column in which the volutes of the capital spring up vertically from the shaft

Alcove, a recess in a room, or a small room opening out of a larger one

Arcading, a series of adjoining arches, employed solely as a decorative feature

Architectural faience, glazed coloured earthenware used as an ornamental facing for facades, shopfronts, &c

Art Deco, architectural and decorative style which flourished between 1925 and 1935 and which was characterised by the use of glossy materials such as tiles, opaque glass, plastics, mirrors, lacquers and veneers. Among the formative influences on Art Deco (also called Art Moderne) were Art Nouveau, Cubism, and Egyptian art as exemplified by the treasures of Tutankhamun's tomb

Art Nouveau, the "new art" which flourished between 1895 and 1910 and which was characterised by flowing and sinuous ornament, largely based on plant forms

Ashlar, masonry formed of squared, flat-surfaced stones, laid in regular courses

Back bar, subsidiary bar of the private or saloon type which, in the late Victorian Scottish pub, was occasionally provided at the rear of the public bar

Backcourt, a courtyard behind a flatted tenement, provided with communal facilities for the disposal of refuse and the washing and drying of laundry

Back-fitment, a wooden bar-fitment which stands against a wall, behind a long, semi-circular, or U-shaped bar counter, and which incorporates shelves, cupboards, spirit casks, etc

Balustrade, a row of vertical members, usually of an ornate character, topped with a rail or coping

Bar canopy, a shelf-like or ledge-like structure over a bar counter

Baroque, a late Renaissance phase of architecture and interior decoration, characterised by richness of detail and dramatic spatial relationships

Bay, a compartment or section into which a structure is divided

Beam, a horizontal structural member used to support a roof or ceiling

Beamed ceiling, a ceiling in which the beams are exposed. In many pubs the beamed ceilings are purely ornamental, as the exposed beams serve no structural purpose

Bearing partition, an interior wall which supports a load set upon it from above

Bed recess, a rectangular alcove in a tenement flat, designed to accommodate a built-in bed

Bevelled mirror, mirror on which the edges have been given a sloping surface

Bodega bar, a wine bar

Bolection moulding, a moulding applied to a panel, projecting in front of the surface of the framing

Bow dormer, a curved window projecting from a sloping roof

Bracket, a projecting support for a beam or a cornice

Brilliant cut glass, glass into which a design or pattern has been cut by means of a rotating stone wheel

Broken pediment, pediment with the apex or crest omitted, a Baroque architectural device which was also adapted for use on furniture

Buffet bar, pub specialising in the supply of snacks and cooked meals

Cabinetwork, fine interior woodwork

Capital, the carved or moulded crowning feature of a column, colonnette, or pilaster

Cast iron, iron which contains a high percentage of carbon and is therefore not malleable, in consequence of which it is shaped by pouring it into moulds

Ceramic, a product of baked clay

Coffered ceiling, ceiling ornamented with sunken panels

Colonnette, a miniature column

Column, a vertical cylindrical shaft which serves as a support for a horizontal feature, such as an entablature

Concrete, a building material consisting of sand and water, mixed with gravel, crushed stone, bricks, or tiles, and combined with Portland cement

Conical roof, roof in the form of a cone

Console, a bracket-like projection, frequently ornamented with reversed volutes, used to support a cornice

Corinthian capital, the most elaborate form of classical capital, ornamented with four volutes and rows of acanthus leaves

Corinthianesque capital, a free variation of the classical Corinthian capital

Cornice, the crowning part of a classical entablature; a horizontal projection round the top of a building; a projecting moulding at the junction of a wall and ceiling

Cornucopia, the ''horn of plenty'' of classical mythology – a horn overflowing with fruits, etc., used frequently as a decorative motif

Cupola, a small dome-like structure, not necessarily hemispherical in shape, employed as a crowning feature on a tower, roof, or turret

Dado, the lower part of a wall, when treated differently from the rest of the wall, i.e. – wood-panelled, papered, etc

Dentil course, tooth-like rectangular blocks, introduced as an ornamental feature in a cornice

Display fitment, see display stand

Display stand, a wooden bar-fitment, either free-standing or positioned against a wall, which incorporates shelves for the display of bottles, glasses, and other items of stock

Dressed stone, stone which has been smoothed and polished

Dressings, blocks of dressed stone, used at the corners of a building, or as a frame for doors or windows

Edwardian Baroque, 1900s architecture and interior decoration influenced by late Renaissance models

Edwardian Classical, 1900s architecture and interior decoration influenced by Graeco-Roman and Neo-Classical models

Elliptical arch, an arch curved in the form of a semi-ellipse

Embossed glass, glass into which a design or pattern has been etched by means of hydrofluoric acid and/or white acid (a mixture of hydrofluoric acid and other chemicals)

Embossed tile, tile which has its surface decorated with a moulded relief pattern

Empire style, a phase of French art and architecture, derived from Egyptian and Graeco-Roman sources, prevalent from c.1804 to c.1820, and subsequently imitated

Enamel, vitrified coating applied to metal or ceramics and fired

Engraved glass, see brilliant cut glass

Entablature, horizontal series of carvings or mouldings, carried on columns or colonnettes

Etched glass, see embossed glass

Facade, the principal face of a building

Faience tile, a tile of glazed ceramic ware

Fanlight, semicircular window with glazing bars radiating from the centre in a fan-like arrangement

Fascia, the lettered panel on the upper part of a shop front or pub front

Fenestration, the arrangement of windows in a building

Festoon, a garland of leaves, flowers, etc., bound with ribbons and suspended from its ends

Fibreous plasterwork, plaster to which hair has been added as a reinforcing agent

Fin de siecle, the end of the 19th century, which gave birth to Art Nouveau

Finial, ornamental feature on top of pinnacle, gable, etc.; terminating ornament on furniture

Flemish Renaissance, Flemish art and architecture of the 16th and 17th centuries

Fluted column or colonnette, column or colonnette ornamented with shallow concave grooves, running vertically

Freestone, stone which can readily be worked by masons

Fresco, wall painting executed on damp plaster

Frieze, a continuous horizontal band of painted, carved or moulded ornament

Frontage, the front part of a building, especially a shop front or pub front

Gasalier, a hanging or standing fixture with branches for gas-jets

Geometric ceiling, a ceiling decorated with designs based on geometrical forms such as circles and squares

Girder, a main load-carrying beam of timber, iron, steel or reinforced concrete

Half-landing, small landing at the bend of a staircase

Ionic capital, capital ornamented with spiral-shaped scrolls (volutes)

Italian Renaissance, the "new birth" of Classical art and architecture in the Italy of the 15th and 16th centuries

Jacobean, Renaissance architecture, interior decoration, etc., of the reign of James I of England and VI of Scotland (1603-25)

Jug bar, in Scottish pubs, a small compartment devoted to off-sales, also called the "family" or "jug and bottle" department

Lantern light, a glazed structure which is raised over an opening in a flat roof to admit light to the area below

Latticework, a network of crossing diagonal bars or strips of wood or metal

Leaded glass, small pieces of clear, coloured, patterned, or textured glass which have been joined together, by means of lead strips and solder, to form decorative panels for windows, doors, screens, etc

Limewash, solution of slaked lime and water, used for coating walls, etc

Linoleum, a floorcovering made from a fabric which has been impregnated with a mixture of oxidised linseed-oil, resins, and fillers, and then cured by heating

Lounge, in Scottish pubs, a comfortably furnished sitting room, generally situated at the rear of the premises

Mansard roof, a roof with two slopes on each side, the lower slope being steeper than the upper one

Matchboarding, see tongued and grooved boarding

Mezzanine, an intermediate storey between the two main storeys of a building, usually between the ground floor and the first floor

Mosaic tile, a tile, developed in the late nineteenth century by Maw & Company, that could be employed to simulate a mosaic floor—i.e., a decorative floor surface formed by small pieces of different coloured tiles, embedded in cement

Moulded capital, capital ornamented with moulded plaster; capital of ornamental cast-iron

Moulded ceiling, ceiling ornamented with moulded plaster decoration or one of the proprietary plasterwork substitutes

Mural painting, a wall painting

Necropolis, nineteenth century cemetery, modelled on the Greek "city of the dead"

Neo-Classical, art and architecture influenced by Graeco-Roman sources

Neo-Georgian, architecture and interior decoration influenced by eighteenth century work

Niche, an ornamental recess in a wall, cabinet, etc

Obscure glass, semi-transparent glass

Oriel window, a projecting upper storey window, supported on brackets or corbelling

Overmantel, ornamental structure, set over the mantel-shelf on a fireplace

Panel, see wood panel

Partition, an interior wall or screen of one storey or less in height

Partition wall, an internal wall

Pediment, an ornamental structure over a portico, door, window, or niche, derived from the triangular spaces at the gable ends of Graeco-Roman temples. As adapted for use on furniture, pediments can be triangular, broken, swan neck, segmented, or semi-circular

Pendant, an elongated ornamental feature, projecting downwards from a ceiling; a hanging ornament in light fixtures, furniture, etc

Pilaster, a pillar-like feature, partly built into, partly projecting from, a wall

Pillar, a vertical structural member, not necessarily cylindrical or of classical proportions

Plinth, the square base of a column; the flat-faced projecting base of a building

Porch, a sheltered approach to a doorway

Public bar, in Scottish pubs of the late Victorian and Edwardian periods, the principal, and frequently the only, drinking space

Quoins, corner stones, frequently of dressed stone, laid at the angles of a building

Raphaelesque, painting, etc., inspired by, or reminiscent of, the manner of Raphael (1483-1520), a leading artist and architect of the Italian Renaissance

Register grate, fire-grate provided with a device for regulating the draught flow

Renaissance, the rebirth or revival of the arts in the Europe of the 15th-17th centuries

Revolving door, door which turns on a central pivot

Rooflight, a skylight or lantern light in a roof

Round-headed window, a window with a rounded top

Rubble masonry, masonry composed of irregularly shaped stones with rough surfaces

Rusticated masonry, masonry of shaped, coursed blocks with roughened surfaces; masonry of flat-surfaced blocks with recessed or chamfered edges

Saloon, in Scottish pubs, a large public room

Saloon bar, in Scottish pubs, a subsidiary bar, usually quieter and more comfortably furnished than the public bar

Scallop shell pediment, pediment ornamented with a carved representation of a semi-circular shell with radiating ridges

Sconce, bracket designed to hold a candle or an electric bulb

Scottish Baronial, a term used to describe the semi-fortified houses built by the Scottish nobility from the 14th to the 17th centuries; a nineteenth century revivalist style based on Scottish Baronial architecture, especially tower houses of the Renaissance period

Scottish Renaissance, Scottish architecture, interior decoration, etc., of the 16th and 17th centuries

Screen, a partial partition of wood, etc., which in late Victorian and Edwardian pubs was usually decorative as well as functional

Scroll, a spiraling and convoluting ornament based on plant forms such as acanthus leaves, laurel, ivy, etc

Second French Empire, French art and architecture, approximately between 1852 and 1871

Segmental or segmented pediment, curved pediment of which the contour is a segment of a circle

Servery, a "service" room adjoining a dining room

Settle, a long high-backed bench

Skylight, a glazed frame which is set over an opening in a sloping roof to admit light

Snug, a small sitting room

Stained glass, decorative glass made by adding metallic oxides to molten glass or by fusing coloured glass on plain glass

Stencil, a pattern made by brushing paint over a perforated sheet of metal or paper

Stock casks, spirit barrels which in the late Victorian or Edwardian pub stood on a stock platform or a back-fitment and were decorative as well as functional

Stock platform, a wooden island bar fitment which was enclosed by a U-shaped, semi-circular, octagonal, or oval-shaped bar counter. The stock platform acted as a support for spirit casks and frequently also incorporated shelves and cupboards

Structural column, a load-bearing column

Structural wall, a wall which is an integral part of the fabric of a building

Sunk storey, a basement storey

Swag, an ornamental festoon of fruit, flowers, etc., in a pendant curve

Terracotta, red-brown, unglazed earthenware. In the late Victorian and Edwardian periods it was frequently used in architectural decoration, as a facing material for buildings, etc

Tongued and grooved boarding, a type of woodwork in which the pieces consist of boards with tongues cut along one edge and grooves in the opposite edge; the matching boards are then joined together

Transfer-printed tile, a mass-produced tile, decorated by means of a transfer tissue which was printed either using a copper plate or by a lithographic process

Turnpike stair, a staircase which winds around a circular column (newel)

Turret, a small tower

Twisted column or colonnette, a column or colonnette which appears to be twisted around its vertical axis

Veneer, thin slices of expensive, interestingly figured or richly coloured wood, applied to a base of cheap, coarse-grained wood or plywood

Vitreous fresco, an obsolete term for a mural made up of faience tiles

Volute, the ornamental spiral scroll which is the principal feature of an Ionic capital

Wood panel, rectangular piece of wood used as wall decoration or as an ornamental feature in bar cabinetwork, etc

Wreath, a circlet composed of foliage, flowers and/or fruit, often featured as a carved or painted decorative motif

Wrought iron, iron which contains a low percentage of carbon, is malleable, and can consequently be bent, twisted and formed by hand

GLOSSARY OF SCOTS WORDS AND EXPRESSIONS

Auld, old

Auld Reikie, old smoky (Edinburgh)

Bailie, city magistrate

Baith, both

Bauld, bold

Birle, spin; spend money freely

Bodle, small copper coin

Bonnie, beautiful; pretty

Bousing, boozing

Bree, liquor

Caddie, street porter

Canny, cautious; prudent; frugal

Catcht, caught

Cauld, cold

Close, enclosed courtyard behind a building; narrow alley; common passage in tenement

Collops, sliced meat

Danderin, sauntering

Deacon, master or chairman of a trade-guild

Doun, down

Dram, glass of spirits

Droukit, drenched

Fley, scare away

Fou, full; intoxicated

Fouk, folk

Gae, Gang, go

Gar, make

Gash, lively; talkative

Gie, give; give way

Gin, if

Haddock Lug, "haddock ear" – i.e., part of the head of a haddock, served as a titbit

Hae, have

Hauf, half; half gill of whisky

Howff, haunt; tavern or public house

Lang, long

Land, tenement of several flatted storeys

Lawin, tavern reckoning

Loup, leap; spring

Lown, lad

Luckie, mistress of an ale house

Mak, make

Mercat, market

Meridian, midday drink of liquor

Mony, many

Mune, moon

Mutchkin, liquid measure equal to an English pint

Our, Owre, over

Pend, wide covered passage through a building

Quaiche, two-eared drinking cup

Rin, run

Rizzared Haddock, haddock dried in the sun

Sang, song

Saunt, saint

Saul, soul

Shoppie, a small shop

Stark, strong

Sune, soon

Tappit Hen, Scottish quart-measure

Thegither, together

Thrawart, perverse

Tinkle Sweetie, bell formerly rung in Edinburgh at eight p.m. (the closing hour of
the shops)

Unco, very

Wad, would

Whan, when

Wharewi', wherewith

Writer, lawyer

Wynd, narrow lane or street; alley

Ye, you

Index

Faculty of Procurators, Glasgow, 33

Fair, George, Glasgow publican and restaurateur, 107

Fairfield of Govan, shipbuilders, 121

Falkirk, as brewing centre, 15

Falkirk Brewery, 54, 104, 125

Falkirk, pub in, 116 – 118

Faraday, Michael, 120

Farmer, George Honeyman, Glasgow publican, 32

Ferrari, Andrea dei, 104

Fergusson, Robert, 10, 12 – 16

Fifty Waistcoats, Kilmarnock, 116, Plate 55

Fisher, Peter, Edinburgh publican, 128

Fisherrow Brewery, Musselburgh, 115

Forbes Mackenzie Act (1853), 7, 20, 36 – 37, 66 – 67, 70, 108

Forrest & Son, glass stainers and embossers, 93 – 94, 107, 116, 118, Plates 19 – 20, 54, 60

Forrester, John, architect, 87, 129

Forrester, John, Glasgow restaurateur, 41

Forth & Clyde Canal, 117

Fortune's Tavern, Edinburgh, 13 – 14

Fowler, John, brewer, 54

Franklin, Benjamin, 120

Frazer, James, Glasgow innkeeper, 18

Fyffe, Will, 84

Gamle Carlsberg Lager Beer Import Company, Leith, 44

Gardner, Andrew, decorative painter, 95

Garibaldi, Guiseppe, 63

General Post Office, 32

Gibb, Alexander, cask merchant, 90

Gibb, Thomas, Aberdeen publican, 133

Gilbert Stewart's Vaults, Barrachnie, 112

Gillespie & Sons, brewers, 55

Gillies, Neil, Glasgow publican, 109

Gilmour, David, Glasgow publican, 27

Gin, 21

Gin shops and gin palaces, 6, 10, 21 – 22, 40, 86, 101

Girgenti, reformatory, 78

Girouard, Mark, 34

Gladstone, William Ewart, 42, 47, 70

Glasgow, as brewing centre, 15, 44 – 45, 55

Glasgow Co-operative Congress (1890), 76

Glasgow Corporation Improvements & General Powers Act (1897), 105

Glasgow, Corporation of, 35, 70 – 71, 78

Glasgow Courier, 18 – 19

Glasgow Cross, 83

Glasgow District Subway Company, 33

Glasgow Exhibition (1901), 90

Glasgow, gangs of, 83

Glasgow Green, 62

Glasgow Herald, 112

Glasgow, inns of, 17 – 18

Glasgow Institute of Architects, 109

Glasgow Journal, 17

Glasgow, licensing magistrates of, 29, 35, 59 – 60, 70 – 71, 79 – 80, 91, 96 – 98, 105, 111, 113

attitude to "disreputable" pubs, 35

enthusiasm for early closing, 79, 81

influence on pub design, 91, 96 – 97, 105, 111, 113

opposition to barmaids in pubs, 29

opposition to free lunches in pubs, 60

opposition to music and games in pubs, 80 – 81, 98

rigid application of licensing laws by, 71, 79 – 81

unsympathetic attitude to licence holders, 33, 35, 80 – 81, 97

Glasgow, magistrates and town council of, 17

Glasgow, municipal chambers, 26

Glasgow, model lodging houses of, 40, 83 – 84

Glasgow Public House Trust Company, 71 – 72

Glasgow, pubs of, 18, 22 – 23, 25 – 28, 32 – 35, 40 – 41, 49, 56, 59, 72, 77, 79 – 81, 83, 86 – 89, 91, 94, 96 – 97, 99 – 100, 102 – 113

Glasgow Rangers, football club, 28

Glasgow, registered clubs of, 37 – 38

"Glasgow School" of painters, 110

Glasgow, taverns of, 17 – 19, 21, 23

Glasgow, tea-rooms of, 40 – 41

Glasgow, temperance party in, 70, 81, 97

Glasgow, town councillors of, 70

Glasgow United Young Men's Christian Association, 65

Glenburgie, distillery, 53 – 54

Globe Tavern, Leith, 129

Golf Tavern, Edinburgh, 123

Gordon Bar, Glasgow, 32, 106, Plate 15

MacPherson, Alexander, of Cafe Royal, Edinburgh, 119

MacSorley, Philip, Glasgow publican and restaurateur, 31, 87, 108 – 109

MacSorley's public houses, 108 – 109, Plates 21 – 23, 26

MacWhannel & Rogerson (Ninian MacWhannel and John Rogerson), architects, 111 – 112

Main Law, 66

Mair & Dougall, bottlers, 58

Mair, Henry, Glasgow publican, 23

Malory, Sir Thomas, 112

Manchester, pubs of, 96

Mannering, Colonel, 11

Marshall, George, Edinburgh publican, 131

Marshall, Thomas, brewer, 54

Marshall's Bar, Edinburgh, see Bennet's Bar

Marwick, Thomas Purves, architect, 128 – 129

Mary, Queen of Scots, 99, 110

Mashers, 29 – 30

Mather, Hugh, Edinburgh publican, 124

Mather's Bar, Edinburgh, 124, Plate 80

Matthew, Father Theobald, 62

Maw & Company, tile manufacturers, 89, 131

McAndrew, Colin, 126

McAnulty, Bernard, Glasgow publican, 112

McCall, David, Glasgow publican and restaurateur, 107

McConnell, Alexander & Company, 95

McCormack, Mrs. M., Renfrew publican, 115

McCulloch, J. & J., spirit brokers, 30

McCulloch, Malcolm, Glasgow publican, 116

McDonald, Alexander, of McDonald & Currie, Architect, 115

McDonald, Peter & Company, 50, 90

McEwan Hall, Edinburgh, 54

McEwan, William & Company, brewers, 55 – 56

McGlashan, John & Company, engineers and bar-fitters, 57, 90

McGonagall, William, 63 – 64

McIntyre, James, Glasgow publican, 28

McIntyre, Malcolm, Glasgow publican, 109

McKay, John, Aberdeen publican, 134

McLay, James, Paisley publican, 113

McLaughlin, Alexander & Company, glass embossers, 94

McLaren, George, of Cafe Royal, Edinburgh, 119

McLennan, John, tile decorator, 112, Plate 36

McLennan, W. D., architect, 113 – 114

McNish, Robert & Company, whisky merchants, 47

McQueen, John, cask merchant, 49

McTavish, J. S., Edinburgh publican and restaurateur, 127

Mechanical Spirit Maturing Syndicate (Limited), London, 50

Meikle, John, Glasgow publican, 32

Meikle, William & Sons, glass embossers, 94

Melline Company Limited, 50

Melvin, Alexander, brewer, 54

Menzies, William, Glasgow tavern-keeper, 18

"Meridian," 12, 105

Metropole Theatre, Glasgow, 33

Metropolitan Bar, Glasgow, 25, 41

Meux, Richard, brewer, 15

Middlemass, Luckie, 15 – 16, 120

Midlothian County Buildings, Edinburgh, 122

Mills, George, Edinburgh publican, 131 – 132

Milne, George, architect, 134

Minton, Hollins, & Company, tile manufacturers, 89, 126

Mitchell, A. G. S., architect, 124

Mitchell, Jane, Partick publican, 111

Mitre Bar, Edinburgh, 127, Plate 86

Moluag, Celtic Saint, 110

Mossman, John, sculptor, 21

Mortimer, J. E. & Company, brewers' agents, 93

Museum Bar, Paisley, 113

Murdoch, Warroch, & Company, brewers, 15

Muir, John, of Whitebait music hall, 20 – 21

Muir, Joseph, Glasgow publican, 49

Nation, Carry, 8, 65, 82, 102 – 103

National Commercial Bank of Scotland, 124, 129